ASK YOUR DEVELOPER

ASK YOUR DEVELOPER

HOW TO HARNESS THE POWER OF SOFTWARE DEVELOPERS AND WIN IN THE 21ST CENTURY

</>

JEFF LAWSON

HARPER
BUSINESS

An Imprint of HarperCollins*Publishers*

HarperCollins books may be purchased for educational, business, or sales promotional use. For information, please email the Special Markets Department at SPsales@harpercollins.com.

FIRST EDITION

Designed by Bonni Leon-Berman

Library of Congress Cataloging-in-Publication Data
Names: Lawson, Jeff, author.
Title: Ask your developer : how to harness the power of software developers
and win in the 21st century / Jeff Lawson.
Description: First edition. | New York, NY : Harper Business, [2020] |
Identifiers: LCCN 2020034250 (print) | LCCN 2020034251 (ebook) | ISBN
9780063018297 (hardcover) | ISBN 9780063018303 (ebook)
Subjects: LCSH: Computer software—Development—Management. | Information
Technology—Management. | Strategic planning.
Classification: LCC QA76.76.D47 L3948 2020 (print) | LCC QA76.76.D47
(ebook) | DDC 005.1068—dc23
LC record available at https://lccn.loc.gov/2020034250
LC ebook record available at https://lccn.loc.gov/2020034251

21 22 23 24 25 LSC 10 9 8 7 6 5 4 3 2 1

TO M & A: I CAN'T WAIT TO SEE WHAT YOU BUILD.

CONTENTS

FOREWORD

BY ERIC RIES

In the twenty-first century, every business is a digital business. Customers have expectations of service and user experience based on the best digitally enabled products out there. Eventually, they'll have those expectations of every company, no matter what the industry. What that means is that every organization that hopes not just to survive but to succeed needs to understand how to innovate by building software, and how to hire and manage the people who build it.

I've spent the last decade helping all kinds of companies, from Silicon Valley startups to Fortune 50 industrial behemoths, increase their chances of building game-changing innovations by adopting the principles outlined in my book *The Lean Startup*. As a result, I've often found myself trying to explain the semiconductor revolution to leaders who don't understand software. Many still believe that this tsunami of disruption will somehow bypass *their* business. I once worked with a group of senior leaders from large hospital trade associations who were desperate to improve patient experience, but throughout our time together they made excuses for why that experience was so dismal. Nothing I said about using digital tools to create the kind of transformation they were looking for got through to them. Finally, I asked how many of them had used Uber or Lyft. When they all said they had, I asked them to take their phones out of their pockets and look at how those apps show there's a car on the way and where it is. I asked them to imagine what it would mean to the patient experience if a patient knew the arrival time of the nurse or a doctor coming to their room to help. Thanks to software, it's just as easy to do that for medical staff as it is for ride shares. Only the delusion that there's no connection between software and patient care prevents that from becoming the norm.

The digital revolution is fundamentally rewriting the rules of general management. Software simultaneously lowers transaction costs, demolishes barriers to entry, and accelerates the pace of change. Companies—and institutions—that cannot cope with this pace and intensity will cease to be relevant. There are few people in the world who are experienced both as software developers and as business executives. That's what makes Jeff so unique: he has feet in both worlds. I've seen executives at great companies unintentionally sabotage their own digital success by doing (and not doing) things that disempower talent and kill innovation.

I once advised a company that made household products. They were trying to figure out how to test a new product through a small pilot program. I suggested creating a minimum viable product, an MVP in Lean Startup terms, or a version of the product that's good enough to allow a company to collect useful feedback about its value from a small number of consumers while still being fast and inexpensive to create. The idea was to use the MVP to gather information as quickly as possible in order to determine next steps in the development process. Normally, this company would have to manufacture a huge quantity of the new product and test it out in a few stores. However, in this case, there was already a lab up and running that had made enough of it that team members were taking it home every day because they liked it so much. This immediately presented itself to me as an MVP opportunity. Instead of the team taking this stuff home, they could give it to fifty customers to test and report back on.

To solve the issue of recruiting these customers and making sure they were continuously supplied, I suggested they do the recruiting online, have customers sign up for a subscription, and then provide them with the ability to text the pilot team when they needed more product. I emphasized that this was a perfect example of how software can enable speed accelerations and cost reductions that give companies an advantage in the marketplace. The idea that the team could set up this kind of system quickly and use it to get crucial information about how to make their product more marketable seemed like nothing less than a magic trick to them. But it's not magic. It's what Twilio does every day for thousands of companies.

Here's another tale. A major corporation I was working with had a CEO excited about digital transformation and providing customers with online browsing and ordering, something this industry had never done before. They launched an in-house startup to build an experimental website, helmed by a super-motivated junior team with no prestige or resources at their disposal, but a ton of commitment to building this MVP. The catch was they had no idea how to build a website or write software. They were in a completely nontechnological field. First, they went to the company's IT department for help, which refused them because this crazy project wasn't part of its purview. Next, they explored hiring an outside agency to do the site, but that was too expensive. Eventually, they recruited a designer, with a budding desire to write code, to take on the project—but that created new problems. Designers weren't "allowed" to write code at this company.

This example showed me that even with CEO support and a hungry team, it still takes a lot of work to set up those teams for success. It starts with having the right players on the field and then empowering them to make progress. *Ask Your Developer* can help companies translate CEO enthusiasm and raw talent into what they're actually looking for—a superior customer experience achieved through digital transformation. Those that embrace the full potential of their employees will reap outsized rewards in the years and decades to come.

I've had the privilege of watching what Jeff Lawson and his extraordinary team at Twilio have built unfold in real time as it has been integrated into our world in countless ways that we never stop to consider. Jeff's long-term vision for the company and his skill at bringing together incredibly talented people are the reasons that so much of the hidden infrastructure our lives now run on works seamlessly and elegantly. Twilio is what allows you to text your Uber driver or order a pizza online. It's built into Hulu and Twitter and Salesforce to help with communication and information sharing. It plays roles in the real estate industry and health care, as well as numerous nonprofits and relief organizations. It's helping businesses that never imagined themselves as digital companies make extraordinary transformations and grow under intense pressure to evolve or face their own demise.

Ask Your Developer begins with why it's so important to actually understand what well-crafted software can make possible. It's that initial leap of imagination that allows leaders to understand the value of software developers. From there, it explains why even if a company hires talented coders, making good use of them is an impossibility without good management to help them realize their full potential. Every company needs to employ people who have the skills to help them build things in order to grow and transform, but they also need to be willing to listen to them about what has to happen in order to reap the full benefit of what they have to offer.

As Jeff details, it's destructive for leaders to sit atop an organization far removed from the people who make its interfaces and user experience work. Building a structure and methodology for ideas to flow not just down but up the hierarchy, as well as across different areas of the organization, is critical not only to survive but also to thrive. Having worked with a large number of companies undergoing digital transformation, I've seen over and over again that the ones that did this kind of management transformation *before* rather than after they attempted digital transformation were more successful at it. This book is essential reading to drive a mutual understanding between managers and company leaders and the software developers they employ so that together they can successfully navigate extreme uncertainty.

Ask Your Developer makes a compelling case for the centrality of software and its uses, and it also offers practical advice for people looking to build the next generation of companies at every level. Jeff's native understanding of what software makes possible, along with his deep knowledge of why organizations attempting digital transformation often run into trouble, is a powerful combination. This book will be key for anyone who knows that digital is critical to their future but doesn't have all the answers for how to get there. It should also be handed to anybody who thinks they're in the clear because they don't run a digital business, in order to help them confront why that simply isn't true and begin to understand what they need to in order to transform.

There couldn't be a more critical time for Jeff's wisdom, experience, and perspective to reach a broad audience, from new startups to enterprise companies on the verge of reinvention, from management to the developers they need in order to thrive. *Ask Your Developer* is an essential resource for understanding the connection between software, the people who build it, and the value they offer in building and transforming the organizations we need in the age of digital disruption.

PROLOGUE
IT BEGINS WITH A BILLBOARD

In early 2015, Twilio rented a billboard in San Francisco beside Route 101. Tech-company billboards have become part of the landscape in the Bay Area, like movie billboards in Los Angeles. Partly it's about building brand awareness, and partly it's a recruiting tactic, a way to be seen by thousands of engineers on their way to work. There's also a bit of super-geek one-upmanship involved, since we all try to come up with something clever, like an inside joke or a reference to something that only Silicon Valley will understand.

So we reserved the billboard. The problem was we couldn't figure out what to say on that billboard. We were having these huge debates. Some people said we should get customer testimonials. We could put up logos from well-known companies that use our cloud communications platform. That would at least address our biggest challenge, which was that we were a successful business that nobody had heard of. At the time, we did about $100 million in annual revenue, and were on the path toward our initial public offering (IPO), yet we weren't a household name. That's because Twilio does not sell products to consumers. We sell a service to software developers that lets their apps communicate with voice, SMS, email, and more. We have amazing customers—Uber, WhatsApp, Lyft, Zendesk, OpenTable, Nordstrom, Nike. But our software hides under the covers, inside websites and mobile apps. In fact, you've undoubtedly used Twilio, without knowing it, if you're a customer of any of those companies or thousands more like them.

So having committed half a million dollars to reserve the billboard for a year (yeah, even billboard real estate in the Bay Area is overpriced!), we needed to come up with our message. And we had a deadline—the day they needed to start climbing the ladder and gluing it up. We hired an advertising agency. They put their best creative team on the project and came up with a bunch of ideas. They interviewed dozens of customers—software developers who'd used our platform to add communications to all those apps. They interviewed lots of our employees—Twilions, we call them—to ask what makes Twilio special. And at the end of several months of work and deliberation, we had the big "reveal" meeting. You've seen this scene on *Mad Men*—the firm pitches the client (us) all the brilliant ideas they've come up with. There were art boards, crafty explanations by very creative thinkers. Big pitch. Yet everything they pitched was kind of boring. We didn't really love any of them. The debate dragged on.

Finally, we were less than a week away from the date when the billboard was supposed to go up—with the billboard firm saying they had to have the artwork in hand—and we still couldn't come up with a pithy, succinct way to explain what Twilio does. By Friday afternoon we were still stuck. And we couldn't leave for the weekend without getting them the artwork. I was with our chief marketing officer, our head of creative, and our chief operating officer, trying to choose which mediocre message to go with—when I blurted out a crazy idea. "Why don't we just say, 'Ask your developer,'" I said. "You know, like those ads on TV where they say, 'Ask your doctor if this medication is right for you.' We're saying, 'Ask your developer if Twilio is right for you.'"

I was half joking. But the more we thought about the slogan, the more it made sense. Developers were the ones spreading the word about us and our product. We didn't do a ton of marketing, and we employed only a handful of sales reps. Most of our employees at the time were engineers. If someone wanted to find out what Twilio did, the best way to do that really would be to ask a developer.

So we put up our bright red billboard with three words spelled out in giant white capital letters: ASK YOUR DEVELOPER. Below that we put our logo and company name. That was it.

The billboard became a sensation—at least, relative to other billboards. "How Twilio Bested Hemingway" was the title of a Medium essay by Andy Raskin, a well-known tech industry marketing consultant. He was referring to a legendary (though perhaps apocryphal) story in which Ernest Hemingway bet someone ten dollars he could write a whole novel in just six words and won the bet with this: "For sale: Baby shoes. Never worn." Raskin said we had done something similar with our three-word billboard, producing "a brilliant illustration of how even stripped-down messaging can convey a powerful, moving story." I'm not sure that Papa Hemingway would surrender the title, but hey, when your billboard garners comparisons to one of the greatest novelists of all time, you accept the compliment and don't quibble.

The message worked because we didn't try to explain what we do. Instead, we provoked a conversation. We caught people's attention. We piqued their curiosity. Later, when they looked us up, they got the message.

What's more, the message operated on two different levels.

On one level we were simply saying that while you might not know what Twilio does, "your developer" certainly does. In our own weird, self-deprecating way, we were admitting that we weren't exactly a household name. Not long after that, Twilio went public and was valued at $2 billion, which soon doubled to $4 billion. *Forbes* magazine put us on their cover, calling Twilio "the sexiest stock in the world" and declaring that "wonky Twilio is the stealth power behind the biggest apps."

As of summer 2020, we have 190,000 customers, and 8 million developers have accounts on our platform. In 2019, we crossed a billion dollars in revenue. We're embedded into thousands of apps and websites. When you text your Uber driver from inside the Uber app? That's Twilio. When Netflix sends you a text message with a six-digit code before it lets you sign in? That's us again. When you order dinner from DoorDash, the notification that your food has arrived is sent via Twilio. You get the point. You probably use Twilio every day but don't realize it.

Our approach has been to win over the hearts and minds of developers who work at every kind of company with powerful, easy-to-learn communications building blocks they could quickly and confidently incorporate into the apps they're building. So the secret of our success has been empowering a type of worker that few vendors actually treat as their customer: software developers. That's why so many developers know about Twilio, while other parts of the company didn't yet know what we did. Thus, *Ask Your Developer.*

But our Ask Your Developer billboard operated on a second level, too. It was a suggestion to business folks that developers can be great company-building partners as well. At so many companies, developers are disconnected from the business problems they're solving and the customers they're serving. Perhaps by their own choosing, or perhaps because of the engineering and management processes the company has constructed, developers just write the code they're asked to write. The cold, dispassionate process of software development common in some companies is a tragedy both for the business and the developers. I see it as a failure to fully realize the potential of this amazing talent.

But at some high-performing technology companies, developers often play an outsized role not just in the code they're writing but also in the product and business strategy. They treat their products more as a craft than a job and, in doing so, delight customers with digital experiences—think Apple, Google, Spotify, and Uber. Companies that operate this way attract and retain top talent, continually wow customers with innovation, and create outsized returns for shareholders. The Ask Your Developer mindset I lay out in this book is a road map to unlocking technical talent as those tech titans have done.

And it's more important than ever.

As I talk to executives at a broad range of companies, I always hear the same thing: every company is striving to build an environment that produces these kinds of digital products and experiences. Building software has become existential for companies across nearly every industry. Digital transformation has gripped nearly every company as the threat of digital disruption has completely challenged how companies operate. And learning from many of the digital-native startups, company after company is realizing they have to build, not buy, their digital future. Thus unlocking technical talent is actually the key for businesses of every shape and size to compete in the digital era—so the Ask Your Developer mindset isn't just a way of making developers feel appreciated, it's a new way of operating to succeed in the digital economy.

When Netscape founder Marc Andreessen wrote "Why Software Is Eating the World" in 2011, he created the catchphrase for the current migration of every business to software. But he didn't articulate how exactly that would work. In fact, you might believe that just buying software was how this transformation would work. Or that the software would just eat the world on its own in some kind of *Terminator*-like hellscape. Nobody wrote the instruction manual for this transformation.

But in fact companies succeed at digital transformation not just by *using* software but by *building* software. Startups like Uber, Lyft, Airbnb, and Spotify have become household names because they're really good at building software. They know how to write software that changes how we live our lives.

Now incumbents in every other industry are learning to do the same. Nearly every industry is transforming because of software. Digital transformation initiatives take top priority at all kinds of companies. But the companies that become really good at building software are the ones that will ultimately succeed at digital transformation and fend off the threats from digital disruptors. Building software is incredibly hard, and building a culture of digital innovation is even harder.

Because we work with customers of every shape and size, in

pretty much every industry, our customers also seek our advice on how to build and operate a modern software development organization like the digital disruptors have done so successfully. Many of these companies are locked in a Darwinian struggle, fighting off disruptive new competitors. No matter what business they're in—retail, airlines, banking—learning to build great software has become key to their survival. But doing so isn't easy.

Why is that?

I think there's often a false divide between businesspeople and software developers. At many companies, there's a disconnect between the way businesspeople think, and what they want to accomplish, and what the software developers in those companies think they're supposed to do. But it's always struck me that business folks and software developers often want the same things—to build awesome products that delight customers, are massively adopted, and make a lot of money. However, businesspeople and developers often speak different languages and have different working styles—and these differences can inhibit the business and the developers from effectively collaborating to achieve their goals.

Ask Your Developer isn't just a skill set—it's a mindset. Over the last decade, I've met so many people who exhibit this mindset, in every function—from finance to customer support, from marketing to operations, from sales to product—who are building the future of their respective companies as digital businesses. All of those people are builders. There's a misconception sometimes that digital disruption is all about developers. It's not. Yes, companies need developers to build software. But really it's about the successful collaboration between all the functions, and the software developers who actually write the code. It takes a village.

I'm a software developer and have been writing code for nearly twenty-five years, but now I'm also the CEO of a publicly traded company with several thousand employees and, as of summer 2020, a $25 billion market cap, more than $1 billion in revenue, and nearly 200,000 customers. I still write code, but most of my time is spent doing public company CEO things. It puts me in a unique position to help bridge these two points of view and working styles, and help create a more harmonious relationship between businesspeople and software developers. That's the purpose of this book: the Ask Your Developer mindset is designed to help businesspeople better understand and collaborate with technical talent in order to achieve those shared goals.

As a business leader, if it feels like you're screaming from the mountaintops about digital transformation, but change isn't happening fast enough—*Ask Your Developer* can help you recruit and mobilize the talent you need to accelerate change.

If you're frustrated at how slowly your software teams are delivering products, the Ask Your Developer mindset can help you unshackle your teams who, trust me, also want to be moving faster.

If it feels like your technical teams are working incredibly hard but somehow overlooking the big things your customer needs, *Ask Your Developer* can help you get to the root of organizational problems that hinder customer understanding.

If competitors are moving faster at delivering digital delight, maybe they've figured out how to unlock their developers. But don't worry, you can, too. The Ask Your Developer mindset can help.

If you know you need to embrace software and help lead your company through a digital transformation, but you're not sure where to start—*Ask Your Developer* is a good starting point because people are at the heart of every big transformation.

If you're having trouble hiring great technical talent, or worse yet, you hire them but they're leaving before they add value—*Ask Your Developer* can help you create the conditions to attract and retain great developers by unlocking their intrinsic motivation to build.

If you simply don't know what questions to ask in this rapidly changing digital landscape—which is completely common—*Ask Your Developer* is a great starting place to understand what's happening at the heart of this digital disruption.

If you're a technical leader struggling to help your business counterparts understand the complexities of building great software, then *Ask Your Developer* can give you the tools to tighten the collaboration and help bridge the gap with a common parlance.

Even if you're far down the path of digital transformation, rocking and rolling, *Ask Your Developer* can challenge your assumptions about what your software teams are capable of.

You get the point—I believe that business leaders, technical leaders, and technical talent at every stage of digital transformation can benefit from tighter collaboration and a set of shared operating principles. *Ask Your Developer* aims to provide that framework. Think of this book as a toolkit of ideas to help business leaders, product managers, technical leaders, software developers, and executives achieve their common goal—how to win in the digital economy.

Company leaders who build industry-changing software products seem to do three things well. First, they understand why software developers matter more than ever. Second, they understand developers and know how to motivate them. And third, they invest in their developers' success. That's why I've structured the book into these three sections, starting with why developers matter more than ever.

Ready? Onward!

PART I

WHY DEVELOPERS MATTER MORE THAN EVER

CHAPTER 1
BUILD VS. DIE

It is not the strongest species that survive, nor the most intelligent, but the ones most responsive to change.
—Charles Darwin, *On the Origin of Species*

In September 2004 I joined Amazon as a product manager, and at the first all-hands meeting I attended, our founder and CEO, Jeff Bezos, said something that has stuck with me ever since.

When we got to Q&A time, someone in the crowd of about five thousand people got up and asked a question about retailing—I don't even remember exactly what it was. But Jeff came back with an answer most of us didn't expect.

"Amazon," he said, "is not a retailer. We're a software company."

That seemed like a strange thing to say, especially given so many Amazon employees at the time came from either Walmart, an actual retailer, or from Microsoft, an actual software company. Both sets of employees were equally surprised. But Jeff insisted it was true. Most software companies at the time sold software pressed on CD-ROMs, packaged in boxes, and even still bought on a shelf at CompUSA.

Jeff's point was that Amazon was just as much a software company as Microsoft or Oracle or Adobe. It just happened that instead of being the product that we shipped to consumers, our software ran behind the scenes, allowing us to ship brown boxes with books or music or just about anything to someone's doorstep.

"Our business is not what's in the brown boxes," he said. "It's the software that sends the brown boxes on their way." We monetized our software not by selling it directly, but by selling everything else—books, DVDs, and CDs. What's more, the quality of our software would determine whether we succeeded: "Our ability to win," Jeff said, "is based on our ability to arrange magnetic particles on hard drives better than our competition."

I still think that's an incredibly cool way to describe what we did. If you have ever wondered how Amazon became such a global powerhouse over the years that have followed that 2004 all-hands—it's contained in that statement. The key to Amazon's success is that Jeff Bezos understood way sooner than everyone else that he was actually in the software business.

In the early 2000s it seemed that retailers would be threatened by disruption from e-commerce. But as the century progresses on, it's apparent that not just retailers are under siege. Why is it that every industry is rapidly becoming a software industry? That's because there's a true Darwinian evolution playing out—I call it "Build vs. Die."

It's likely that your industry and your company are changing rapidly due to the threats, and opportunities, posed by what software can do. When Amazon is mentioned in the context of your industry, does everybody in the room tense up? That's why digital transformation is a hot topic at so many companies, but how to navigate this change is not well understood. If you're like many leaders responsible for driving this change, you're bombarded with software app vendors or consultants who promise to solve it for you. You're inundated with promises, but you're skeptical that just cutting a big check will solve all your problems. And you're right.

It's not as easy as just buying a digital disruption strategy from a software company or a consultant. Great companies learn to *build*. Let's see why.

FROM COST CENTER TO STRATEGIC CENTERPIECE

For a long time, most companies considered IT something that supported the business—software and servers that ran the back office, or the PC on every desk. You had big software to manage the financials, and an even bigger enterprise resource planning (ERP) system to keep tabs on inventory, shipments, and other kinds of complex logistics. But essentially this was all bookkeeping—of money and materials that mattered mostly to the bean counters. IT also ensured employees had computers to do their job and printers to, well, print things. In the 1980s and '90s, these were all cost centers, meaning they cost the company money and did not, in and of themselves, make money. So it made sense for many companies to cut corners as much as possible and outsource this function, often to offshore firms where talent was less expensive.

When a chief information officer of a company was looking to implement a new solution, they would often undertake the well-known "Build vs. Buy" process to ask whether they should buy a piece of off-the-shelf software or build their own. Sometimes companies decided to build, but that was difficult and risky, so for the most part, companies chose to buy a vendor solution. After all, the vendors had a good point. Why would any company build their own financial software or ERP system when they could just buy one off the shelf? The upside of building your own was limited. No customer ever cared what ERP system your company used. And if you tried to build your own and screwed up, the consequences were dire. You couldn't track your inventory, or you couldn't report your financials to Wall Street. There was a famous saying: Nobody ever got fired for buying IBM. So pretty much every company just bought software and went along their way.

But along came the web, and then mobile, and suddenly the interface that most companies had with their customers became digital. Software went from the back of the business to the front. Instead of just automating back-office chores, software became the face that a company presents to the world. Instead of walking into your bank, you used an app. You didn't walk into a store, you shopped online instead.

This had two critical implications for the world of software:

First, customers suddenly did care about the software that companies used because the customers directly interfaced with it. If you had a better website or mobile app than your competition, it would be a good reason for customers to pick you.

Second, it meant that new competition could enter the market more easily. To become a bank or a retailer, you didn't need to open up a branch or store on every street corner. You just needed an app and a warehouse somewhere.

These two trends became apparent in the early 2000s. Suddenly startups that were great at building software, and had no legacy infrastructure or storefronts to deal with, began springing up. These digital native companies focused their early energy on creating great customer experiences, and they used their software-building expertise to their advantage. The new playing field was digital, and they brought an A-game.

Uber and Lyft, without owning a single taxi, in less than five years used software to completely overhaul how people get around cities. Airbnb challenged the global hotel industry without owning the real estate.

One of my favorite examples is Casper, the mattress company. Casper makes mattresses and distributes them directly to consumers via their website. I was always intrigued with how Casper could be considered a tech company, raising substantial money from Silicon Valley venture capitalists and fetching tech-like valuations in the process. Could there be an industry that feels less like technology than the pile of springs and fabric you sleep on?! But indeed Casper is a tech company. The technology isn't about the product itself, but about how they acquire customers, how they distribute the product, and ultimately how they make the customers feel throughout the whole process of buying and using the product. Because of technology, they can do it at scale with minimal investment. They use digital engagement strategies to grow incredibly fast. Just five years since their founding, they're doing nearly $500 million in revenue with fewer than one hundred employees. By contrast, Tempur Sealy, the largest mattress company in the world, employs seven thousand people to generate $2.7 billion in revenue. Think about the leverage that technology is giving Casper—Tempur Sealy is doing five times as much revenue, but has *seventy* times as many employees. Whether Tempur Sealy will ultimately beat Casper at their own game is yet to be known, but the war is on.

This is repeating in every industry. Take razors: startup Harry's has started to challenge the incumbent Gillette. In investing, startup Robinhood is challenging Fidelity, T. Rowe Price, and other century-old institutions for your brokerage account. Opendoor is shaking up the real estate business by changing the way houses are bought and sold. In industry after industry, digital native companies are using technology to bring a new kind of product to market, faster, cheaper, and with a better customer experience than the incumbents.

Another way to think of this: *Software has moved from being a cost center to the profit center.*

That's how the ferocious and relentless Darwinian competition kicks in. Suddenly, software isn't a liability to be outsourced. It is the source of competitive advantage. Digital natives—the startups that know how to build software—start to win market share. In response, one of the incumbents, intent on fending off the upstart, reverses the IT-outsourcing trend and starts assembling their in-house software teams to compete. One by one, every player in the industry (the ones that intend to survive, at least) becomes a builder. It's unavoidable. It's mandatory. That's why I call this a Darwinian evolution of every industry. It's no longer a question of Build vs. Buy. Rather, it's the existential question of Build vs. Die. It's natural selection driven by customers, who pick the companies that serve them better in this digital era.

Take mattresses again. In response to Casper, Tempur Sealy launched "Cocoon by Sealy," which offers an end-to-end online experience similar to Casper. Take that! The Empire Strikes Back! Think about your bank. It probably offers the same things that every other bank offers. Checking account, savings account—it's a fiercely competitive business. So what differentiates one bank from another? It used to be about the experience inside the bank branch. What did it look like? Was it recently remodeled? Were the employees well dressed and friendly? Did they give you cookies? Did they give your kid a lollipop? But now, you don't walk into a branch, you open an app. So banks need different skills—software skills. And they can't just *buy* all this software from a vendor. To be sure, there's no shortage of companies that will claim to sell the software that banks need to perform a digital transformation. But if all the banks just bought the same bank software, they'd all be undifferentiated again. So ultimately, they have to listen to customers' needs and answer those needs with software by learning and iterating quickly.

Companies that adapt to the new digital landscape will serve customers better, and will survive. Those that don't will die. It may not be overnight, but it's inevitable. It's as simple as that. It doesn't matter what business you're in. Banks. Airlines. Automakers. Insurance companies. Real estate. Retailers. Health care. Sure, you also have to deliver a great product or service at a competitive price. But in every market, the company with the best software will eventually win. As Jeff Immelt, the former CEO of GE and a member of our Twilio board of directors, once told his executive team at GE: "If we don't become the best technology company in the world, we're doomed. We're dead. There's no Plan B."

"It's a quest for survival," says Werner Vogels, the legendary chief technology officer at Amazon and one of the chief architects of Amazon Web Services, the world's biggest cloud computing platform, with dozens of data centers girdling the globe. Vogels is a huge guy, six foot six and built like an NFL linebacker. He has a doctorate in computer science and spent more than a decade in academia before joining Amazon.

These days a big part of his job involves traveling the world and helping traditional companies adapt and survive. He also stars in a video series called *Now Go Build*, which Amazon launched to celebrate companies that are building software. Helping customers also helps Amazon. "Our whole cloud would be useless if people don't know how to use it. We have to help them get good at organizational change, as well as the cultural change, and then show them how to adopt the technology," Vogels says. Most companies have embraced cloud computing, but they struggle with how to become software-centric organizations. "It's the most asked question," Vogels says. "Customers will ask us, 'How do we do this?' They're really trying to learn from companies like Amazon."

One big hurdle is staffing up. Giant multinationals that spent the 2000s outsourcing most of their tech operations are now unwinding those deals and bringing software development back in-house. "The larger enterprises know that digital is becoming their lifeblood, so they need to take control over it instead of turning to outsourcers. But it's also their biggest challenge," Vogels says.

Another challenge is speed. Digital natives can turn a great idea into production code in a matter of weeks—or even days. They roll out new iterations every day. For traditional companies, keeping up means speeding up. "You can no longer afford to spend six months or twelve months in development before you launch," Vogels says.

Don't believe me? Ask Blockbuster. Ask Borders. Ask Nokia. Ask Yellow Taxi. They're victims of the digital revolution, because they didn't adapt quickly enough—the dodo birds of digital Darwinism.

HOW SOFTWARE PEOPLE THINK

To truly thrive in the digital era—either as a disruptor or those fending off the disruptors—you need to think like a Software Person. Now, a Software Person is not necessarily a developer—it's anybody who, when faced with a problem, asks the question: "How can software solve this problem?" That's because being a Software Person is a mindset, not a skill set.

Software People are the ones who see the world through the lens of software. They are endlessly optimistic, because they believe that any business problem can be solved once it's brought into the domain of software. Bringing more and more of the world's problems into the domain of software is exactly what technologists have been doing for the last seventy years.

If you think about what a computer is—it's a machine that performs mathematical calculations, with a set of sensors (inputs) and actuators (outputs) attached. Those sensors and actuators are the only way we know what's happening inside the machine, and you can look at the history of computers really as the continual progression of more and more sophisticated sensors and actuators that allow us to "compute" on more and more of the world. The first two decades of computing—the 1950s and '60s—were about mathematical calculations, and we used punch cards to get numbers into and out of computers—so we could apply software to them. We used computers to calculate missile trajectories and the national debt, but not much else. In 1960, only a few thousand computers existed in the world. But then we advanced our sensors and actuators, enabling them to get text into and out of computers—so we could apply software to textual problems—and the next two decades were about computing on text, not just numbers. With keyboards and printers, the 1970s and '80s were about word processing, desktop publishing, and spreadsheets, and every desk got a PC. Then we advanced those sensors and actuators again, enabling them to digitize audio and video. Computers got sophisticated graphics and sound cards, and the 1990s and 2000s were about multimedia—bringing us MP3s, PC gaming, and *Jurassic Park*. Now, however, with always-connected smartphones in our pockets, we're carrying an array of sensors and actuators, constantly connected to the Internet—bringing the rest of the world into the domain of software. Thus the 2010s and 2020s are about computing on just about everything else. That's what's made the last decade (and will make the next decade!) so exciting. The category of problems to which we can apply the software mindset is exploding.

It's not just software itself—it's the fundamental agility of software that drives Software People. It starts by listening to customers, rapidly building initial solutions to their problems, getting feedback, and then constantly iterating and improving. With this progression of computation, Software People can apply this software process to more and more of the world's problems. I particularly enjoy seeing it arise in traditionally hardware-centric fields because when you see a Software Person running the playbook in the field of hardware, you can see the evolution play out physically in plastic, metal, and glass.

Consider what Apple did to the TV remote control. Before Apple released Apple TV, set-top boxes came with a remote control with a hundred buttons. Some even advertised the number of buttons as a selling point! Next to each button was a label: Volume Up/Down, Channel Up/Down, Favorites, PiP, Source, Menu, and so forth. The first Apple TV remote had only seven buttons. Why? Because all the smarts of the Apple TV resides in the software running on the device. That means Apple can learn from customers and update the software constantly with new features and functionality. Developers can't iterate on things that are fixed in plastic and metal—once the gizmo leaves the factory, its functionality is set for life. So the decision to remove the buttons isn't just aesthetic, it's incredibly strategic. When I first saw the minimalist Apple TV remote, I thought: *Oh, this is a software game now.*

This is the same thought process Steve Jobs brought to the iPhone in 2007. He mocked all the phones with physical keyboards because, he correctly noted, the keyboard was always there whether you needed it or not. You could never update it, you couldn't change languages, and you couldn't get rid of it when you didn't want it. The real estate on the device was always and forever a bunch of keys in the arrangement and language that the device shipped with. The iPhone keyboard is software. It disappears when you don't need it, which is most of the time. It can change to an emoji keyboard when needed, or another language if you're multilingual, which means Apple can ship one SKU worldwide. The language you need is just software, not something that has to be fixed at the factory.

Another example: the Square credit card reader. Traditional credit card machines are big hunks of plastic, with screens that look like they're taken from a 1990s-era scientific calculator, and a handful of buttons. When a new method of payment comes around, or screens with more than a hundred pixels become available, you have to throw the whole thing away. Everything that credit card reader could do was fixed at the factory in plastic and silicon. By contrast, the Square reader is just the minimal interface needed to bridge the physical world (a magnetic stripe reader) and the software world. Everything else can be done in software—which Square can update every week. The software grows smarter with every revision, getting new features and fixing bugs. Square can iterate and learn at the speed of software, because its developers pushed absolutely everything into software, leaving only the minimal bits of plastic needed to get the job done. With contactless payments, more physical bits are starting to disappear. The less hardware you have to work around, the more software people can do their software thing.

Another example is the Tesla. The average car has dozens of buttons on the dashboard. Most Tesla cars, by contrast, have just four buttons and two scroll wheels in the steering wheel. Everything else is software running on that giant screen. The buttons in a Tesla don't even have labels. That's so everything can be treated as software and updated constantly as Tesla gets customer feedback. That can mean fun things like the infotainment system, where they've added things over time like Caraoke (yes, an in-dash karaoke system) and YouTube, but also critical safety advances.

In October 2013, a Tesla owner ran over a bit of debris on the freeway, which punctured the car's battery and started a fire. The Model S alerted the driver to the issue, and he safely pulled over and got out minutes before the car was engulfed in flames. But it was a PR disaster for Tesla. To make the car safer, Tesla decided to make it ride an inch higher at highway speeds. At most companies, this would have required a recall—costing the automaker tens or hundreds of millions of dollars, and creating a huge inconvenience to owners. But Tesla just issued an over-the-air update, modifying the suspension to increase the ride height at highway speeds by one inch—problem solved. That's the software mindset at work.

I love how obvious the software mindset is on display in these kinds of hardware companies—you literally see how they remove every bit of glass and plastic imaginable, so that only the absolutely required physical interface to the world is left. But even if your business isn't hardware, the lessons are the same. How much of your industry is digital versus analog. What would happen if you could iterate on your key experiences and workflows on a weekly basis? That's the software mindset at work, beginning by digitizing your physical reality, and then applying the software mindset to problem-solving.

Every kind of company can become a software company—all you have to do is internalize the value of rapid iteration. You don't need to be Elon Musk or Jack Dorsey; you just need to believe in the power of iteration, and Darwin will be on your side. But of course, to iterate, you first need to build. You can't iterate on something you've bought off the shelf.

That's why it's Build vs. Die.

WHY BUYING SOFTWARE NO LONGER MAKES SENSE

The problem is that, by definition, a one-size-fits-all piece of software doesn't suit anyone very well. And if every company buys the same software, no company can differentiate itself. They are all just the same as their competitors, at least as seen through the digital lens—which is increasingly the only lens that matters.

One of our customers said it incredibly well: with off-the-shelf software apps, you have to change your business to match the software—which is crazy! Really, you should change the *software* to build the business your customers need.

You might be able to customize off-the-shelf applications, but it will never be a perfect fit. Worse, you will have to wait for the software maker to deliver upgrades. And even when a new version ships, it will take what feels like forever to roll it out across your organization. As for special features—customization that isn't on the menu—well, you can submit requests to the product team, then wait and hope.

The problem gets magnified when an organization is managing a bunch of programs from different software makers. You can try to stitch programs together, but they will never work seamlessly with one another. And if you change one, it might throw off the others. When something goes wrong, the software makers start pointing fingers at each other.

The worst thing is that everything takes too long. The purchase process itself takes forever, beginning with a "request for proposal," or RFP. You will spend months reviewing proposals and listening to sales pitches from software vendors who hope to win your business. You'll run "bake-offs" to compare the products. Meetings are held. Opinions are solicited. Presentations are given. Sweeteners are added: *Buy our HR software, and we'll throw in our CRM package at a discounted rate.* Then you spend months negotiating the contracts, and finally the winning software company sends in a squad of consultants who spend months, sometimes even years, installing the software. By the time it's up and running, you have a piece of software that meets your needs . . . from two years ago! Awesome!

You could almost get away with this when all of your competitors bought software this way. But now your competitors are shipping updates on a weekly basis, maybe even daily. There's no way that some clunky, crumbly, duct-taped, off-the-shelf app can do what theirs does. It's like a drag race between a tractor and a Tesla.

You don't have to be in Silicon Valley to see the Build vs. Die battle play out. In fact, you just need to look to the Netherlands.

BUILD VS. BUY IN BANKING

One of my favorite stories about a Darwinian struggle for survival involves two banks in the Netherlands. One is ING, a traditional organization that is radically overhauling every aspect of its business with a software mindset. The other is Bunq, a mobile bank headquartered in Amsterdam that has no physical branches—it's basically a bank made entirely out of software, stored on the cloud and viewed on mobile phones.

Bunq's founder and CEO, Ali Niknam, has been writing software since he was a kid. He doesn't even think of Bunq as a bank, but rather as a software company. Because Bunq writes its own software, instead of buying off-the-shelf banking apps, they create incredibly tight feedback loops between developers and customers. The developers constantly solicit feedback from customers about what features they want or which things they don't like. The developers fire back new features almost overnight. Users are dazzled—and loyal.

Ali was born in Canada. His parents are Iranian. They moved to the Netherlands when he was seven. At nine, he began coding. At twelve, he started investing in stocks, and at sixteen he started a company. In 2003, at age twenty-one, he started TransIP, which grew to become the third largest domain and hosting provider in the world. (Think of it as the Dutch version of GoDaddy.) Four years later Ali founded the Datacenter Group, the largest data center operator in the Netherlands. Then in 2012, at age thirty, he had a revelation: "I figured out that I love to create products that people love to use and that I wanted to do something for the greater good, something with a social impact."

He looked at various ideas and realized that when it came to technology and innovation, "banking was stuck in the Dark Ages." He figured the entire industry was due for an overhaul. Most banks were still running ancient mainframe computers from the 1970s. Their websites and mobile apps were terrible. They all offered the same things at the same price. Nobody was innovating. Customers were stuck. "There was no real freedom of choice in the financial sector. There was more choice in buying ketchup than there was with something as important as your money. Something needed changing," he says.

Instead of trying to make a slightly better version of what banks were doing, Ali says, "I went back and figured, if you could start fresh today and build a way to purchase things, and save money, and transfer money to a friend, what would that look like?"

Bunq's user interface looks and feels like a modern social networking app—simple, clean, and personalized, with bright vertical stripes in rainbow colors with the word *bunq* in lowercase letters and the company's simple slogan: BANK OF THE FREE. The app looks at home next to Uber, Waze, Spotify, and the other apps on your iPhone or Android device. That doesn't seem like such a huge accomplishment, but comparing Bunq's user interface to most banks' apps, you'll see the difference.

Setting up a new Bunq account takes just a few minutes. Just like with a social app, you create a profile with your photo, name, and nickname. It's easy to set up shared accounts and sub-accounts. A couple can have a shared account for household expenses but personal accounts for their individual hobbies. Customers can create many sub-accounts—one for groceries, one for the soccer team, another for the school fund-raiser. To switch accounts, you just enter a different PIN code.

Bunq offers cool travel features. If you're going on a trip with a group of friends, you can set up a "Slice Group" to keep track of who paid for what. When you get back and want to settle up the expenses, you tap a button and it's done. Most Bunq customers get a debit card, but Bunq also offers a Travel Card, backed by MasterCard, that charges no monthly fee and no extra fees for currency exchange. The card acts like a debit card and draws on your account but can also serve as a credit card. Because some customers don't want to take on debt, Bunq sends "realtime balance checks" so people can keep track of how much money they have and stop spending (or replenish the account) instead of running up credit card charges.

Bunq's customer demographic (so far) skews toward younger people who care about social causes. Bunq offers a service that lets customers choose what Bunq does with the money they deposit. If you don't want your money invested in companies that oppose climate change legislation, Bunq will follow your instructions. In a similar vein, Bunq offers a "Green Card," and for every hundred euros you spend, the company will plant a tree.

Ali has bankrolled the whole project himself, investing €45 million to date. His biggest hurdle wasn't technology; it was regulators. In 2012, no company had gained a permit for a new bank in the Netherlands for thirty-five years. "It had been so long that nobody knew how to hand out a permit anymore," he says. It didn't help that Bunq was "a new player with twenty people operating from a vacant building in the middle of nowhere." On the other hand, regulators realized the banking sector needed an infusion of new ideas. After three years, Bunq received a permit in late 2015. "It was magical that we actually pulled it off," Ali says.

It took a year to write the first version of the software, with Ali writing 20 percent of the code himself. In 2016 Bunq opened for business, and by the end of 2019 it was operating in thirty European countries. The entire customer experience was a mobile app—they didn't even have a web version until 2019. Bunq operates entirely in the cloud, using Twilio, Amazon Web Services, and others. They also run incredibly lean, with fewer than two hundred employees. Yes, you read that right. This is the thing that should terrify incumbent banks—the scale and efficiency of software is unprecedented. The culture is so engineering-driven that Ali doesn't even describe Bunq as a bank but rather "a tech company that happens to have a bank attached to it." Now that Bunq is gaining momentum, it's the model of a digital disruptor, and the incumbents are taking note.

...

One of those rivals is located just across town—ING, whose roots reach back to the 1700s and which manages more than $1 trillion in assets. It's about as far from a startup as you can get, and it competes in an industry that is notoriously stodgy, risk-averse, and highly regulated. Yet ING has become one of the most innovative software development organizations in the world. Over the past few years I've had the pleasure of working with ING and becoming a part of its transformation. One reason that ING has succeeded is that the change began at the very top of the organization, with Ralph Hamers, a tech-savvy executive who was promoted to CEO in 2013.

A few years ago, ING radically overhauled its culture. Part of that change involved allowing developers to operate with tremendous creative freedom. Starting at the top with Hamers, they've adopted agile processes. But it wasn't just the software engineering organization—the entire company, down to the brick-and-mortar branches, started operating with agile practices. There's even a video titled "The agile way of working at ING" on their corporate website, describing the company-wide transformation. Every unit organizes into small teams, operates on two-week sprints, and holds stand-ups. That's how they're fighting the onslaught of new digital disruptors, like Bunq. It's Build vs. Die playing out live in the banking industry. I've been privy to seeing the results of this transformation firsthand, as Twilio worked with a small team of ING developers who pulled off a project so ambitious that it absolutely blew our minds.

In 2015, an ING engineering manager named Theo Frieswijk reached out to us looking for help building a new contact center system. Theo manages forty engineers who support contact center systems used by more than ten thousand support agents at ING locations all around the globe. Over the years ING has grown by acquiring banks. They all used different contact center systems. All told, ING was running seventeen different systems developed by seventeen different commercial software companies, running in all sorts of on-premises data centers. Maintaining this hodgepodge was a nightmare. "Nine months out of the year we would have to work on upgrade projects simply because the vendor would no longer support the previous version, and upgrading one component meant that you also had to upgrade another component and yet another and yet another, so this would very quickly turn into very big projects," Theo says.

Not only was this concoction of legacy systems a pain for the software engineers to maintain, but it also meant the bank's 38 million customers were not getting the best possible service. Over the years, when the existing solution didn't have some needed functionality, they'd bring in another solution. That's why their contact centers had bloated unsustainably. Management wanted Theo's team to choose one of those contact center solution vendors and make it the standard for all of the company. Theo pitched management a different idea. Instead of buying yet another monolithic system and hoping for a better outcome this time, why not let his team build their own contact center system from scratch, which would allow them to build as needed to solve each incremental problem or try each new idea. It would be an investment but ultimately let them become more agile, which was one of the company's top priorities. Leaders were curious, if not skeptical at the onset.

Theo and his team argued that no matter which off-the-shelf commercial package the bank chose, it would still be a lowest-common-denominator solution. The software would be generic, meant to appeal to the largest number of potential clients and not a perfect fit for any single company. Building in-house meant ING could create a bespoke system that did exactly what ING needed.

At first glance this seemed not just audacious—but insane. Contact center systems aren't very sexy, but they are incredibly complex. Most are sold by companies like Avaya and Genesys, which have roots in the telecom industry. These companies have been building contact centers for decades, yet here were these developers in the IT department of a bank claiming they could create something better than what these giant specialized software makers produce.

Not only that, but Theo vowed his team could create an entire contact system from the ground up in less time than it would take the bank to select a commercial software vendor and roll out its software, and for less money. Most important, ING would own the code, so developers could improve their system as often as they wanted, rolling out new code every day if need be, instead of waiting for a commercial vendor to ship an upgrade maybe once or twice a year.

Theo wasn't making this bold proposal based on instinct. He had been doing research. In 2014 he started tracking new software companies, like Twilio, that don't sell finished software applications but instead sell the building blocks that developers can combine to build their own applications. (I describe this shift in Chapter 2.)

In 2015, Theo and his colleagues traveled to San Francisco to attend our SIGNAL conference. They asked us if they could use Twilio to build a contact center. A few months later a team of Twilio engineers flew to Amsterdam and ran a three-day hackathon with ING engineers. "We just worked on a number of scenarios that in an ideal world we would be able to do but were difficult in the old world," Theo says. "In three days we created a lot more than we actually had expected we would be able to do. That got us really enthusiastic. After that hackathon we were convinced that we could build a contact center and move toward architecture that uses APIs and microservices."

This experience gave Theo the courage to pitch his idea to management. Maybe it was not as insane as it seemed at first glance. But it was still a huge gamble. In fact, it's the kind of bet upon which IT careers in the old world are ruined. That's another reason why big corporations are so reluctant to change and why they continue to lag behind startups—because the top brass has a "shame and blame" culture, and the people who run the tech group don't want to take risks. The safest bet has always been to go with some big commercial vendor. Sure, the software might not be great. But when things go wrong, the vendor takes the blame, not you. Tech department decision makers might be fully aware that buying more off-the-shelf software is a terrible move. They know the company should be making radical changes. But who cares? It's easier and safer to just kick the problem down the road. Let the next person deal with it.

That mindset arises from the way many cultures respond to failure. The norm is that if you launch a big initiative and it fails (in any department, not just tech), it would certainly limit your career. In more agile cultures, failure isn't punished. Instead, it's a learning opportunity. The mindset of embracing risk and tolerating failure is a huge part of the software ethos. It's also one of the biggest things that old companies avoid—even those with leaders who claim, as many do, that they want to become more like a startup.

This brings me to an important point:

If you want to become a software builder, you need to start by changing the mindset of the entire organization.

It's not enough to just hire a bunch of new developers, or to change the way developers do their jobs. None of that will work unless you also change the culture around them. Otherwise, you're just planting a new tree in barren soil. One reason Theo got the green light is that ING itself was in the midst of its radical company-wide overhaul. This kind of innovation might not have been possible prior to CEO Hamers's intense focus on agility.

As for the risk, Theo says he thrives on that. "I want to make a difference. I want to achieve something. For me this was a big opportunity. And you're not going to be happy if you don't take any risks."

In the spring of 2016 the engineers started working on the project, dubbed "Contact Center 2.0." Many companies had added Twilio to their contact centers, but nobody had built a complete brand-new contact center quite like this. "There was nothing we could point to. The combination of all this functionality is something that nobody had done before, and for me that's actually something that I liked." The engineers were enthusiastic and believed they could succeed, but "quite a lot of people were skeptical that we could pull this off," Theo says.

In summer 2017 the engineers began pilot-testing Contact Center 2.0 in a few locations, and quickly expanded to all the contact centers in the Netherlands. By the end of 2019, Contact Center 2.0 was being used by eleven thousand agents in seven countries; the global rollout is expected to be finished by the end of 2021.

The bet began paying off immediately. Engineers make constant tweaks and upgrades, pushing code every week and constantly getting feedback from "customers," meaning ING's support agents as well as the bank's end users. "Things are fast. Things are real-time. We don't need downtime for maintenance. We can deploy new changes as often as we want," Theo says.

Also, the code is more reliable, and agents can resolve calls faster, which has reduced wait times. The system is so good that other companies now visit ING to find out how they can build something similar. Even our engineers at Twilio are constantly learning new things about our own product by watching what ING does with it.

ING's next big push is to get its developers from all over the globe contributing to the platform. In 2019, developers in Amsterdam launched a pilot program with developers at an ING subsidiary in the Philippines. That subsidiary has no brick-and-mortar branch locations and runs only on mobile phones. Developers there are experts at creating cool features for mobile phones. They also have tweaked the contact center software to suit their very different needs. They share their new features with the core team in Amsterdam, which integrates them into the core platform.

That means instead of having a small team in Amsterdam doing all the work, ING can harness the creativity of dozens more developers around the globe—which accelerates the development process.

"In the next couple of years we're going to see an exponential increase in our speed of innovation. That's what we're aiming for with this platform. The first rollout is focused on replacing the existing telephony systems. But the big advantage is yet to come."

The success of the Contact Center 2.0 project is a testament to the skills of the engineers at ING and proof that "regular IT people" can transform into ace developers who build world-class software. These world-class software builders are everywhere. Companies need to find them and turn them loose. Make them feel like owners. Theo says the project has been the highlight of his career. Ever modest, Theo credits his engineers as well as the top brass at ING, which dared to let his group take a big risk. "I'm two levels below the CIO, but I feel that I can be entrepreneurial and try things and even make mistakes," he says.

In a Build vs. Die world, ING Bank is the model of evolution.

I happened to pick a banking example to demonstrate Build vs. Die in action. It's hard to imagine an industry more immune to disruption, given the high stakes (people's money!) and the byzantine regulations involved. Yet even banking is becoming a software industry. I'm not even talking about the potential impacts of Bitcoin and other cryptocurrency; I'm just talking about the basics of how to run a retail bank, acquire customers, and keep them happy.

These dynamics are playing out in every industry, all around the world: in Munich, at Allianz, the world's biggest insurer; in the United States, at Domino's, Target, and U-Haul. Whether they are cooking pizzas or writing insurance policies, renting trucks or delivering tulips—no matter what their business, they're all becoming software companies.

Build vs. Die is becoming a natural law of business, just as evolution defines organic life on earth. This is simply survival of the fittest, where fitness is defined by how well companies can arrange magnetic particles.

To gauge how prepared you are for the new Build vs. Die reality, you might consider asking your senior technical leaders how they make Build vs. Buy decisions. What technologies are table stakes, and should be bought, and which digital innovations are the differentiators between you and your competition? Dig in on the answers—many of the factors people perceive as differentiating have become table stakes over the last decade. What analog bits of your business should you invest in digitizing? What off-the-shelf software solutions are holding you back? How often do you hear "We can't do that"? Instead of accepting the answer, ask your teams what changes or investments could change the answer to "Yes, we can build that!"

CHAPTER 2

THE NEW SOFTWARE SUPPLY CHAIN

What matters isn't how you *use servers*,
but rather how you *serve users*.
—Me, 2010

As I noted in Chapter 1, I believe every company that's going to survive and thrive in the digital economy needs to build software. Thus, your supply chain matters. If your digital supply chain is better than your competitors', you'll be in a much stronger position to succeed. Conversely, if your supply chain is lagging or nonexistent, and your competitors are getting better every day with a supply chain that's accelerating their lead, you'll always be behind. Chances are, your digital supply chain is not a commonly discussed idea at your company—it's a brand-new concept. But understanding the emergence of the digital supply chain, and how to best leverage it to build your lead, is critical to success in the digital economy.

Think about industries that produce physical goods—things like cars, refrigerators, houses. They have mature supply chains. Auto manufacturers don't create every piece of a car themselves. They buy steel from a steel company, leather from a leather company, seats from a seat company, speedometers from a speedometer company, and so on. All those Camrys and F-150 pickup trucks zipping past you on the highway contain parts provided by hundreds, maybe thousands, of major suppliers. Those suppliers in turn draw from hundreds or even thousands of smaller part makers along the global supply chain. As industries mature, so do their supply chains, allowing many companies to specialize in parts of the process, making the entire industry more efficient and productive.

Until recently, the software industry had no such thing. Most software companies—think of companies like Microsoft, Oracle, or SAP—pretty much wrote all of their own software end to end. That worked when software was a highly specialized field and there were relatively few software companies, right up through the 1990s and into the 2000s. That notion was especially true when software companies sold products as downloads or CD-ROMs.

But now every company is becoming a software company, and most companies can't build everything from scratch. They need a supply chain—just like Ford and Toyota—that divides the industry into areas of expertise and allows each company in the ecosystem to specialize on its core competency. But the software supply chain looks different. Instead of specializing in speedometers or steering wheels, software supply chain companies deliver reusable chunks of code that developers bring together to make finished applications. These are Application Programming Interfaces (APIs). Each API supplier provides only a piece of the solution. Amazon Web Services delivers the data center. Twilio provides communications. Stripe and PayPal enable payments. Modern apps integrate dozens of these small components into a unique value proposition for the customer. This shift to component software is the next big leap in the evolution of the software industry.

I call it the *Third Great Era of Software.*

This trend—from solutions to building blocks—was best predicted by a 1990s-era IBM commercial. A raggy-haired consultant is showing a business owner their first website, which seems to have been made without much input from the business owner. The consultant finishes by saying, "Now you have a choice . . . between the spinning logo or the flaming logo." The upper left corner of the website (where the logo always stood back on those days) had the company's logo, cheesily spinning in circles, or animated with amateurish flames. The nonplussed businessman responds, "Okay, but can it optimize my supply chain?" This idea was that packaged software with only cosmetic flexibility would never satiate the needs of a fast-moving, complex business. And now, more than twenty years later, that commercial has proven incredibly prescient. But, as is often the case, the incumbent is not the company that made it a reality.

A BRIEF HISTORY OF SOFTWARE

To understand the new way of thinking about software, we need to look back at how the software industry began and how it has evolved.

At first, companies ran mainframes. Many still do—more than you might imagine, in fact. Then came minicomputers, Unix workstations, and finally the PC. Anyone under the age of thirty might not remember this, but when the personal computer came out, the software programs literally came on floppy disks. Later they shipped on CDs. Software literally came in boxes! You drove to a brick-and-mortar store like Babbage's, Egghead Software, or Software Etc., and you took it off a shelf. Seriously, those stores were rad.

From mainframes to PCs, the computers kept getting smaller, the operating systems changed, but the software industry pretty much used the same business model. A software maker would invest

R&D dollars to create an application, then sell it to individual users or to huge enterprises. Selling to consumers was a good business. But selling to enterprises, the way Microsoft, SAP, and Oracle did, was a great business. From the standpoint of profitability, selling packaged software to big corporations might be the greatest business in history. You built software once, and incurred practically no incremental cost for each unit sold.

But for these business customers, the whole scheme was a huge pain in the neck. Each company had to have its own IT department, which would rack and stack servers, and install and maintain this infrastructure. Most of the software programs were ones that ran back-end office chores, like financials and ERP. These big enterprise software projects were notoriously prone to failure—at one point, more than 70 percent of these big installations were never actually completed successfully. These projects took so long to implement that oftentimes multiple generations of company leaders would come and go before they were completed.

And importantly, companies weren't using all this software to deliver better experiences to customers or differentiate themselves in the market. They just used software to run their internal operations—accounting, enterprise resource planning, and the like. And if you were a line-of-business owner inside a company, such as a head of sales or HR, and you wanted software to run your department—well, you had to send a request to IT and then get in line.

This problem got solved when the second era of software—Software as a Service (SaaS)—began, about twenty years ago. The company that pioneered this model is Salesforce. Its founder and CEO, Marc Benioff, interned as an assembly language programmer at Apple (translation: he was a hard-core coder) and after university joined Oracle, where he quickly became a legendary salesman.

He won Rookie of the Year and was promoted to vice president while in his mid-twenties, the youngest ever at Oracle. In 1999 he launched Salesforce with the slogan "The End of Software." Of course it wasn't actually the end of software—it was just a new way of delivering software.

With SaaS, line-of-business owners who needed a new software program didn't need to send a request to the IT department and then get in line and wait for them to undertake a huge multimillion-dollar, multiyear initiative. Instead, the head of sales could just go to Salesforce, fill out some online forms—and almost instantly have their whole department up and running on a best-in-class sales automation software product. The sales chief didn't need to know anything about IT, and didn't need to rack up servers or install software or hire IT staff to maintain the system. Just fill out a form, and you were in business.

Over time, SaaS companies sprang up to serve every line-of-business owner. The chief financial officer (CFO) reached out to NetSuite, provider of SaaS financials software. The chief marketing officer signed up for Marketo, provider of SaaS marketing automation. The chief human resources (HR) officer signed up for Workday, provider of SaaS HR information software. You paid based on the number of employees who were using the software. You didn't have to worry about data centers or per-CPU licenses anymore. In fact, many products were so inexpensive to get started that a small team could just put it on a credit card and expense it.

The model also came to be known as cloud computing, which became possible because of high-speed Internet connections and what's called "multi-tenant" software. Once we had superfast Internet backbones, people realized you could zip bits from a server located thousands of miles just as quickly as you could from a server down the hall or across campus in the company's own data center.

(Or at least the difference was so small that people using the program couldn't tell the difference.) In cloud computing, you no longer needed to run your own data centers. And individual employees didn't need to run local versions of a program on their PCs. They could just do everything they needed to do via a web browser. That made life easier in all sorts of ways. If a software program had a bug and needed to be updated, or if the software vendor released a new version of the app silently, customers didn't need to send IT guys to everyone's desk and install the new version. Those fixes and upgrades just happened—out in the cloud. To the user, this was all invisible.

Another change involved the business model. Instead of paying to license a program based on how many servers you deployed—including a big initial payment up front and then paying annual maintenance fees—you just subscribed. When you stopped needing the software, you ended your subscription, not unlike a magazine subscription.

When Salesforce started out, in 1999, a lot of people thought Benioff was nuts. Why would anyone pay for software but never actually take possession of it? What would happen if the Internet went down? Remember that in those days the Internet wasn't speedy and reliable enough for SaaS. By 2001, only 6 percent of Americans had broadband Internet access. Most connected via squonky dial-up modems, according to the Pew Research Center.

But Benioff knew the Internet would get better and more robust. As high-speed Internet became the norm, Salesforce took off, growing into one of the largest software companies in the world, with 2019 revenues of $17 billion in its 2020 fiscal year. But they're not alone—many multibillion-dollar SaaS companies arose over the years since the turn of the millennium, representing tens of billions of dollars in revenue, and hundreds of billions of dollars of market cap.

But as good as SaaS companies are, the fastest-growing software company in the history of the world didn't look anything like Salesforce or Workday.

AMAZON WEB SERVICES CHANGES THE GAME

I joined Amazon in 2004 in the early days of Amazon Web Services (AWS). Once I joined, my boss explained the mission. Amazon was going to build enormous data centers and rent compute-power and storage capacity not as applications, but as *building blocks* that developers and other companies can use to build their apps. This would enable any developer and every company to leverage Amazon's mastery of web-scale infrastructure. The service would be flexible, able to scale up and down on the fly. If your traffic surged for a few days, the "Elastic Compute Cloud" would simply throw extra computer horsepower at your website. When the surge ended, your virtual data center would shrink back down. You paid only for what you used. You paid a monthly bill, just like you do for your mobile phone and your electricity.

The pay-for-what-you-use model was a huge breakthrough—maybe as significant as the technology itself. The old model of buying hardware up front was ridiculously expensive and wasteful. For decades companies bought way more capacity than they needed and were vastly overprovisioned. CPUs sat idle. Storage space sat empty. Utilization rates for disk storage systems could dip as low as 30 percent. Servers typically sat at 10 percent utilization. Each application needed its own dedicated servers and storage—enough to handle the maximum load it might ever experience.

The capacity from one application often could not be shared with the others. A retailer's point-of-sale system might need extra capacity during the busy holiday season but could not borrow the idle capacity and empty storage space in the HR system sitting right next to it. Instead, you had to buy enough horsepower to handle the load experienced during the holiday season, even though for the rest of the year you didn't need it. Software makers developed programs that let IT systems share resources, but that became yet another piece of expensive software that you needed to buy and required another team of IT workers. Fixing one headache just created another. Switching to AWS meant not only that you no longer had to buy expensive hardware—you also didn't have to hire a huge 24-7 IT department to manage all that hardware. That was another huge cost reduction.

With AWS it seemed as if Amazon had waved a magic wand and made all of those headaches go away. Sign up, and you need never think about how to run hardware and storage ever again—just pay for what you use.

The difference between this model and the first-era model was like the difference between generating electricity with your own diesel generator and buying electricity from a utility company. You have no idea where your programs are running, or what kind of computer they're running on. And you don't have to care. It's all happening out in "the cloud." (Factoid: in the early days, "the cloud" pretty much meant Virginia.) Someone else is taking care of it. The only thing you care about is that when you flip the switch, your data center is there for you, as much or as little as you need. Big companies jumped on this. They started moving applications from their own data centers to the Amazon cloud.

Other implications of AWS were not immediately apparent. One was that AWS would drive down the cost of launching a new company—to almost zero. Before AWS came along, when you started a tech company you needed to buy expensive servers, storage systems, routers, and database software. You might spend a million dollars buying and installing hardware just to stand up version 1 of your idea.

With AWS and its pay-as-you-go model, an entrepreneur could spend maybe a hundred bucks and launch in a few minutes—the time it took to fill out a form and tap in a credit card number. The implication of low startup costs was that there would be a lot more startups. Those startups also could get to market faster. They could go from an idea sketched on the back of a napkin (or in Twilio's case, the back of a pizza box) to shipping product in a matter of months. They could expand and grow without any friction from infrastructure. They could move fast and build things.

The realization I had while working inside AWS was that the AWS platform would unleash a new generation of startups that would be so much faster and leaner than traditional companies as to seem almost like a new species. Those nimble little superpredators would start disrupting companies across every industry. And then those big companies would start building software, further accelerating the pace of software innovation.

But to me, the most interesting implication of AWS was that it changed not just the way computing power was bought, but *who* was buying it. In the traditional world, IT decisions were made by people near the top of the organization—the CIO or the CFO. That's because these were high-stakes decisions, with years of work and millions of dollars being decided. At AWS, however, a lot of customers were just ordinary developers. Individual engineers or department managers could spin up a server and storage capacity at AWS just by entering a credit card number. When the company started using that application the IT department didn't move the code back to their in-house data center. They left it on AWS. As their usage went up, so did their monthly bills. And because of it, developers gained much more influence over how companies bought infrastructure.

The result of these trends is shown in the business results of AWS. Its sales have grown from practically zero in 2007 to an annualized $40 billion as of the first quarter of 2020. From zero to $40 billion in twelve years, which is pretty much unprecedented growth. That's why it's obvious that this business model—the platform business model—represents the next big thing in software.

But AWS isn't the only company driving the Third Great Era of Software. Microsoft, Google, and Alibaba have also developed their cloud offering to compete with Amazon, providing compute, storage, and more as services developers can integrate. Microsoft Azure booked $37 billion in revenue in 2019, and Google Cloud $9 billion. These are the giants leading the field. My company, Twilio, provides APIs for communications, and we've grown quickly to reach $1.1 billion of revenue in 2019. Private company Stripe, which provides payment APIs, hasn't disclosed its sales numbers, but private investors have valued it at $36 billion as of their April 2020 fund-raise. There's a lot of value being provided to customers, and being created for investors, in this Third Era.

HOW'D WE GET HERE?

Even more interesting than the "API economy" that's developed over the past decade is how it came to be. It's not obvious how a bunch of tiny APIs, each priced in pennies per use, would rack up tens of billions of dollars in revenue and run the apps we all use every day. But the genesis story of APIs is intricately tied to many of the other aspects of the software playbook I detail in this book. It all starts with small teams.

In 2000 Amazon had a giant monolithic mess of engineers and code powering the fast-growing retail business. Engineers were stepping all over each other, and the coordination energy to get anything done was massive. Things were slowing down, so Bezos wrote the "two-pizza team" memo proposing that they divide the company into small teams in order to move faster. (The idea was that you could feed the whole team with two pizzas.) But they had a problem.

How can you organize a company into a bunch of small, independent teams when their work is all intrinsically tied together in the code they write? They can't truly perform independently when the changes one team made to the code broke the code other teams were working on. It just wouldn't function.

The answer turned out to be keeping the code and the teams together. As Amazon split the organization up into small teams, they also kept carving up the code into small pieces so the teams could "take it with them" and operate it independently. These teams and their respective code needed a way to talk to each other, and "web services" turned out to be the answer. Instead of each team shipping code into some giant repository that somebody else would deploy and run on servers, each team would run their own code as a service that other teams could interoperate with. Because each team was small, the surface area of their service was typically somewhat limited as well. Over time, these became known as "microservices" because each individual service typically did one thing, and did it well.

These microservices were delivered not as a pile of code, nor as a website, but as a web-based API. APIs are well-defined interfaces that enable code to talk to other bits of code. Once a team builds and exposes an API to others, it's important that they teach other teams how to use it via documentation that's accurate and up to date. So at Amazon, an internal culture of API documentation arose. One team could find another team's API documentation and start using their services, often without even needing to talk. This enabled the teams to effectively work together, solving the coordination problem.

The next problem, though, was how to measure the effectiveness of each of these services, and how to account for where the business was spending money. If one team ran their service on ten thousand servers, was that good, or was that horribly inefficient? And what business purpose should that cost be ascribed to? So Amazon started ascribing a cost to using these services, even internally. Some people call this transfer pricing, but in fact it's a system of doing two things: holding teams accountable for their costs, and deciding where to put more resources in budget cycles.

Small teams are accountable for the efficiency of their service, because they have to effectively publish a "price" for internal customers, and those internal customers have to pay the costs out of their P&Ls. If those "customers" aren't happy with your costs, then you have work to do. The internal system of accountability aligns everybody's interests and creates a natural incentive to drive for greater efficiency over time. Internal pricing also enables leaders to make good budget decisions. Imagine you have two customer-facing products in a typical company, and one is doing $100 million of revenue and growing quickly, while another has $10 million of revenue with slow growth. Which one would you be likely to reward with more budget to keep going? The answer is obvious when you have revenue as a scorecard. The same goes for internal services. When an internal service is used extensively by internal customers and is growing fast, you should probably feed it more budget. But without an equalizing scorecard across your initiatives, it wouldn't necessarily be clear what teams need more investment.

So that's why adding a pricing function, even for internal customers, is tremendously useful.

But here's where it gets even *more* interesting. Once you've divided and subdivided the business into small teams that specialize in particular areas, offering microservices for each other to use, with well-documented interfaces and pricing that represents the true costs of delivering those services—well, why develop all of those microservices internally? Why devote your own developers to microservices that you could instead buy from other companies? Why write your own microservice for calculating currency translation on international sales when you can just buy that microservice from a vendor that specializes in currency translation software? So your developers start plugging in pieces from specialist providers, and boom—you have a software supply chain. Does it really matter what company's logo these microservice providers have on their business cards?

Soon people started figuring out that you could make a business out of building microservices and selling them to others. New Relic launched in 2008 and developed software that monitors website performance. Stripe developed payment processing services. Twilio developed a cloud communications platform. Another example is Google Maps. With just a few lines of code, developers can pop that service into their websites. That's a lot better than doing it themselves, spending years driving cars with roof-mounted cameras down every street in the world, and then creating mapping software with aerial views and street views and all the other features that Google Maps has. The value proposition is pretty obvious.

Each of us took a problem that was a real pain to solve, spent a few years coding up a solution, and now we provide that service to others. Our service is a black box. Customers don't know or care how it works. They just plug our code into theirs, write a bit of their own code, and off they go. In total, Twilio now operates more than one thousand microservices. We sell them on a pay-for-what-you-use basis, the same way Amazon sells its computing power.

Cloud platforms are the new building blocks for modern developers. They've made it much faster and cheaper to develop applications. They can scale up to support billions of users. All of this would have been unimaginable ten years ago.

BUILD AND BUY

There are many benefits of the Third Great Era of Software, but also a new set of questions to answer. Developers and company leadership are constantly deciding which microservices to buy from third-party cloud suppliers, and which ones to build themselves. Decision makers need to stay up to speed with the Cambrian explosion of new microservice providers that are racing into the market. Each microservice is continually and rapidly changing and improving.

"Tech companies are constantly debating" which microservices to build and which to buy, says Ashton Kutcher. He has invested in dozens of startups and chalked up some big wins, most notably Airbnb, Spotify, and Uber. "I think what you don't build is as important as what you build. The only things companies should build themselves are the things that are core to their business. A lot of times people end up building things where there's already a product you could buy or license for a relatively low cost. Should you build your own benefits and payroll system? I would never try to rebuild Twilio, or Slack, or Gusto."

My rule of thumb is that for anything that gives you differentiation with customers, you should build. Software that faces your customers, you should build. Anything where your customers will be saying, why doesn't it do X, and your answer is, well, the thing we bought doesn't do X. That's a problem. When your customers care, you need to build. There may be cases where it also makes sense to write your back-end software. You may be in a business where you can gain a competitive edge by how well you manage your inventory. In that case, sure, go build your own supply chain software.

But for most back-end operations, and for things that won't give you any differentiation with customers, you should buy. You aren't going to build your own email. Or your own database software. HR software, ERP programs—those are areas where you probably can't gain any competitive advantage by writing your own code, so you're well served buying an app from a SaaS provider. But let me repeat the rule of thumb again: anything that is customer-facing, you should build.

Because *you can't buy differentiation. You can only build it.*

But the good news: building has become a lot easier. Back in the day, before the maturation of the software supply chain, the answer was usually to buy solutions because the lift to build was so great. You had to be as good at software as Microsoft or Oracle to build software. But now, thanks to the Third Great Era of Software, and the digital supply chain enabling companies to build with unprecedented ease and speed, it's not just possible for companies to build their own software—it's required. Competitive dynamics dictate it.

You tie together these building blocks into the end-to-end experience, which you imagine, build, and own—because that's your competitive advantage. But the pieces that make it up are taken off the shelf and rapidly integrated and integrated upon. You'll add into the mix many of your own microservices, but instead of recreating the wheel, the services you build are those that represent your "secret sauce" areas of competitive advantage. Maybe it's a proprietary pricing algorithm, or a logistics algorithm that's unique to your system of distribution. But by taking off-the-shelf building blocks wherever possible, you can put all of your energy toward your unique areas of differentiation.

The good news is that more and more of these off-the-shelf building blocks are gaining maturity all the time. Cloud platforms are replacing legacy infrastructure in nearly every category. These commercial microservices are the raw ingredients of almost every app you use. Behind that user interface, apps are actually a patchwork comprising hundreds or even thousands of microservices, some created by a company's own developers and some from commercial providers.

Today, there are still many places where developers have no choice but to build microservices from scratch because off-the-shelf alternatives don't exist yet. But the beauty of the microservice model is that it's possible to swap out a microservice without interfering with the rest of the code in your app. As new commercial microservices emerge, it's not uncommon to remove the homegrown pieces over time and replace them with commercial alternatives. That's because those commercial services are getting massive investment by vendors and getting better every day, whereas the home-built versions often stagnate over time. Take Twilio, for example—we have (as of the time of writing) more than one thousand people on our R&D team improving our communications platform every day. Our customers get the benefit of that investment as our app gets better every day.

In theory it might one day be possible for a software company to produce an app without writing any code of its own, just by assembling a bunch of microservices created by other companies. In fact, people have theorized about the "one-person unicorn," meaning a company that is valued at $1 billion or more but is run by one person—a developer whose app sits on top of all those commercial microservices. This hasn't happened yet, but it might be only a matter of time. The process that we think of as "writing software" might become largely a process of snapping together chunks of code—the way Dell assembles commodity off-the-shelf components to make a PC or a chef takes (literally) off-the-shelf ingredients to make their special dish. It might in fact become so easy to write software that anyone can do it, without any special training in computer science.

For now, we have a hybrid model. You buy the common stuff where you can and write the rest. The "value add" of your company might be the way you integrate the pieces, and how well you develop the customer-facing software that sits on top of microservices. Apple's iPhone contains commodity pieces, like memory chips and flash drives that any company can buy. Apple doesn't design or build its own versions of those parts because that would not differentiate its product. Apple does, however, design its own special microprocessor for the iPhone, because that chip enables Apple to do things better than other phones. Apple also writes all the software that goes onto the iPhone. Apple's secret sauce involves knowing which parts to buy and which to build; knowing how to integrate those parts in unique ways; and, most important, hiring some of the best developers on the planet to write great software. They've also always been good at telling their story and selling their brand—that's another area where they've decided to differentiate, and it's paid off.

Just like Apple, software developers now blend their own bespoke software with off-the-shelf microservices provided by others. Uber is a good example. What you think of as "the Uber app" is actually a patchwork of about four thousand microservices—

some developed by Uber engineers, and many provided by external cloud platform operators. When a passenger calls a driver, their command zips from the Uber main screen to our Twilio servers, and we route the call to the driver. But that's all invisible to both of them; as far as they're concerned, Uber is letting them talk to each other. Payments are handled by a different microservice, while currency and exchange rate translations are delivered by a microservice, Tincup, that Uber developed internally.

This is how all new companies in Silicon Valley create their software, and it is rapidly becoming the standard in traditional companies like banks, retailers, airlines—everyone.

ASK YOUR DEVELOPERS WHAT SERVICES YOU SHOULD BE BUYING

Some companies believe that services like compute, storage, payments, or communications are core and can't be outsourced. I know of some retail businesses, for example, who in the early days of the cloud, refused to use AWS because Amazon's retail business is a competitor. However, companies with this attitude are falling by the wayside. Exactly when competition is growing more fierce is when companies must focus all of their internal development effort on the differentiating parts of the business. Buying the table-stakes capabilities offered in this Great Third Era of Software, even from your fiercest competitor, is what enables you to have a shot at winning. That's why you see Netflix, which competes with Amazon Prime Video, as a large and public customer of AWS. That's why at Twilio, we see large carriers leverage our services for contact centers, customer notifications, and more. Oftentimes, these decisions to not leverage cloud services are made at the top because . . . strategery. I think this is foolish.

Executives should look to their developers and technical talent to help make these decisions. Organically, this is already happening. Developers are building on AWS and Twilio, and expensing it on their credit cards. Instead of scolding them, leaders should see this organic traction as a signal and hop on board.

I'm reminded of the story of Joe McCorkle, vice president of telecom at RealPage, a large public software company that serves the multifamily property rental industry. They offer dozens of SaaS products for companies that own and operate real estate properties such as apartment buildings. They're also quite acquisitive. They've made dozens of acquisitions over the last ten years. In 2012, after they'd acquired several startups that were Twilio customers, the bills started landing on Joe's desk to approve, because he was responsible for all communications spending. At first he ignored them, but then the COO of the company asked Joe to "figure out what this Twilio thing is, and how we can get rid of it," presumably by replacing Twilio with services they were already buying from a carrier or a telecom hardware company.

Joe came to our annual customer conference in 2012, then called TwilioCON, with the goal of figuring out what Twilio did, and how he'd rip us out. While there, he met hundreds of other customers and got a flavor for how many different companies were using Twilio to innovate for their customers. He started drinking the Kool-Aid, and on the flight back, he wrote a memo. In summary, he said, "We're not getting rid of Twilio, we're moving everything to Twilio." Over the past several years, they've been doing just that.

It's a great example of Joe following the lead of his developers, who were in the know with the latest and greatest. As you build your software development team, the fundamental ask of your developers, your architects, and your technical leadership is to pick the right areas to build. Deciding which areas are core competencies—an oft-discussed question of corporate leaders—now extends down to the microservice level. I don't expect that most corporate executives will gain an expertise or desire to inspect down at this level—but executives should understand that their technical teams are making these decisions pretty frequently. Executives should understand the ecosystem of available services at a high level, and strongly encourage teams to adopt a "building block" approach that will accelerate building value for customers. We should also be constantly asking our technical teams where we could redeploy their talents to more valuable areas because common, off-the-shelf building blocks will serve us better. That's not just an up-front, Build vs. Buy decision. With microservices, the answer to that question is likely to change over time. It's worth revisiting the question with regularity.

Developers are usually the first to know what's new and interesting in this digital supply chain. You might consider asking your developers how free they are to adopt modern APIs, or what restrictions the company puts on adoption. How can you balance the need for things like security and purchase orders with the desire to let your developers use the most up-to-date services? Ask your team if they're secretly buying these services of the digital supply chain, and expensing it. If so, don't punish them. Understand why, and figure out how to formalize their ability to do so. Ask your developers what strategic rationale they use to decide what services to buy versus which capabilities are truly differentiating for your company.

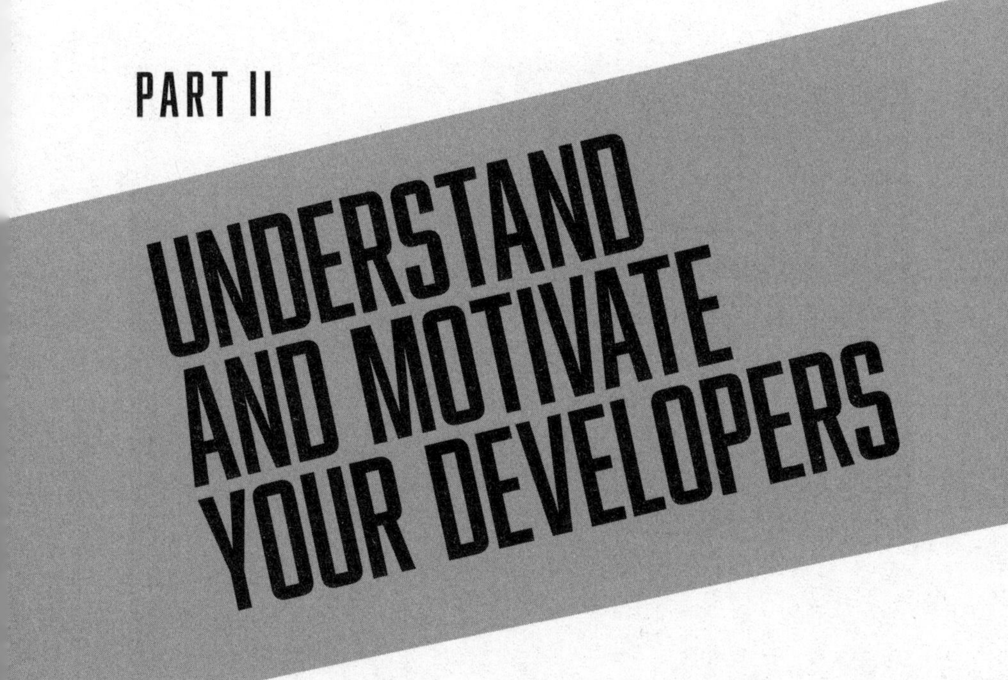

PART II

UNDERSTAND AND MOTIVATE YOUR DEVELOPERS

So you've read the first two chapters about how you need to build software for your company to survive and thrive in the digital age. But that really wasn't newsworthy, or else you probably would have never picked up this book. No, the most important part is how you're going to accomplish that. And it starts with understanding what drives developers to do their best work, and what you do as a leader that either motivates or accidentally demotivates developers. Part II is all about getting into the head of developers, starting with myself.

CHAPTER 3
HI, I'M JEFF, AND I'M A DEVELOPER

Every two weeks, we onboard the newest group of Twilio hires, and I do a thirty-minute session with them—and I kick it off like this: "Hi, I'm Jeff, and I'm a software developer." They all know me as the CEO and founder, but I actually self-identify as a software developer. In so many companies, there's a gap between executives leading companies in the digital era and the software developers actually implementing their digital transformation. My hope in writing this book is to bring these perspectives together—giving developers, managers, and executives a common language to improve their collaboration. As a public company CEO, and a developer, my perspective is different than most executives as well as most developers. I've seen the challenges and the successes of collaboration between managers and developers from both sides. To understand the Ask Your Developer methodology, it's helpful to understand my journey. While I'm a CEO today, I started life as a tinkerer and a builder. I want to highlight the turning points in my life that led to the Ask Your Developer mindset.

I was raised in the suburbs of Detroit, in a town called West Bloomfield. My mom was a math tutor and my dad was a radiologist. In the early 1980s, radiology was all analog. When the hospital received the raw, unexposed film from Kodak, it came packed with a piece of white cardboard between each piece of film, a dozen or so per box. The hospital would just throw away the cardboard—mind you, this was before recycling was in full swing—so my dad started bringing it home, building a stash of white cardboard in his den.

On weekends, when we were bored and tempted to watch TV, my dad would say, "Let's do a project!" We'd pull out the box full of various sizes of cardboard and he'd say, "What do you want to build?" I'd say things like "Let's build a robot!" or "Let's build a VCR" or "Let's build an X-ray machine!" and we'd get to work. We'd form some cardboard into a box roughly the size of a VCR, for example, and then, with a Magic Marker, I'd draw on the buttons—Play, Pause, >>, <<, etc. I'd draw a slot for where the Beta tape would go in. (Yeah, we were a Beta house!) And every time, when we were all done, I'd ask the question my dad always feared: "Dad, how can we make it *really* work?" If there were some kind of Geppetto-like power he could have mustered, I'm sure he would have. He'd have done anything to bring the VCR, robot, or whatever we were making that day to life. But he couldn't, which was frustrating for both of us.

Nonetheless, I got the itch to build. I fell in love with the idea that just by taking out your tools and supplies, you could create something. Even if that something didn't work . . . yet.

Around 1983 we got our first computer, an Apple IIe, and I discovered BASIC—a simple programming language you could use to ask the computer to do things you wanted it to do. Starting with stupid stuff like:

```
10 PRINT "Hello World"
20 GOTO 10
```

But then came more advanced stuff. I remember building a simple address book application. It was a nice toy, but ultimately not very useful. Nonetheless, my parents feigned being impressed, as they're required to do.

In 1990, the family got our first PC: a 20-MHz 386DX from a company called CompuAdd. It was a beast—an enormous beige box that weighed at least thirty pounds. Over the years, I dug into the guts of that machine, upgrading components, upgrading from Windows 3.0 to 3.1. Periodically, I would brick it by doing stupid stuff, like deleting c://command.com or monkeying with c://autoexec.bat—luckily my uncle Jerry lived down the block, and I could run down there and copy his autoexec.bat and be back in business.

I became the kid who "knew about computers." When somebody would ask me why their mouse wasn't working or why their computer wouldn't boot, I generally never knew the answer outright. But I knew I could just dive in and "figure it out." Heck, I probably wouldn't make it worse! With that 386DX computer, I learned to dig in and monkey around. I learned that even if you thoroughly messed it up, you could always fix it. And that, in many ways, is the essence of building.

But it wasn't until I got to college that my appreciation for programming really took hold. When I arrived at the University of Michigan in 1995, most kids were excited about the usual eighteen-year-old spoils of freedom: parties, alcohol, girls, boys. But what really got me excited was the Ethernet jack in my dorm room! For the first time, I had access to a 100Mbps, always-on Internet connection, which was a far cry from the 28,800kbps dial-up connection I'd had at home. The first thing I did after saying good-bye to my parents was to FTP down a copy of Netscape Navigator 1.0.

Good-bye, AOL; hello, "real" Internet. This was literally weeks after the Netscape IPO that took the world by surprise, and I was one of the millions of people discovering the Internet for the first time in those months.

I remember seeing the usual static websites of the day—marketing pages for companies, researcher pages from academia, personal home pages detailing people's hobbies, and more. You could click around for hours, learning just about anything. But even more amazing than early web content was that you could "View Source" on any web page, and see the code for how the author had made the page. There were no secrets, nothing magical behind the scenes. You could literally look at how anything on the Internet was made, learn from it, and build upon it. It was amazing.

Even more interesting, though, were these "dynamic" websites that were starting to appear around that time, which did more than just display content. Amazon.com let you browse books, and even buy them! Yahoo, Lycos, and AltaVista let you search for things. MapQuest let you find anywhere on the planet, and get turn-by-turn directions!

What was most amazing about these sites was that somebody could write a program. But unlike in the era of the Apple IIe, anybody else on the Internet could interact with the code. Instead of an audience of my parents, I could write something that millions of people could use. Suddenly, it felt *real.* It wasn't a toy for a kid to play with; this was the real world.

I took computer science classes, learning the fundamentals of how computers work, like how CPUs function, how memory works, and even the theoretical aspects of modern computation, like why binary is the chosen underpinning of computers, and more. I also started learning the basics of software development, writing sort algorithms in C and C++, loops, functions, and structures. This was all very interesting, but, as you've probably guessed by now, I'm more of an *applied* kind of person. I wanted to build more than just sort algorithms that had been built millions of times before by millions of other students.

In the summer of 1997, after a couple of years of computer science courses, I landed an internship at Citysearch in Pasadena, California, nestled in the mountains just northeast of downtown Los Angeles. Citysearch was one of the first big websites. Their product was a "city guide" telling you all the things to do in your town. Just before I arrived in June 1997, they had rebuilt the Content Management System (CMS) that let them update the website, and the new version had a new file format. (Yes, the data was stored in files, not even a database!) On my first day, my manager welcomed me to the company and outlined my task: I needed to convert the files from the old format to the new format. He gave me my company-issued computer, descriptions of the old and new file formats, and showed me to my desk.

I wrote a program in C that read in the old files and spit out the data in the new format. At around lunchtime, I returned to my manager's desk to let him know I'd finished my first task. He was stunned. That, apparently, had been my job for the *whole summer*. He figured that I would spend the days copy and pasting data from one file to another—for thousands of files—and that this would make for a great internship. I asked what I should do with the rest of the day, and he said he'd get back to me. Turns out, he didn't have anything for me to do—not just for the remainder of that day, but for the entire summer. That was the first time I realized there was this big disconnect between managers and what software developers really do.

So I came in every day, sat at my desk from nine to five, and futzed around on the Internet. I learned a new programming language that was gaining traction for building Internet apps—Cold Fusion. I returned from that summer to Ann Arbor with a newfound desire to start something of my own.

I've always thought that the best way to learn something new was to commit yourself to "customers" and force yourself to learn. So I got together with a couple of friends, Brian Levine and Michael Krasman, who both shared my fascination with the Internet, and we started brainstorming products we could build. We came up with a handful of ideas, but one stuck with us.

Plastered around campus in Ann Arbor, there were signs advertising for note-taking companies. These were small outfits, with names like Blue Notes, Superior Notes, Grade A notes, that operated out of copy shops around campus. For about $50 per course per semester, you could buy the notes from some very bright, studious person—you know, the person in the front row—and study from their notes instead of your own crappy ones. After paying the $50, you trekked across town in the snow after every lecture to pick up your notes, which were physically photocopied. These services were fairly popular, especially for those in the large, 101-style introduction courses where a thousand incoming freshmen might all be taking the same course.

Brian, Mike, and I figured that instead of trekking through the snow multiple times a week, wouldn't the Internet be a better way to get these notes? You could sit in the convenience of your dorm room and pull up your notes online. With the concentration of students in relatively few mega-courses (Psychology 101, Economics 101, etc.), we could hire just a small handful of note takers and cover the needs of nearly every incoming freshman: nearly five thousand students at a school the size of the University of Michigan. These services existed at pretty much every college and university. We did the napkin math and figured the entire lecture note "industry" was a whopping $15 million market. So we decided that instead of selling the notes, which in 1997 would have been very hard to do on the Internet, we'd just give them away for free. The advertising market was much bigger than the "lecture note" market so we'd monetize by putting ads for local and national businesses on the notes.

We decided to call our venture Notes4Free.com, registered the domain name, and adopted an unofficial tagline: "We don't condone skipping class. We just make it easier." As you might imagine, the service was very popular. What student wouldn't want free lecture notes you could get without even leaving your dorm room? Soon we expanded to a second campus—Michigan State—and then to the entire Big 10.

The fall of 1998 brought the dot-com boom. The opportunity to participate was too big to pass up. My cofounders and I dropped out of school to build the company full-time. We raised a $1 million seed investment round from friends and family and expanded our office three times in six months, continually taking on more space as it came available, since we were hiring all of our college friends and even some legitimate adults to join us on the mission. We renamed the company—thankfully—to Versity.com. In the summer of 1999, we raised $10 million of venture capital from Venrock Associates, a prominent Silicon Valley venture capital firm, and moved the company—then fifty people—from Michigan to Silicon Valley. We kept growing. We hired a "professional" executive team, who, in retrospect, were primarily interested in selling the company. Which we did. In January 2000, we sold Veristy.com in an all-stock transaction to another company courting college students—CollegeClub.com—which had just filed to go public. CollegeClub withdrew its IPO filing to complete the acquisition of Versity, and by the time they refiled—in April 2000—the IPO window had closed, the party was ending, and they were burning about $30 million per month. Instead of an infusion of IPO cash, the company ran face-first into the wall, declaring bankruptcy in August 2000. Our stock was worthless.

In just eighteen months we had gone from a side project during our college studies to a company valued by investors north of $150 million as part of a company on the verge of an IPO—to worth nothing again. It was the canonical dot-com roller-coaster story. In retrospect, I'm sure that company was an absolute shit show. We were twenty-one years old, running around with no business model and millions of investor dollars. In the entire life of the company we spent more than $10 million in venture funding and generated about $14,000 in revenue. But revenue was never the goal—investors weren't asking about it, board members didn't fret about it. All anybody cared about was building an audience—eyeballs. That part, we did. We garnered an audience of millions of college students, who'd visit our site weekly or even daily. When it came to building the college student audience, we'd nailed our plan and then some. Despite the failure to create a valuable dot-com business, I got the itch for entrepreneurship but also learned that in failure, you can learn a ton and set yourself up for what's next. Was my career over? No, it was just starting.

Right around that time, Jeff Fluhr, a friend of mine, had just written a business plan for a company called Idrenaline Inc. The idea was to build a website where people could buy and sell event tickets—like sporting events, concerts, and more—in a much safer and easier way than buying them for cash on the street corner from a scalper. Jeff and his cofounder, Eric Baker, had a business plan and were starting to find some investor money, although 2000 was no time to be raising money for your dot-com idea. Jeff and Eric were both bankers and had never run a company. It sounded interesting, and I had no desire to stay at CollegeClub, so I agreed to join as the first chief technology officer, helping them build the site, build the technical team, and get the company off the ground. We knew we needed a better name, so Jeff picked the name Liquidseats, which always sounded to me like some kind of diarrhea situation. My friend Dave Bruan, who had run marketing at Versity, also joined Idrenaline as the head of marketing. He had the idea for the name StubHub. Jeff also hired Matt Levenson—an important figure in the Ask Your Developer story, whom I'll get to later in this chapter—as the chief operating officer.

It was mid-2000, and we were trying desperately to launch in time for the start of the NFL season that fall. It was a mad dash. We started figuring out how we'd get initial supply of ticket inventory, how we'd find buyers, where we'd launch. Using my old video skills, I produced a launch video in an attempt at viral marketing. I'd never built a commerce site before, written the code to take a credit card online, or thought about how auctions work, but that's what made it exciting. I dove in and assembled a small team to take the site live in September—going from the first line of code to launch in about six weeks. The frantic grind to get StubHub launched was a blast. I loved how we could take this idea, build the first version, and get it in customers' hands so quickly. With that speed, we were able to iterate constantly.

However, while StubHub was a great business opportunity, it wasn't calling to me. I wanted to spend my days building something I viscerally loved, and tickets just weren't the product category that got me out of bed in the morning. So eventually, I began searching for my next opportunity.

That was when I had lunch with Kevin O'Connor, the founder and CEO of DoubleClick, the leading Internet advertising network of that era. They basically invented the banner ad, and represented the first wave of monetization of the Internet. Kevin had been an angel investor in Versity, and we'd kept in touch. During lunch, I told him I was interested in starting something new, and he said he'd be interested in collaborating on coming up with an idea. I tapped Matt Levenson, who'd worked at both Versity and StubHub, to join me.

We brainstormed nearly a thousand ideas, researched about fifty that had merit, and wrote probably twenty business plans—but at the end of all that, an idea came out of left field. Matt had grown up in Santa Barbara, California, and had seen the popularity of extreme sports—skateboarding, surfing, snowboarding, and BMX biking—explode. Yet, for those sports, the only retail options were small mom-and-pops. Those small independent shops are great when the sports are niche, but as these sports were gaining mainstream traction, Matt hypothesized that shoppers would want a big-box retail experience—predictable store hours, good return policies, wide product selection, like what REI provides for outdoor sports. We got to work wondering what such a store would look like for extreme sports. If REI was for the granola-eating sports, we would do it for the Pop-Tart–eating sports.

Of all the thousand ideas we brainstormed, fueled by big technology trends happening on the Internet and mobile, the only idea we could all agree on was this brick-and-mortar retail idea. Odd, although it was also a sign of the times. In the wake of the dot-com crash, the idea of a business where you buy goods for X and sell them for more than X sounded pretty nice in contrast to the crazy business models of the Internet, which all seemed to be imploding in 2000–2001.

However, I had my misgivings. I asked Matt what a software developer like myself was doing opening an extreme sporting goods retailer, given that I didn't do any of those sports. We discussed the technology that would fuel the customer experience and the benefits of starting a retailer from scratch in 2001, with no legacy technology to deal with. This meant we could build whatever we wanted to delight our customers and build efficiency into the stores. That idea intrigued me, so I got in the car with Matt and we moved ourselves back to sunny California—this time Los Angeles, which is the epicenter of all things extreme sports.

Matt and I got to work. We settled on the name Nine Star, which I didn't love, though it was better than our working title: Rough Riders. After securing the real estate, Matt and our team focused on building out the physical store and getting products in, while I focused on building the software we'd need to power the store. For me, it was the opportunity of a lifetime to figure out how all that technology at retail stores worked, and build something even better than most stores had. I'd been in countless retail stores in my life, seen cashiers ring up purchases with a laser scanner, swipe my credit cards with the swipey device, and print receipts a thousand times. Now I got to dive in and learn how all that stuff worked. What happens when the laser hits the bar code on the sticker? What information is encoded on your credit card's magnetic strip anyway? How does the cash drawer know when to open?

I built all that as a web application, because, well, the web was what I knew. In the language PHP, I wrote a complete point-of-sale system, the software that retailers use to ring up sales, take cash and credit cards, print receipts, and more. Better yet, because I'd written the whole thing, I could build it and change it in any way I wanted. When we decided we wanted a member program, I built it all into the point of sale. When a new customer was checking out, we'd ask if they wanted to become a member. If they said yes, the cashier would take their name and email address and use a little webcam to snap a photo. Within thirty seconds a full-color member card popped out of the register. The kids ate this up! It was like their own Nine Star credit card for preteens. We decided members would get 20 percent "kickback" from all the money they spent in a year, available as credits to spend in February (when we were trying to clear our leftover holiday inventory). I built a "kickback bucks" system into the point of sale.

I wrote code in the back of the store, and when it got busy, inevitably somebody would come back and grab me and I'd work the register. At first, it was great. I got to use the software I was building every day. I'd find a bug or some improvement to speed up the cashiers, and go into the back and emerge a half hour later to deploy the improvement. The feedback loop was tight, and incredibly gratifying. But deep down, I knew I was sitting in the back of a skate shop, surrounded (literally) on all sides by shoeboxes and skateboards. My coworkers were skate kids and surfer dudes, and I was "the computer guy."

As a developer, you need deep concentration to hold the entire system in your head. People call it flow—that state where your mind is enveloped in a problem and you get an incredible amount of work done. Diving into a codebase, remembering how a particular part of the code worked well enough to make changes, takes incredible concentration. And concentration was in tight supply working in the back of a skate shop. We'd made every surface of the store skatable so kids in the store could treat the store like a skate park. They loved it. I hated it. I was constantly distracted by loud noises and the shouting of store employees.

One day, one of our store employees ran into the back while I was deep in concentration. He tapped me on the shoulder. "Yo, dude. Is the website down?"

I took off my headphones, irritated by the interruption.

"Are you *asking* me, or are you *telling* me?!" I growled.

The skater dude backed away slowly, and I realized what I had become: I was the grumpy computer guy in the back that nobody wanted to talk to. That's when I realized I didn't belong there.

While I was building all this cool tech at Nine Star, I was watching Google rise out of nowhere to become a tech giant. Amazon was growing every day, adding new product categories to the site. The companies that survived the dot-com implosion were starting to define our lives. I wanted to be back in tech, not in the back of a skate shop. It was also financially difficult at Nine Star. All of our cash went into buying product for the shelves. Matt and I hadn't taken a salary in three years, and the impact of that was showing in my very negative bank account and maxed-out credit cards. The Subway across the street from Nine Star had a two-for-one promotion every day after 5 p.m. I'd buy a $3.99 sub for dinner and keep the extra sub for lunch the next day. At one point Baja Fresh, the Mexican chain, had a coupon on their website for a free burrito bowl. This was still early in the web and apparently they didn't realize that you could print a web coupon as many times as you wanted. Matt and I ate free burrito bowls twice a day for about three months until they caught on. Such is entrepreneurship.

As I thought about what I might do next, I realized that I'd been involved in three early-stage startups. I'd been there at the inception, when we were a few people in a garage (or a skate shop, as the case may be) trying to make something out of nothing. But I had no experience at a big company, other than my summer (but really half a day) working at Citysearch. If I wanted to create a meaningful company one day, I needed to learn how big companies operated. What worked well? What should I emulate with my next startup? What stopped working when companies got big? What pitfalls should I avoid? I needed to learn how business worked, how to manage, lead, and scale a fast-growing organization. At startups, you just ran as fast as you could, but how did *real* companies work? I wanted to find out. It also wouldn't hurt to get a paycheck and recharge the coffers.

In the fall of 2004, I took an offer from Amazon Web Services (AWS) and moved to Seattle. I'd always worked in scrappy startups with whatever talent and budgets we could muster. It was a totally different story working at a world-class company, with world-class talent. I learned how systems worked at scale. I learned about technology they were inventing to deal with the scale of Amazon—distributed systems, consistent hashing, idempotency, the CAP theorem—far beyond anything I'd dealt with. When I arrived, there were about thirty people on AWS, where I was a product manager, working from the sixth floor of the Pacific Medical Center—or PacMed for short—the old art deco hospital that had been converted into Amazon's headquarters. Jeff Bezos worked on the seventh, and if you were near him, it meant he cared about what you were working on. AWS was his pet project, thus our presence on the sixth floor.

We were building products not for consumers, but for developers like myself. The people I was working with were truly inventing something new. Everything had to be rethought. The products, the marketing, even the pricing. My office mate, Dave Barth, was the first product manager on a budding product called the Simple Storage Service, or S3 for short, destined to disrupt the market for digital storage. I'd been assigned to a product that later was named the Flexible Payment Service (FPS). The goal of FPS was to enable developers to accept payments in their apps. Just like S3 gave developers access to Internet-scale storage, FPS would give developers access to the same payments infrastructure that powered the largest e-commerce site in the world. We used to joke that there was a reason S3 was called the *simple* storage service, while FPS was the *flexible* payments service. Our product was ultimately too complicated and struggled to launch. But nonetheless, it was an amazing experience. Despite the fact that Amazon seemed to me like a *huge* company, it felt like a startup. The whole company was divided into small, two-pizza teams, each operating like a tiny startup. There was urgency. There was energy. What we were doing mattered. We were inventing the future—that's the feeling you want your technical talent to feel.

One of the things that struck me at Amazon was how much influence and decision-making ability developers had. The most senior leaders on many of these projects at the time weren't business leaders, but technical leaders. S3 was informally led by Al Vermeulen, Amazon's CTO. My project, FPS, was led by an engineer named Vikas Gupta, who had built much of Amazon's retail payment systems. Business leaders like Andy Jassy provided leadership guidance and wisdom, but really created an environment for technical leaders to flourish and add business value, not just code. This experience cemented my belief in developers as great potential business leaders—a foundational element of the Ask Your Developer mindset.

Working at Amazon had fundamentally changed how I looked at the world, and at Internet-scale opportunities. I'd also learned a ton about company culture—the things you do as leaders that create the environment for great people to do their best work. I saw the great things Amazon had done in its early years, and also some things I'd do differently.

Moving to Seattle was life-changing. So was meeting my (now) wife, Erica. She had just finished medical school at Washington University in St. Louis, and had moved to Seattle to start her intern year in pediatric medicine at Seattle Children's Hospital.

After a couple of years, I felt the urge to take the knowledge I'd gained at Amazon and start my next company. This time I promised myself I would build a company whose customers I could truly identify with—not secondhand ticket buyers or skateboard kids. I was determined to learn from my past mistakes and build something that I needed and the world needed. I also vowed to take what I'd learned about scaling from Amazon and build a company that held that amount of energy and drive at every step of the way.

When I left Amazon in mid-2006, I didn't have a plan, except to find my next idea. I downsized my apartment to save money, moving from the downtown waterfront with a beautiful view of Puget Sound to a musty old place in the U District, the part of town where students at the University of Washington reside. Student rents were much more affordable to somebody without a paycheck. My experience at Amazon showed me how easy it was becoming to build a software startup. If I didn't need a data center or servers anymore, then I'd need to raise far less money, and hire fewer people than before. All of my entrepreneurial energy could then focus on the thing that matters the most: the customer, and what problem I could solve for them. There were a bunch of ideas floating in my head. One was for a new way of doing computer backups. Another idea would help people stream video from far parts of the globe via peer-to-peer networking. I had to decide what idea to pursue next, and talking to prospective customers was the way I made the decision.

When you pitch a new product idea to potential customers, one of two things happens, especially when they're an acquaintance. If they genuinely like the idea and it seems to solve a pain point in their life, they ask you questions. Does it do this? Does it do that? They're trying to match your solution to their problem. That's a good sign. If they don't see your idea as solving some pain point they have, the conversation goes differently. They try to be polite, and say: "Oh, that sounds nice . . ." as their voice trails off. After a few moments of awkward silence, they'll change the subject. "So, how 'bout them Tigers?" Not a good sign.

A lot of my pitches led to conversations about the Detroit Tigers, but I only spent a few weeks and no money pursuing them, so it was okay.

This is how innovation works: *experimentation is the prerequisite to innovation.* The more quickly and cheaply you can run experiments, the faster you'll eventually find something that works. So I kept looking for ideas.

One thing struck me—at each of my three prior companies, we were using the power of software to build great products and great customer experiences. Even though each company was very different—a lecture note company, a secondhand ticket marketplace, a brick-and-mortar skate shop—they all involved figuring out how we could build software to delight our customers. The superpower of software to me was how quickly you could take an idea and get it in front of customers. Once customers could play with your idea, they'd give you feedback, and tell you what was good and what was bad. That would inform the next thing you built, and so forth. You could release a new version every day if you wanted to. That iterative spirit is what makes software so powerful. Think about how we launched StubHub in six weeks, or how I could improve that Nine Star point-of-sale system in real time while I was working in the store.

But there was another common thread between all three companies: at every company, we'd come across instances when we needed communications to close the loop with our customers, or build better operations. At Versity, if a note taker had forgotten to upload their notes, and after an email reminder or two still hadn't completed the task, we wanted to automate a phone call to their home. If you bought a ticket on StubHub and had to rendezvous with a courier delivering the ticket, you needed to make a phone call to find each other outside a crowded event. At Nine Star, customers would call all the time to ask if their surfboard repair was ready, and we had to pull a sales rep off the floor to look it up in the computer, a task that should just be programmed.

Communications was deeply integrated into our product or our workflows and always came up as something the business needed. Yet as a developer, I didn't know the first thing about communications. Making a phone ring somewhere, thousands of miles away? That felt like magic.

Every time these problems arose, I would call the companies who knew how this stuff worked, like Cisco and AT&T. If I could get a call back from their sales team (we were small peanuts to them), they'd say that they could make it work, but we'd need to run copper wires from a carrier to our data center, then rack up a bunch of gear, then buy a bunch of software. But that technology didn't do what we wanted right out of the box. We would need to hire a bunch of contractors with expertise in telecom and Cisco certifications filling up their business cards to build it. All told, it would cost millions of dollars and take twenty-four months to build. We never ended up building the things we wanted.

The world of communications was diametrically opposed to the ethos of software. The communications industry was built upon a century of physical infrastructure investments: digging millions of miles of ditches and laying down wire, launching satellites into space, or spending billions buying wireless spectrum from governments. These were big, high-risk activities, so they moved at a slow pace.

Yet how we got value out of communications wasn't about the physical stuff anymore. We take for granted all those wires we've wrapped the planet in, and now we have the luxury of thinking about what we build on top of that in software, with innovation happening in days or weeks, not months or years. Build, test, iterate. That's what I'd needed at all three of my prior companies. Then I thought about what we'd been building at AWS—infrastructure as Application Programming Interfaces (APIs) that developers could invoke with a few lines of code, and for pennies per use. Modernizing communications for the software era seemed like a big problem, and I thought there was a way to solve it: by turning communication into APIs for software developers.

I talked to prospective customers—software developers. I'd ask, "What if you had an API that let you initiate or receive phone calls from your app, and do things like play audio, or read back text, or bridge multiple callers together—would you have a use for it?"

At first, they'd say, "Oh, that's interesting . . . How about them Tigers?" But then, about a minute later, they'd circle back. "Wait, that idea you had about the phone, could I . . . notify people when their package ships?" And I'd enthusiastically say, "YES! Yes you could!"

This experience happened over and over. You could almost hear the gears start turning as developer after developer connected this idea with some feature they'd recently wanted to build but couldn't because they didn't know the first thing about telecom.

In late 2007 I contacted John Wolthuis—my first hire at Versity, and then again at StubHub—to see what he was up to and if he shared an interest in this problem. Then I contacted Evan Cooke, one of my teaching assistants at the University of Michigan, whom I'd stayed in touch with and with whom I'd discussed entrepreneurial ideas from time to time. We were all excited about the idea, and customer interviews kept proving that there was interest, so in January 2008 we started focusing on it exclusively.

First, we needed a name. I'm a big believer in having a unique proper noun for the company that can be owned completely. We started making sounds with our mouths—literally just expressing syllables that sounded remotely like *telephone*. "Teliph." "Telefoo." "Telapia." Nope, that's a fish. We kept making sounds. It must have been hilarious to listen to, but we didn't care. After about twenty minutes, I said: "Twili. Tweli. Twilio." The last one had a ring to it. Amazingly, Twilio.com was available for seven dollars, so I bought it. That was that. We'd named our company.

Writing software that could interact with the telecom system turned out to be an insanely difficult challenge. Telecom is a weird, complicated world, full of arcane technology and terminology with loads of cruft and crust that has built up over the decades, plus a litany of rules and regulations. On top of that, the carriers are notoriously slow moving and difficult to work with. But as we dug in and realized how hard it truly was, that encouraged us even more. The worse the legacy world was to deal with, the bigger our opportunity was to simplify it and improve the customer experience.

At first, we were just figuring out the basics of how the telecom system works, and then writing the first version of Twilio. Our software would abstract one hundred years of complexity that the industry had accumulated and present it as a simple API for developers. An API lets web developers do things over the telecom system without having to learn how to speak telecom. They just write some code in common languages they already know, like Ruby, Python, JavaScript, or Java, and use it to build apps that can make and receive phone calls.

Remember all those developers who had the lightbulb go off when we described it to them? As we were building the first version of Twilio, we circled back to them and gave them access to the early versions of it, and just asked them for their feedback. Even though we were very early in the development, their excitement for what they could build was palpable.

When we showed prototypes to venture capitalists, however, they weren't impressed. We got turned down twenty times. Money was so tight that in 2008, when Erica and I got married, we sold our wedding presents and put the money in the bank. Investors might not have believed in Twilio, but I did, and so did my cofounders. We were not going to give up. We were convinced that we had come up with something that customers would love, in a large market.

It turns out now that the response I got from those dozen or so developers at the beginning was representative of millions of developers worldwide. Developers, and the companies they work for, were indeed looking for a better way to engage with their customers as they built out new, digital experiences. That demand has been our tailwind as we've continually expanded our service—initially just voice calling in the United States—to now more than dozens of products, all of which span the globe. Twelve years in, I'm incredibly proud of what we, and our customers, have built.

THE ORIGINS OF THE ASK YOUR DEVELOPER METHODOLOGY

Looking back now, the particular experiences I've had, and the people I've worked with, have led me to see the interplay between business and software, between businesspeople and developers. First, having built four startups, I've learned that building software is actually pretty easy but building the *right* thing is hard. So rapid iteration, experimentation, and close contact with customers are the prerequisites to innovation. Second, having seen big companies like Amazon as well as tiny startups like StubHub, I've learned that the key ingredient to unlocking innovation is cultural more than anything else, and that culture starts at the top. And third, and most important, I've realized that the relationship between developers and businesspeople is not well understood, but is critical to solving business problems with technology. That last point is the most important takeaway from this chapter.

I first realized the unique power of a great businessperson/developer relationship back in 2004, at Nine Star, that extreme sports shop in Los Angeles that I started with my former Versity and StubHub colleague, Matt Levenson. At Versity, Matt had been the head of campus operations. His job was to manage the enormous field operation across dozens, then hundreds, of campuses. He hired the campus managers, then enabled them to hire note takers and field marketing teams. At our height, this was nearly fifteen thousand people in total, all of them college students, who are notoriously difficult to employ and who turned over almost completely every semester as the courses changed. Making this whole operation scale was clearly a job for software. But Matt was a total technophobe. When he joined Versity, I gave him a laptop and an email address and he told me he had no use for them.

"Matt, you're going to manage thousands of people across the United States. How are you going to do that without email?"

"I'll just, like, call them," he said. (At least, that's how I remember the baffling conversation.)

How could a guy who refused to use a laptop and email work at a tech company? Well, Matt did it, via a unique way of working together we developed that I would later come to think of as the Ask Your Developer methodology.

Every so often Matt would come to me with a business problem he needed to solve. At Versity, he was trying to turn the campus managers—typically a grad student running the show for us to make a few extra bucks—into great managers. With ten thousand student note takers to manage, and hundreds of thousands of lecture notes coming in every semester, that was a hard problem. But it started with knowing which note takers were doing a good job, and which were not. I was then the CTO, so he came to me one day and asked: "How could we figure out which notes our users think are good?" With that simple question in mind, together we brainstormed a rating system, similar to what eBay had to rate buyers and sellers. (Today, rating things on the Internet is commonplace, but back then it was a pretty new concept.) Within days, we had a widget on each set of notes, letting users rate the notes on a five-star scale, which stored the ratings in a database and produced a real-time report of which notes were great and which were lousy.

Then he asked, "If we know the rating of each set of notes, can we recommend to the campus manager each day what action they should take to manage their note takers?" We took the note rating, and some other signals, and produced a daily screen with all the key metrics for their fifty-some note takers, and a "recommended action," which ranged from "Do Nothing" to "Send Praise Email" to "Send Feedback Email" to "Fire Them." The recommended action was preselected, and after the campus manager took a look and approved it, the system would execute the actions on their behalf. Except, of course, for firing the note taker—for that, the system managed a list of people to call and personally break the bad news to. (We weren't monsters!) We even had about a dozen templated emails in the system, so the note takers never got the same "praise" or "feedback" email twice. We called it "RoboManager," and it allowed our campus managers to manage their team in about five minutes a day.

This kind of back-and-forth continued at Nine Star. One day Matt asked, "Hey, you know what? I'm trying to incentivize the store managers on how much they convert visitors to the store into buyers. Could we somehow measure how many people walk through the door, using those infrared people-counters? And then could we correlate that with the point of sale and try to figure out what our conversion rate is in this physical store?"

"I think we could," I said. "I don't know how, exactly. But that's really interesting. Let me figure something out."

So off I went to learn about people-counter systems, those gizmos where you put a light sensor at the door of the store. I discovered that those systems have an API. That meant I could write an application that could talk to the sensors and pull data from them. I wrote another program that pulled data from our point-of-sale system, then connected the two programs. Voilà! We had a rudimentary system for calculating the conversion rate in our physical store. Next I wrote a program that made the conversion rate data accessible to our employees on our store's intranet. Now we had a new statistic that we could use to measure our performance.

We just kept doing things like that. Matt wanted a way to figure out which merchandise we should return to vendors. I built a system that let us assign categories to items. For example: shorts; polka dots; blue; large. I coded up an interface so buyers could tag new merchandise with category information, and every month we would figure out which merchandise wasn't selling and send it back.

This dynamic meant we could work together on the problems of our business even though he was a complete technophobe and I was a hard-core, true-believer, tech-loving computer science major. That working style exposes a truth that seems simple but is actually rather profound and surprisingly rare: the key to getting businesspeople and developers to work well together is for the businesspeople to *share problems, not solutions.*

Matt didn't tell me what code to write. He didn't know what kind of app he wanted. He didn't write lengthy specs. He would just say, *Hey, wouldn't it be cool if we could do X?* Or, *Dude, is there some way we could do Y?* He didn't know anything about software, a fact that ended up being a boon because when he asked me to solve a problem, I became more engaged.

Unfortunately, this is not how most companies treat their developers. How we build software, or really get anything done, is about whom we ask, and what we ask of them. This book, as well as the Ask Your Developer mindset, isn't really about software. It's about people—the software developers and businesspeople who need to work together to hear customers' needs and answer them.

CHAPTER 4
CODE IS CREATIVE

If you want to build a ship, don't drum up the men to gather wood, divide the work, and give orders. Instead, teach them to yearn for the vast and endless sea.

—Antoine de Saint-Exupéry

If you're an executive, you probably spend a bunch of time with your sales team, and you understand how your salespeople do their work and what motivates them. You probably realize that salespeople like to win, and the way you structure your sales process and sales compensation helps create a game that lets them compete. Salespeople who "make it rain" are lauded as heroes, and executives know them by name. Yet I've found that few executives have the same understanding of what makes software developers tick. Like most people, developers like to win, too, but the game is different. If you're wondering why it's hard to recruit and retain great developers—the kind that Facebook, Amazon, and Google employ—start by understanding what motivates developers. If you wonder why "simple" changes to your website or mobile app take so long to make, then start by understanding the interaction between developers and managers. If you create an environment that lets developers scratch their itch, they'll amaze you with what they can build. But it starts by understanding what makes developers tick—and contrary to popular belief, it's more about creativity than calculus. That's because code is creative.

Thirty years ago, if you wanted to make music, you had to "get discovered"—signed by a record label so you could afford expensive studio time, press CDs, and get radio airplay. Only a handful of acts got discovered in any given year, and odds were low that your music career would pan out, even if you were an insanely talented musician. Most people kept their day jobs. Same thing in the film industry. Aspiring filmmakers would move to Hollywood and wait tables for years, looking for their big break. Hollywood only produced about one hundred feature films a year, and competition was fierce for the creative roles involved in making them. Even very talented filmmakers would be rejected by this system, and most moved back home, their dreams of "making it in Hollywood" dashed.

But over the last few decades, personal computers, low-cost software, and the Internet have disrupted and broken open these fields, making it possible for anyone to record and distribute music or movies. Cheap, professional-quality tools and low-cost or free distribution channels have lowered the barriers to entrance, empowered individual artists, and smashed the gatekeepers who previously controlled access.

For $299, any aspiring filmmaker can buy Final Cut Pro, the same software used to cut major Hollywood motion pictures, and reach a billion people on YouTube. For $199, musicians can buy the same Logic Pro X software that Beyoncé uses to record her albums, and then distribute their music on SoundCloud for free.

That's happening all the time. Montero Lamar Hill, aka Lil Nas X, a twenty-one-year-old kid, bought a beat online for thirty dollars, rapped lyrics over the beat, and in December 2018 released a song, "Old Town Road," on SoundCloud. It blew up and has now been streamed more than a billion times. It also set a new record for the number of weeks in the number one spot on the *Billboard* charts, and was voted Song of the Year at the 2019 MTV Video Music Awards. Other examples include comedian Joe Rogan, who launched a free podcast in 2009 and in 2020 inked a $100 million deal with Spotify; and eight-year-old Ryan Kaji, who earns $26 million a year (according to *Forbes*) with a YouTube channel, Ryan ToysReview, where he—you guessed it—reviews toys.

The same thing is happening for another group of creative artists—software developers. Software infrastructure used to be incredibly expensive, but now it's cheap or even free to get started. You don't need to buy massive servers or rent space in a data center anymore. There's a whole toolkit that you can take down off the shelf and use to build your apps—Amazon or Microsoft for servers and storage, Google for Maps, Twilio for communications, Stripe for payments. Any kid has access to the same core building blocks as the largest corporations in the world.

The same goes for distribution. Developers no longer have to strike a deal with a software publisher, get shelf space at CompUSA, or land a coveted spot preinstalled on a mobile phone. Anyone can put their app on an app store, just like anyone can put their video on YouTube. A web developer can buy ads on Google using their credit card, for as little as pennies a click.

There has never been a better time to be a software developer. The only limit is your imagination. But there's an often-overlooked reason software has so many parallels to the music and film industries:

Code is creative.

Pop culture depicts developers as science and math nerds. Characters like Steve Urkel on *Family Matters*, Sheldon Cooper on *The Big Bang Theory*, and Dennis Nedry from *Jurassic Park* all create a picture of social misfits, man-children, more comfortable with a slide rule than a conversation. The media loves those stereotypes, but they're incredibly misleading.

Writing software is more similar to making music or writing a book than it is to doing math or science. And just as YouTube and SoundCloud have spawned success for a new breed of creative people, developers are using their creative power to build impressive products and companies, sometimes reaching bigger audiences like those superstars of music, film, and podcasting.

Two engineers founded Instagram and sold it to Facebook for $1 billion, when the company still had only thirteen employees. Two developers invented WhatsApp and employed only about fifty people when they sold the company to Facebook for $19 billion. A few years ago, two developers went to a hackathon in New York with an idea to code up a group messaging app. Using Twilio, they wrote the first version in a single eighteen-hour sprint. They named the app GroupMe, and fifteen months later sold the company to Microsoft for $80 million.

These are the stories that inspire developers—not just because of the staggering amounts of money, but because they show what amazing things a handful of engineers can do when they're turned loose and allowed to dream and solve real-world customer problems creatively.

Many developers take this as an article of faith. "I've always thought that engineering is one of the most creative jobs in the world," Amazon's CTO, Werner Vogels, says. "Every day you get to create something new. Engineering is an extremely creative profession. Not all engineers are trained to become creative players. But it can be taught over time."

Yet most companies don't understand this, and don't create an environment where developers can exercise this creative muscle—

and everybody loses. Developers don't do their best work, and they dream of quitting to start their own company. Companies lose because some of their best talent goes underutilized. Customers lose because the products are the sad results of a dispassionate software factory. To solve this puzzle, companies must first start by recognizing that code is creative, that many developers are in fact creative problem solvers—and should be treated as such.

IT'S NOT ABOUT PING-PONG

Companies from outside Silicon Valley spend a lot of time studying the way tech companies operate. They send teams on "silicon safaris" to visit startups and tech giants like Google and Facebook, and build innovation labs out here. I've met with a bunch of those executive teams on their trips, and there's one thing I like to emphasize—they need to let their developers lead the way. But too often I witness executives leave Silicon Valley, taking away the wrong lessons. It's easy to latch on to the superficial stuff that is evident when you walk around tech offices, like free food, or letting people wear T-shirts and hoodies, and bring dogs to the office. After visiting enough Silicon Valley offices, it would be easy to assume that if you litter your office with enough Ping-Pong tables and colorful tricycles, then great software will somehow emerge. Sure, you should let developers wear T-shirts and hoodies if they want to, but that's definitely not the point.

Casual observers of innovation often overlook the thing that matters most, which is that developers are given responsibility and freedom. Not just freedom in working hours or what to wear, but freedom in terms of creativity.

When you think of software developers, instead of Urkel, Sheldon, or Dennis Nedry, think of Patrick McKenzie, Ryan Leslie, Leah Culver, and Chad Etzel.

Patrick McKenzie works at Stripe and is better known on the Internet as "Patio11," the screen name he uses on Hacker News (the most popular website for developers to discuss the trade), where he has long been one of the highest-rated commenters—for good reason. On his website Kalzumeus.com, he's penned some of the most insightful and entertaining essays ever written about being a software programmer. Patrick lives in Japan, where he once worked as a corporate programmer before striking out on his own, creating two simple online businesses—a bingo card generator app for teachers, and an appointment reminder app—that made him financially independent. He's a classic polymath. He speaks Spanish and Japanese, can geek out about arcane aspects of U.S. tax code, and once wrote passionately about how well Japan's emergency response systems performed during the 2011 earthquake. "That this happened was, I say with no hint of exaggeration, one of the triumphs of human civilization. Every engineer in this country should be walking a little taller," he wrote.

Ryan Leslie is a Grammy-nominated rapper and producer, an entrepreneur, and yes—a software developer. At age fourteen he scored a perfect 1600 on the SAT. He left high school early to attend Harvard, where he studied political science and macroeconomics, and graduated at age nineteen. Along the way he taught himself music production, and after graduation landed a recording deal with Universal Motown. His 2009 release, *Transition*, reached #4 on the U.S. R&B charts. But when he asked the label for a list of his fans, they just shrugged; they had no idea. What kind of company doesn't have any relationship with its customers? Not one that hopes to survive in the digital economy, that's for sure. Here was a business that was ripe for disruption, and Ryan figured he was the one to do it. He learned to write code, and created a software product called SuperPhone that lets artists engage directly with their audiences.

SuperPhone lets Ryan publish his phone number at concerts, on his website, and in his social media; when people call or text the number, Ryan adds them to his list of millions of fans. SuperPhone is basically a customer relationship management app based on text messaging. When Ryan puts out a new single or announces new concert dates, he can text his fans directly. That software code has helped him generate millions of dollars from albums and merchandise! Better yet, SuperPhone has become a booming business in its own right, with funding from some of the best venture capitalists in Silicon Valley and a staff of twelve people. SuperPhone has about two thousand customers, ranging from entertainers like Miley Cyrus and 50 Cent to large electronics retailers and luxury watch brands—all of them using SuperPhone to build intimate one-to-one relationships with their customers. Ryan isn't just a rapper; he's also a developer, a venture-funded entrepreneur, and a Software Person who uses the power of code to solve problems. "It's been a wild ride," he says. "It's really been life-changing. We're really passionate about the value that we think this can deliver."

Leah Culver finished her computer science degree at the University of Minnesota in 2006, and moved to Silicon Valley. So far she has founded or cofounded three companies. The first two were acquired, and now she's running Breaker, a seven-employee company that sells podcasting software. Between startups she worked as a developer at Medium and Dropbox. As an entrepreneur, she says she gets to exercise her full brain. She's learning new skills, like developing products, managing employees, and running a business. "What I like about startups is that it's hard. A lot of normal software jobs are too easy. I don't feel challenged. The reason people get into engineering is because it's challenging, and it's fun. I like having different things to do every day. It's the challenge of not knowing how to do something, then learning it, and then mastering it." That notion of constant learning, and expanding horizons, is something I hear consistently from great developers.

Chad Etzel is one of the most creative developers I've ever met. He excels at listening to customers and turning what he hears into interesting software. He's spent the past five years as an iOS engineer at Apple, the first place where he's felt at home after bouncing through several employers (including Twilio) in his first nine years out of university. He has creative facial hair, often wears a jaunty cap, and goes by "Jazzy Chad," which was his AOL screen name when he was a kid. (He plays saxophone well enough that he has done some gigging in San Francisco jazz clubs, and he sometimes brings his instrument to the office with him.) Like Patrick, Chad has a keen sense of humor, strong opinions, and nearly zero tolerance for any kind of BS, corporate or otherwise. His favorite job was one where he started his own company and worked for himself. "I had total autonomy," he explains. "Forging something from nothing is where I get my greatest fire and energy. The moment someone tells me how to do something, or says, 'These are the three things you need to do, and don't worry about the big picture,' that's really demotivating." Chad says the reason he's bounced through so many jobs is that until he landed at Apple, it was very hard for him "to find a company that allows this sort of autonomy or freedom so I can give my full self."

Developers like Patrick, Ryan, Leah, and Chad are incredibly creative. They're adept at applying the craft of software to serving customers and solving problems—and building businesses. Yet at most companies, an executive or perhaps a product manager would be responsible for meeting with customers, designing the product, and generating specifications documents for the developer to build to.

In spring of 2020, Twilio surveyed approximately one thousand developers around the world, asking them about how they, and their managers, viewed their role in the company. The results were telling. More than 66 percent of developers reported believing they had above-average creativity, but only 50 percent reported needing above-average creativity for their jobs. Hrm. So how are developers using that excess of creativity? Many find outlets outside of the job: 48 percent reported hobbies where design is central (such as architecture, furniture, web), and 32 percent reported producing fine art (painting, sculpture, ceramics) in their free time. (Oh, and another stereotype-busting result: developers are athletic! 36 percent are runners, 33 percent are cyclists, 28 percent play basketball, and 25 percent are hikers!)

For developers like these, handing them a "Product Requirements Document" detailing exactly what to build wastes most of their potential. That's why my biggest piece of advice to those executives who travel the world to visit Silicon Valley is this:

Share problems, not solutions with your developers.

Then watch with amazement what happens. The quality of the software improves, cycle times shorten drastically, users are happier, and your developers stay at the company longer. I've never met a business executive who didn't want all of those things.

ASHTON KUTCHER AND THE POWER OF HACKATHONS

What happens when you let developers be creative? Ashton Kutcher and Demi Moore have built a tech-fueled nonprofit, Thorn, by doing just that.

In 2012, Ashton and Demi watched a documentary about child sexual abuse that shocked them into action. It led them to cofound Thorn, which builds technology to defend children from sexual abuse. Thorn's software tools are used by law enforcement agencies around the world to find child sex trafficking victims faster and eliminate child pornography, aka Child Sexual Abuse Material (CSAM), from the Internet. To date, Thorn's software has helped identify more than fourteen thousand child sex trafficking victims and remove roughly two thousand children from a situation where their abuse was being documented and distributed as CSAM.

Several years ago Ashton asked Twilio if we would run a hackathon and help Thorn develop communication features for their software. We were proud to participate and contribute to such an important mission.

Ashton has a deeper understanding of how engineers work—and how to motivate them—than most venture capitalists (and definitely than most actors!). That's part of why the venture fund he cofounded in 2010, A-Grade Investments, has grown from $30 million to $250 million (according to *Forbes*), earning Kutcher a reputation as a standout VC. His keen eye has led him to invest in success stories like Warby Parker, Spotify, Skype, and Airbnb. One of his best investments was $500,000 that he put into Uber in 2011.

None of this is surprising when you learn that Kutcher once studied biochemical engineering at University of Iowa. "When I was in engineering school," he told me, "one of my engineering professors used to say, 'Scientists *find* problems, and engineers *fix* problems.' That's always been my outlook on software engineers. They're problem solvers. They sit down and look at a problem and then find the most efficient way to solve it."

At first, Thorn turned to other tech companies in the San Francisco Bay Area for help. "We knew what we didn't know," Kutcher says. "We didn't know necessarily how to solve the issues. But we went to a bunch of bright developers and said, 'Look, it seems that this crime [child sex trafficking] has moved online. We need to figure out how to make it a bad criminal business online. In order to do that, we are going to need to build tools. But we need to get inspired about what tools to build.'"

That led to the company's ongoing hackathons. Periodically, Thorn holds hackathons in different cities and invites developers to spend a weekend solving problems. Developers arrive knowing little or nothing about the problem of child sex trafficking, but they know that it's an important issue that needs solving. Ashton and other Thorn leaders educate them on how technology is worsening the problem of child sex trafficking, and ask the developers how technology can be used to stop it. They're given some background on what tools and data are available and then they let the developers run with their ideas. Ashton and Thorn leaders are available to help brainstorm, bring their domain knowledge, and answer questions the developers have.

The idea was born of necessity—like most nonprofits, Thorn didn't have deep pockets. Hackathons became part of Thorn's R&D lab. "We just introduce four or five problems, and say, 'Okay, go fix it. Solve the problem,'" Kutcher says. Thorn continues to use hackathons to expand upon its work, and has also built out its own dedicated engineering and data science team, 100 percent dedicated to advanced tools to end online child sexual abuse.

More interesting, from my perspective, is what this reveals about developers themselves. The people who participate in these hackathons often work for companies that treat them like code monkeys. Thorn invites them to spend a weekend trying to solve an important and difficult tech problem—how to wipe out child sex trafficking—and gives them complete freedom. And guess what? They shine. These mild-mannered cubicle dwellers turn into superheroes. Imagine what might happen if their employers knew how much good these people are capable of doing.

Think about it. Do you voluntarily do your day job on the weekends, for free, out of passion? Do most accountants do hobby accounting on the weekends? Maybe there are some who do, but probably not many. Do dentists play with some creative dentistry ideas on the side? (God I hope not!) For developers, code is more than a job—it's a creative outlet. When developers can't express that creativity at work, they find other areas to do it. Many have outside projects and even startups on the side.

Kutcher's engineering background makes it easy for him to trust developers and to realize that they are great at solving business problems. But what if you're not an engineer? Well, this approach also works if you're the president of the United States.

PRESIDENT OBAMA ASKS DEVELOPERS

After leaving Twilio in 2014, Evan Cooke, my friend and Twilio cofounder, got a call from Todd Park, the outgoing chief technology officer of the United States. Todd asked Evan if he would be available to take a meeting, no details provided. Evan was intrigued, mostly by Todd's @whitehouse.gov email address, and so he submitted his personal information (over an archaic and insecure email system) for a background check, and on the appointed day he showed up at the Hotel Fairmont in San Francisco wearing a pair of tan jeans and a cheap blazer, the closest thing he had to an actual suit.

He and a few others (who he would later learn were senior-level engineers from Amazon, Apple, and Facebook) were taken to a penthouse suite with stunning views out over the San Francisco Bay. They were met by Todd and Megan Smith, a former Google VP who had just succeeded Todd as CTO of the United States. Todd and Megan explained that they were building a new organization, the United States Digital Service. They wanted to recruit a small number of top technologists from Silicon Valley to move to Washington, D.C., and overhaul critical parts of the digital infrastructure of the government—a sort of technology SWAT team.

Then, framed by the setting sun over the Bay Bridge, they saw Marine One and a V22 Osprey approach the city and land at Crissy Field.

This was February 2015, and the past eighteen months had been excruciating for the White House. In late 2013 the government had rolled out the HealthCare.gov website with great fanfare, only to have the system collapse. This was a huge black eye for the government and especially for President Barack Obama, who had made health care reform the flagship issue of his presidency. Todd and his colleagues had recruited several Silicon Valley engineers to support the recovery effort and had managed to stabilize the site.

But the experience had made everyone aware of just how important the government's often-outdated tech infrastructure had become in delivering key administration priorities. The problems were everywhere—the Pentagon, the Small Business Administration, the Department of Education, Health and Human Services, the General Services Administration, Homeland Security. There were thousands of systems, and billions of lines of code, a hodgepodge of hairballs and patches and workarounds, much of it so old that nobody remembered where it came from or who created it.

The government was facing the same challenge that companies are facing—that more and more of what the government does depends on software, and that, thanks to companies like Spotify, Uber, and Facebook, citizens have high standards when it comes to what their user experience should be like across the board. In addition, there were massive issues of inefficiency and poor quality when it came to acquiring and implementing new software. Multibillion-dollar contracts were routinely awarded to the usual suspects, who took years to deliver a project that was often not what had been promised, even as the tech industry had long since figured out how to deliver high-quality software quickly and inexpensively. The new "thousand-dollar plunger" was the billion-dollar website. But at least the plunger worked!

Which was why Evan and the others had been brought to this meeting.

Todd and Megan needed to win them over, and they didn't have a lot of leverage. These developers could work anywhere they wanted. They could not be won over with money, as the government couldn't match their Silicon Valley salaries.

So Megan took a different approach. She went to the window and pointed across the bay to the Richmond Shipyards. Right over there, she said, was where the United States built Victory-class cargo ships, engineering marvels that could outrun German U-boats. She said that Evan and the others in the meeting were like the engineers who had designed those Victory ships, and had enabled the country to triumph in World War II.

Then the door to the hotel suite opened and in walked President Obama with a simple, powerful message: "Your country needs you." He went around the table, addressing each person individually. "Give me one good reason why you can't come to Washington and serve your country," he said. "Is there an issue with your work? Do you want me to call someone? I will call anyone." None of the five asked Obama to make a phone call. None came up with a good reason why they could not take the job. Then they snapped a quick group photo, and Obama vanished out the door with his entourage.

Two months later, Evan arrived in Washington, D.C., for his first day of work at the U.S. Digital Service, located two blocks from the White House. He would spend the next three years with the U.S. Digital Service, and says it was one of the best experiences of his career.

Now think about what Obama did and didn't do. He didn't tell Evan and the others to come to D.C. and grind out code. He shared a problem, and a big one at that. *The U.S. government needs to be fixed, and I want you to do it.* Now *that's* sharing a problem. He appealed directly to the developers' creative side: How would they go about building tech in government? What kinds of problems could they solve if they had the president's backing? He made them see that what he wanted was their minds and their imagination, not just their coding skills. There were so many opportunities—"A target-rich environment," Evan likes to say.

BASECAMP: ASSIGN PROBLEMS, NOT TASKS

Ashton's company, Thorn, turned to developers for help out of necessity. Obama reached out because he was in a crisis. But great companies embrace the Ask Your Developer mindset as an everyday practice, freeing their developers to be creative all the time. A great example of how to do this is Basecamp, a small but thriving software company in Chicago with about sixty employees.

Jason Fried and his cofounder, David Heinemeier Hansson, run Basecamp almost like a laboratory dedicated to studying new ways of working that will make employees happy and enable them to do their best work. David, known as DHH, is a software developer who became famous after creating Ruby on Rails, a widely used web development framework. But he and Jason also do a lot of thinking and writing about the subject of work itself. Together, they've published two books about software development and three books about the modern workplace, titled *Remote*, *Rework*, and *It Doesn't Have to Be Crazy at Work*. They love sharing their ideas. They even offer one-day seminars where they teach people how to adopt Basecamp's somewhat unorthodox approach to running a company.

Fried says their method is to share problems. "We just say to a team, 'Here's the idea, here's roughly where we want to go or want to build. It's your responsibility to take that and figure that out.' There's a lot of agency here, a lot of autonomy. They decide how they want to attack the problem. We might go back and forth, but the project is theirs. We could detail something out and figure out there need to be forty-two steps and then . . . giv[e] someone forty-two tasks . . . but then you're telling them, 'Don't use your brain, just do what we tell you.'" They provide a backstory to explain where the idea came from and why it's important. They might give the team a rough sketch with markers on a whiteboard illustrating their preliminary thoughts, but that's about it.

This has been Fried's policy since he cofounded the company in 1999, originally under the name 37signals. "I've never believed you should just put work on people's plates," he says. "Anything creative, you have to let people do it. That's why you hire them. If you want to direct every little thing, you end up hiring people who don't use their brains. Who's going to do great work that way? I'd rather hire people who are capable and let them solve the problems."

Fried and DHH have never released numbers on how big

Basecamp's business is, but they have about half a million Twitter followers combined, they just wrote a book about how little they work, and DHH is known for his race car collection—so I think they're doing pretty well. If trusting developers with their most important problems works for them, I bet it can work for you. It has for me.

SHARING THE PROBLEM IN A PINCH

In the early days of Twilio I learned a lesson about how creative developers can be, and how quickly they can get things done when you just get out of their way and let them do their thing. In this case, one product manager and one engineer managed to produce something in two weeks that might otherwise have taken nine months.

When we started Twilio, our first two products were Twilio Voice and Twilio Phone Numbers. Developers needed to make the phone ring, thus our voice product, and they needed phone numbers to make and receive calls—so we have an API to purchase phone numbers, originally in zip codes all around the country and eventually in one hundred countries around the world. Of course, some customers wanted to bring a phone number they already had, so we allowed customers to port their phone number from their existing carrier to Twilio. You've probably "ported" your phone number if you ever changed mobile carriers, for example.

Behind the scenes, porting a phone number from one carrier to another in the United States is extraordinarily messy. The system was hastily put in place by the carriers in 1997, in response to the Telecommunications Act of 1996—and never improved much. It's generally a manual process of people at carriers going back and forth. And since one carrier is losing business when a number is ported out, they have every incentive to make it difficult and drag their feet.

In the very early days, the operationally intensive job of handling phone number ports for customers fell to our first ops hire, Lisa Weitekamp. Lisa was our jack-of-all-trades employee. I'd hired her from the Wells Fargo FOREX desk, where she coordinated foreign exchange trading. Whatever problem I threw her way, she figured out like a champ. In the early days of a company, there are tons of those problems. For us, porting was one of them.

Eventually, Lisa hired a young guy—let's call him Tim—to take over porting. She showed Tim how it worked, and gave him a spreadsheet to keep track of the status of the ports. Our collective attention went elsewhere, and we trusted that Tim would keep trucking along with the ports. Which he did, for a while.

In the spring of 2012, we started seeing complaints from customers that ports were taking forever. First it was a drip on our support email, then more started coming on Twitter, and then personal emails to me, and then even emails to my board members. First one complaint, then two, then it seemed like a barrage of these complaints were rolling in. It crescendoed suddenly one day when we realized 90 percent of our customer complaints were about porting. So we investigated.

As it turned out, our volume of requests to port phone numbers into Twilio was going through the roof. As our business was taking off, so were the number of phone numbers to port. Tim was keeping up as best he could, but there were way more ports than he could deal with. He kept adding them to the spreadsheet, but they were coming in faster than he could process them. Because he was young and a junior employee, he was too embarrassed to tell anybody. So the port requests were just piling up.

It was like that old *I Love Lucy* episode where she's working at the candy factory. As the conveyor belt is moving faster and faster, she starts eating the candy, then shoving the bon-bons down her shirt. It was hilarious when Lucille Ball did it, not so much when it was happening in my own company.

It became obvious that this whole porting workflow shouldn't be a manual process powered by a spreadsheet anymore, but needed to be rewritten in software and automated as much as possible. And it needed to be done yesterday.

Since Lisa knew how the process worked, she had the knowledge needed to automate it. Chris Corcoran was a new engineer on the team, but he had shown an amazing ability to work problems end to end. Even though he'd just graduated with a computer science degree from UMass Lowell two years prior, he had done internships at NASA, been a student developer at Google, and been a computer tech all through his high school and college years. People had started calling him Ozone because his initials were CFC, and CFCs are the destroyer of the earth's protective ozone layer.

I grabbed Ozone and Lisa, and reserved one of the few precious conference rooms in our office for two weeks. I met them in the conference room, told them about the problem with our porting workflow, and challenged them to build the software needed to automate it—in two weeks. Lisa had all the knowledge on how to do ports, and Ozone knew our codebase inside and out. Lisa would share everything she knew with Ozone and let him figure out how to build it. And then I left.

First, they were overwhelmed. But then they got to work. Lisa walked Ozone through a few ports, operating all the bits and pieces with him at her side. Then she handed him the keyboard and had him perform a dozen ports—an example of what we call taking a walk in the customer's shoes. Only after he had experienced the problem himself did she ask him: "Okay, how do we do this with software?"

Ozone began modeling out the problem with data structures, asking Lisa, "Does this seem right?" By the end of the first day they had the basics of the data model in place. With that understood, Ozone could build the form that customers would use to submit their port information. One thing they noticed was that often customers submitted the wrong information, which required a lot of back-and-forth. That problem could be easily solved in software. By the end of the second day, they had a working form to properly collect the needed information.

Then Lisa observed that if you could let the operator batch up the work into ports in different phases, it would speed up their job considerably. Ozone says that in a more typical software development process, adding this feature could take a few months. But in this case, he was able to build a working implementation in an hour.

Of course, it would have been better if we hadn't created this hot mess in the first place. But such is life sometimes at a startup that is scaling fast. To be clear, I don't advocate making a habit of developing software by locking a developer and a product manager in a conference room for two weeks and sliding proverbial pizzas under the proverbial door. That's not the best management practice. The story just shows what developers can do when they're motivated. And to Lisa and Ozone: I'm sorry. And thank you.

The porting software project represents a great example of sharing a problem in order to solve it not just well, but efficiently. Enabling the developer to deeply understand what the user needs, and then letting them meet it, is what sharing problems is all about. Lisa helped Chris understand why people needed the code he was writing, and how it would help them. After he built empathy, the act of writing this simple workflow application was trivial.

USER EMPATHY = BETTER PRODUCTS, FASTER

The truth is that most software is pretty simple. It's what developers call CRUD applications: Create, Read, Update, Delete. Most apps online are forms that let the user input data, modify data, report out data, or delete data. Nearly every website or mobile app you've ever used is 95 percent CRUD operations. This isn't rocket science.

What that means is that the real difference in how long it takes to solve a problem, and how well it's solved, comes from the developer understanding the problem, as Ozone did. When developers actually *care* about their work, intrinsic motivation kicks in and unlocks new and even more creative ideas. When a developer is merely reading a specification document, they become isolated from the people who will use the software. The code becomes clunky and error prone because the developer didn't know how people were going to use it. Not only that, but the act of writing the code takes forever because the developer feels no passion and has no intuition for how to get it done.

This is why, if you've ever worked with developers or had teams build software for your business, there's often a struggle to get things built quickly. It always seems to take longer than the business wants. Chad Etzel—aka Jazzy Chad—views this as the natural outcome of a flawed process in which managers tell developers what solutions to build rather than including them earlier in the process, when they are defining the problem that needs to be solved.

"The managers are getting pressure from executives on the business or financial side of the company. So they come up with an idea and commit to a deadline, but they're beholden to engineering to make that happen. And that can be a difficult feeling as an engineering team when somebody just comes by and says, 'Do this, quick, by this deadline,' and then runs away."

Including developers earlier in the discussion isn't just about being nice and not hurting their feelings. It also creates real advantages. How can managers commit to deadlines when they don't understand the actual work that needs to be done? What if the specified solution can't be built in the time frame given? Either features will get cut, work will be hastily implemented, or the developers will burn out and quit. None of which are good outcomes.

Instead of presenting engineers with a solution that's already defined, product managers can share the problem and ask engineers to help figure out the fastest way to solve it based on how the existing systems—data structures, code paths—are constructed.

"Every time I hear phrases like 'This should just be a quick thing,' or 'You can do this in a day,' it drives me crazy," Chad says. "Because unless you understand how things are put together, unless you know how the infrastructure is built, you have no idea how long it will take. I think that's what sometimes causes a struggle between managers and engineering."

Chad points out that many developers "have some deeper insight into the integration or feasibility of some products or some features, where the product manager says, 'We need feature X,' and engineering says, 'Great, that'll take six months, because the way that the infrastructure is built, we can't add that easily.' But then the manager may not understand completely why it's so hard."

Finding the shortest technical path in context is what engineers do for a living. It's what they're trained to do in computer science classes. There's actually something called Dijkstra's algorithm, which finds the shortest path between multiple nodes—and we've all learned it. But instead of harnessing that short-path-finding brainpower, most companies tell developers to turn *off* that part of their brain. It's almost criminal.

Jazzy Chad is such a talented developer that I still regret that while he worked at Twilio, we never figured out how to get the most out of his creative imagination. He's found a home at Apple, where he's been for more than four years, working on iOS, the operating system inside the iPhone and iPad.

How did they hook him? By asking him to solve problems and getting out of his way. When he joined, they placed him on a team with a bunch of AI talent, but no mobile developers like him. Then they gave him this challenge: figure out how best to get Siri to do more than just voice control. Chad owns all the "Siri Recommendations" on your iPhone. Chad loves the freedom. Instead of telling him, "This pixel goes here," his manager just said, "Figure out how Siri should add more value to iPhone customers."

One of the things Chad points out is how managers have the power to connect developers with customer needs, and help them facilitate a solution. Great product managers are not a layer between customer needs and developers. In fact, they actually remove layers, eliminate preconceived solutions and erroneous presumptions, and streamline communications. Great product managers don't abstract the developer from the customer needs; instead, they facilitate understanding of customer problems. The more layers there are between people who use a product and people who create the product, the worse things get. It becomes like a giant game of telephone, where the message gets relayed through so many people that developers have little way of understanding the people who will use the software they're building.

WHY SOUL-CRUSHING SOFTWARE EXISTS

One of the most extreme cases of the "too many layers" problems comes from Patrick McKenzie (aka Patio11), who was working for a Japanese systems integrator that provides software development outsourcing services to Japanese companies, primarily educational institutions. Its business model amplifies all the issues with "sharing solutions" to an almost astronomic level. One particularly bad project involved so many leaps of telephone tag that it caused Patrick to quit not just the firm but the corporate world for more than fifteen years.

A university in Japan had a manual billing system that it wanted to automate. In the manual system, a worker sat at a desk with a pile of invoices on the left side of the desk and a pile of bank statements on the right. The worker matched invoices with statements, stamping invoices that had been paid. Naturally, they wanted to do this with software. So a business owner at the university passed the request to a buyer at the university who dealt with firm's sales reps, who passed the spec to a project manager, who passed it to another product manager—and finally to the engineers.

The solution requested: Design a computer program that has a virtual stack of invoices on the left side of the screen, and a virtual stack of bank statements on the right. The operator will click on an item in the left pile, then the corresponding item in the right pile, and then click enter. Over and over again. Literally mimicking the manual paper process, but on a computer screen.

"Our sales guys were like, 'Yup, we can build that.' Then it gets to the developers and we're like, 'This is, well, not to put too fine a point on it—crazy.'"

Clearly, a computer could just match up bank statements and invoices automatically, in milliseconds, without needing a human operator at all. But developers had no way to reach back through all of the hand-offs and explain this to the people who would be using the system.

"So we end up making a system that shouldn't exist, which will be harder to build than the computer-does-all-the-work system, at a higher cost to the clients. Not to mention that there's going to be an actual human who spends months of their life doing click, click, click, click, click, click on this," recalls Patrick. "Everything described in this task could be done by a computer—faster, cheaper, better, and without being soul-crushing."

After experiencing this kind of dysfunction too many times, Patrick decided he'd had enough and ventured out to build his own company. Realizing that teachers were an underserved market for low-cost software they could use to run their classes, he designed Bingo Card Creator, a website where teachers could subscribe for a few bucks a month and create custom—you guessed it—bingo cards. Apparently bingo cards are a big educational tool. Teachers in elementary schools make custom cards based on the lessons they're teaching, such as phonics or sight words. But they were making them all by hand. When you have a class of thirty students, you need thirty unique bingo cards, which is a lot of labor. Patrick's site lets you specify words, numbers, or pictures—and presto, you download however many bingo cards you need, all for $30. Eventually he had more than eight thousand customers, and in its peak year the Bingo Card site generated $80,000 in revenue and $48,000 in gross profit. Obviously it didn't make him rich, but when he calculated the amount of time it took by that point in the product's life cycle, his wage was over $1,000 an hour. Not bad for an audience and a need that most people probably never thought of.

Next, he set his sights on a different customer: professionals running independent businesses. No-show rates for doctors, dentists, and hairdressers cost them a huge amount of revenue each year. For a small, often solo, business, the old adage "time is money" couldn't be more true. Patrick created AppointmentReminder.com, another SaaS site, to power automated, low-cost—again you guessed it—appointment reminders via phone so clients would be less likely to miss their appointments. By the time he sold the business, it was generating mid–six figures in revenue and profits. It was a problem he loved solving, because he knew he was making life better for customers.

The magic of the Internet is that unlike in the bygone era of boxed software, Patrick could not only build the sites himself but also market and sell them to a global audience via Google and Facebook ads. He paid a little to Google to acquire customers, wrote all the code himself, did customer support, and was a one-man company. He made enough to pay the bills, and blogged regularly about his learnings along the way. He completely eliminated all those layers of people separating the product from the customers, showing why it's so powerful to do that. But more important, he showed that a developer is more than a code monkey. This made him something of a celebrity with entrepreneurs—he gave the finger to "the man" and supported himself and his burgeoning family by bootstrapping two businesses.

Back in the early days of Twilio, Patio11 became one of our biggest fans. He built Appointment Reminder entirely on top of our APIs to perform the phone calls and text message reminders.

But then a funny thing happened. Patio11, one of the most famous independent developers in the world—if not *the* most famous—got a phone call from Patrick Collison, the cofounder of Stripe. Stripe is an API, just like Twilio, but they provide payments instead of telephony. With a few lines of code, a developer can collect money for the software they build. In fact, Patio11 had used Stripe to collect the revenue for Appointment Reminder. But even though Patio11 had said privately and publicly he'd never work for "the man" again, Collison made him an offer he couldn't refuse.

Collison and the team at Stripe had been working on a new initiative, called Atlas, to solve a problem that many of his customers had: it's too hard for most people to start a company. Stripe had an interest in solving this problem because its mission is increasing the GDP of the Internet, and every additional Internet company founded means more transactions happen online; Stripe collects a small piece of many of them. Collison asked Patio11, a guy with a passion for starting and running his own businesses, to join the team alongside Taylor Francis, who had led the initial Atlas effort. The goal was to make it easier for *anybody* to start and run their own business, by making incorporation as easy as filling out a form online. With that, Stripe snagged the Internet's most eligible bachelor, so to speak. (In case you're wondering, yes I'm jealous that I didn't figure out how to hire Patio11.)

Atlas is an easy-to-use application that makes it simple to incorporate a company, "removing lengthy paperwork, bank visits, legal complexity, and numerous fees." In twenty minutes, an entrepreneur can form a Delaware C-Corp, open a bank account, get set up to receive credit card payments online, and even get startup credits for popular startup services like Amazon Web Services and Google Cloud.

Would Patio11, the consummate independent developer, have joined a big company if they asked him to grind out code? Not likely. But Collison shared a big, giant, hairy problem and asked him to solve it, while providing him with the resources of a well-funded Silicon Valley startup and the support of its founders. For a developer like Patio11, that's an exciting challenge.

CALL FOR STARTUPS

Paul Graham cofounded Y Combinator, one of the most successful Silicon Valley incubators and early-stage investors. Since its founding in 2005, Y Combinator has funded more than two thousand startups, including Airbnb, Stripe, DoorDash, and Dropbox. The combined value of the startups funded by YC exceeded $150 billion as of October 2019. Paul is himself a developer, entrepreneur, and computer scientist. He's a logical thinker who relies on principles to teach budding entrepreneurs the ropes and then set them free.

One way Y Combinator finds or even helps spawn new startups is by posting a list of problems that need to be solved. Y Combinator calls this its "Request for Startups," describing it like this: "Many of the best ideas we've funded were ones that surprised us, not ones we were waiting for. There are, however, some startups that we're very interested in seeing founders apply with. Below is an updated Request for Startups (RFS), which outlines some of those ideas in general terms."

The list doesn't specify exactly how to solve the problems. That's a job for the entrepreneurs, usually technical, to tackle. It's not uncommon for Y Combinator to fund multiple companies all tackling the same problem, albeit in different ways.

Here are some recent RFS entries:

BRICK-AND-MORTAR 2.0

We are interested in seeing startups that use brick-and-mortar commercial or retail space in interesting and efficient ways. Amazon is putting malls and big-box stores out of business. Rather than fight a losing battle with Amazon, brands need to rethink how to use retail space in ways that play to their strengths. Tesla, Warby Parker, and

Peloton, for example, use brick-and-mortar locations as showrooms that complement their online sales channels. Without the need to store inventory, retail space can be used much more efficiently.

CARBON REMOVAL TECHNOLOGIES

The Paris Agreement set forth a global goal to limit the earth's temperature increase to 1.5°C this century. Just switching to renewables isn't going to be enough to reach that goal. We will also have to remove carbon from the atmosphere.

CELLULAR AGRICULTURE AND CLEAN MEAT

Recent scientific developments have changed the way we think about producing protein. For the first time, we can now produce food that is scientifically indistinguishable from animal products like meat and dairy, using only cells and not harming any animals. Growing real animal meat directly from cells is a revolutionary science. We would love to fund more startups taking this science to market. We also want to fund startups specializing in the scaling phase of cellular agriculture. The world will massively benefit from a more sustainable, cheaper, and more healthy production of meat.

SAFEGUARDS AGAINST FAKE VIDEO

Fake videos are on the rise. The tech to create doctored videos that are indistinguishable from reality now exists, and soon it will be widely available to anyone with a smartphone. We are interested in funding tech that will equip the public with the tools they need to identify fake video and audio.

Paul and his team are investors, and like many other business leaders they face pressure from their own investors—limited partners—to produce returns by delivering innovation and commercial success. They do that by turning to developers and entrepreneurs. It's a brilliant approach.

Imagine if all business leaders used the same tactic inside their companies. Define the hairiest, scariest problems that a business faces, and do a "Call for Solutions" inside the company. Not every solution will be correct or worth pursuing, but by framing the big problems, you give developers the opportunity to think about the same things you are.

For better or worse, we all fall in love with our own ideas. What better way to instill that sense of ownership than to enable people to come up with their own solutions? When we do that, people will run through walls. That's what Paul, Ashton, and Obama are tapping into.

SHARE PROBLEMS, NOT SOLUTIONS

There's an old story about NASA trying to develop a pen that astronauts could use in space. It was tricky to get ink to flow upside down, and pens kept failing. We spent millions of dollars trying to come up with a space pen, until someone realized how the Russians solved the problem—they used pencils. Unfortunately this story is an urban legend, but it still gets told a lot in the software world. Like all good fables, this one illustrates a common mistake—the one where people set out to solve the wrong problem. The problem NASA needed to solve was not "How can we make a pen that writes upside down in zero gravity?" The real problem was "How can we write in space?"

At its core, *Ask Your Developer* is about empowerment. People in any field rise to the expectations set for them. *Ask Your Developer* is about setting high expectations for developers—not how much code can they grind out, but how well can they use their ingenuity and creativity to solve the world's biggest problems. They can do this only if they're empowered and given a wide enough berth. The most important thing is to *give developers problems, not solutions.*

While Ping-Pong tables and tricycles are nice, I'm convinced the key to building a world-class engineering culture is bringing developers into the big problems you're trying to solve, and leveraging their full brains. It's not too hard to tell if that's happening in your company. When you see a developer, ask what they're working on, and what customer problem it's going to solve. Do they know? Ask when they last interacted with a customer, and how it made them feel. Did it motivate them? Ask what they learned that surprised them. Based on their answers, you'll get a sense for whether developers are truly brought into customer problems, or whether they're just asked to implement solutions.

CHAPTER 5
EXPERIMENTATION IS THE PREREQUISITE TO INNOVATION

If you're actually inventing something, you shouldn't know what you're doing.

—Caterina Fake, cofounder of Flickr

If you're like many people, you stand in awe of achievements of great human ingenuity like space flight or the advent of the iPhone. And you dream of leading teams who could accomplish such things. As an executive, I bet you'd like your teams to bring you big, bold ideas that have the potential to transform your company, your industry, maybe even the world. Or maybe you bring those ideas to your teams, and you get pushback for all the reasons why it might not work. If you've experienced either or both of these frustrations, they stem from the same fundamental root cause: people are afraid to fail. It's natural, and very human, to want to succeed and to avoid the negative stigma associated with failure. However, tolerance for failure—both personally and organizationally—is the primary key to unlocking innovation. Smart, well-meaning managers often make small errors in leadership that discourage this kind of risk-taking. Building an organization that encourages and rewards incremental achievement of big goals increases your chances of successful innovation, and reduces the costs of inevitable missteps. That's the essence of experimentation. With software, it's never been easier, or more necessary, to build a culture that's good at experimentation. Let's see why.

In his 2016 biography of the Wright brothers, David McCullough details the process by which two bicycle mechanics from Ohio came to be the first to achieve powered human flight, one of the greatest accomplishments of the twentieth century. They weren't the best funded—Samuel Langley had received money from the War Department to develop a heavier-than-air flying machine. But he spent too much time doing whistle-stop press tours and not enough actually building.

The Wright brothers won because they ran experiments—lots of them. And they were willing to fail spectacularly, even when their own bodies were on the line.

In their Ohio bicycle shop back in 1899, they took an idea and built a prototype flying machine. The next summer they took it out to Kitty Hawk, North Carolina, which was a miserable place with biting flies and no facilities. But it had great wind. They attempted to fly their machine. It crashed. They fixed it and made some tweaks. They attempted to fly it again, and it crashed again. They repeated this cycle until either the machine or they were too broken to go on, and they'd pack up and go home for the winter. Taking all the measurements and data from the season, they'd build the next version of their flying machine. Then summer would come again and they'd go back to Kitty Hawk for more tests, repeating this whole miserable process. In 1903, many broken bones, near deaths, and twisted wrecks of flying machines later, they finally figured out the combination of wing shape, stabilizers, control systems, engine power, and more to enable the first powered manned flight. The rest is history.

This is an inspiring story. Every fiber of their physical beings must have been telling them to stop getting in those godforsaken contraptions. When they failed, they risked imminent death, yet they kept trying until they finally found success. If the Wright brothers could commit to experimenting relentlessly until they found success, so can the rest of us.

Experimenting with software works the same way—but luckily, it's easier, faster, and a lot less likely to kill you than experimenting with heavier-than-air flight. You know all those apps on your phone? They're all updated weekly. Many websites are updated daily, or even hourly.

What you may not realize is that there are experiments running within many of those apps and websites. New features are turned on for 0.5 percent of customers to see how they like them. If the response is good, the company rolls the new feature out to more people. If something is wrong—a technical glitch or just plain dislike—the company rolls it back.

That's the essence of experimentation. It's also the essence of the Lean Startup revolution started by Eric Ries, who wrote the foreword to this book. If you can try things in a low-risk way and quickly learn about your customers' needs, why wouldn't you?

Rapid experimentation in software development is the most powerful aspect of Build vs. Die. It's also why I describe it as a Darwinian process. As soon as one company starts adopting rapid experimentation and innovating at a faster clip, the rest of the industry follows. The fierce competition for survival means that overall progress accelerates. As the cost of experimentation goes down, the number of experiments grows. You get a Cambrian explosion, a huge burst of innovation.

There's an old joke that goes like this: A woman goes to church every week and prays to God to win the lottery. Week after week, year after year, she prays. Finally after decades of this, God finally answers: "Meet me halfway, and buy a lottery ticket!"

Innovation is kind of like that—experiments are buying lottery tickets for the chance of a breakthrough innovation. The more lottery tickets you buy, the better your chances. However, I don't like the lottery ticket analogy, because no amount of skill can increase your chances of winning. With experimentation and innovation, you can get better and better at it with practice. This chapter is about how to get good at experimentation to increase your chances of building the answer to your customers' biggest problems.

EVERY BIG IDEA STARTS SMALL

I remember a conversation I had with Eric Ries a number of years ago that was similar to the woman going to church every week. Eric described experiments as planting seeds in the ground. You don't necessarily know which ones, if any, will grow into giant trees. But you do know one thing: if you don't plant any seeds, you won't get any trees. Often, in his work advising companies on the Lean Startup methodology, he meets executives at large enterprises who want to kill small experiments—saplings in this analogy—because they don't yet "move the needle," meaning they're not generating, say, $100 million in revenue, enough to make a difference for the business. They're not yet giant trees.

Eric points out, sure, the experiment is not yet generating that level of revenue, but it's impossible to know which new experiments will be the next big $100 million line of business. "If you knew which ideas would be hits, of course you'd only do those. But of course, nobody knows ahead of time, so you have to be willing to plant a lot of seeds and watch them grow." When they start to sprout, don't step on them, citing how small they are. Rather, water them and give them sunlight. Or, in corporate-speak, invest more.

Like trees, every big idea starts small.

Sometimes ideas come from teams on the front lines, and sometimes leaders might have the ideas. Wherever the idea comes from, the next steps should be the same.

First, vet the idea. This doesn't need to be exhaustive; there should be low activation energy for starting a new experiment. What you really want to know are just two things:

1. What assumptions about customers, the problem, or the market are you making, and how will your experiment prove or disprove those assumptions?
2. If you are wildly successful, will it be a big outcome? The point is to grow a big tree, so ask whether the seed you're planting has that chance if it's successful.

The only reason I would have for declining an experiment is if (a) the opportunity is too small and therefore a successful outcome is meaningless, or (b) the team doesn't yet know how to measure progress.

But if the answers to the two questions listed above are reasonably good, then start with a small team. Maybe it's a new team, or maybe it's part of the work of an existing team, but five people should be sufficient to get the ball rolling.

Don't set them necessarily on a "great idea," but do set them on a customer segment and a problem that needs solving. Don't necessarily tell them what to build, but do tell them which customer to focus on and which (hopefully) valuable problem you can solve for that customer. Those are the customer and mission parts of the team definition.

Next, agree upon metrics of success. Eric Ries is great at this, so read his books *The Lean Startup* and *The Startup Way* to learn his in-depth methods for what he calls "Innovation Accounting." But in short, the small team needs a set of metrics to define what a successful experimental outcome looks like. Note, these aren't long-term business metrics; these are short-term experimental outcomes. Eric calls it validating your blind-faith assumptions.

When the team originally validated the opportunity (question #2 above), they likely built a model that projects out five or ten years and has some math that says, "If we had one thousand customers paying us $500,000 in five years, that would be awesome." That's likely how you agreed that the experiment was worthy of investment. But the next step isn't building the $500 million business; it's validating the legitimacy of the assumptions in that model, namely: one thousand customers and $500,000 in revenue each.

Your experiment might aim to (a) figure out if one customer will indeed pay you that much to solve the problem; and (b) validate that the problem is applicable to a sufficient number of customers that you could reasonably find one thousand in the next five years to bite.

If you can't even get one to bite, then that's a problem. Or if you do, but they'll only pay $1,000 per year instead of $500,000, that's a problem. Or if they do pay the right amount, but you realize there are only ten companies in the world that have this need, then that's a problem.

These parameters are designed so that you can learn as quickly and cheaply as possible whether the inputs to your model that define success are actually going to be true. Scaling them up is a job for later. Right now, you're just trying to prove the hypothesis.

Another key point is that the hypothesis isn't a technical or scientific one. To understand this, think about some famous experiments. Thomas Edison in the lab, trying to get the lightbulb to work, had a scientific hypothesis: he could make light by putting electricity through a filament. He tested more than three thousand materials to prove the hypothesis. The Wright brothers also had a technical hypothesis: that the shape of a wing was the thing that enabled flight. They had assumptions about various curves and how they might impact airflow and lift on a wing. These things needed to be proven by experimentation in the field.

Those are scientific hypotheses. With software, the answer to the *scientific* or *technical* hypothesis—"A computer program can do X"—is almost always yes, we can totally build that. The hypothesis you're actually trying to prove is the *business* hypothesis, which is "Customers will pay for a computer program that does X" or, more broadly, "A computer program that does X will make us more money."

Every spreadsheet projecting out business prospects for a new product or initiative is a hypothesis—literally made-up numbers, full of assumptions. Those assumptions get tested on a small scale, while minimizing costs. In the Build vs. Die world, you're not really conducting experiments on software—you're conducting experiments on the company itself. How can we grow? What products should we make?

The Wright brothers had a technical hypothesis about a wing shape. They did not have business hypotheses for how to build commercial aircraft, or develop an airline industry, or create airports in major cities to turn flight into a system of mass transportation. They built a minimum viable aircraft, a modified glider with a motor. (Once they proved the technical hypothesis, they did turn to business, and they built a company to manufacture airplanes, but neither had much interest in or aptitude for business. Their greatest innovation involved technology, not business. In contrast, Henry

Ford did both; he was an innovative designer of gasoline engines and other aspects of automotive technology, but he subsequently produced business innovations that were perhaps even more remarkable.)

One common mistake companies make is not having a hypothesis that predates the experiment—meaning, they invest in testing out a technical hypothesis and even building prototypes without stopping to find out whether there is sufficient demand for the product. Someone says, "Hey, wouldn't it be cool if we could . . ." Or sometimes an executive falls in love with an idea and commands engineering to pursue it.

That enthusiasm is cool, and great things often start there, but you shouldn't proceed before developing the idea into a business hypothesis. Without that, you won't know what your experiment is measuring. Success or failure will be ambiguous, and you're just left with "Is it moving the needle yet?" To which the answer will almost always be no.

Having a hypothesis, and a set of assumptions to prove or disprove, is great—but you need it in writing so you can track progress. At Twilio, one of our core values is "Write it down," and experiments are a great place to exercise such a practice. It's not uncommon for people to forget the original hypothesis, so keeping it in writing, as well as the results, keeps everybody on track. It's probably the reason why scientists and inventors keep detailed lab notebooks. I've noticed that when the experiment, and its progress, are not properly documented along the way, people (especially us executives) tend to forget the context—and revert back to "Why isn't it moving the needle!?!"-type conversations. Writing it down, reminding people of the experiment's purpose, and updating them on the progress is a great way to keep the experimental mindset alive and supported.

THE MORE EXPERIMENTS, THE BETTER

Experiments themselves are a Darwinian process we can learn from. This is what nature is doing when it throws out genetic mutations. Many fail, but a few produce organisms that adapt better, perform better, and thus survive. Rapid and constant experimentation and iteration is a basic process, fundamental to all of life. Mother Nature doesn't weep or get embarrassed about all the millions of mutations that fail. She just keeps spinning them out.

At Twilio we're always trying to run as many experiments as possible. We ship new versions of our product over 120,000 times per year—more than 300 times per day. With every one, we're incrementally adding new features and functionality, fixing bugs, increasing performance, and running experiments.

In 2019 we recruited Chee Chew as our chief product officer, asking him to help us find ways to accelerate that process. Chee has bachelor's and master's degrees in computer science from the Massachusetts Institute of Technology. He's a veteran technologist with experience running very large development organizations inside three of the world's most iconic software companies: fourteen years at Microsoft, eight at Google, and four at Amazon. I've never met anyone who has thought so deeply and so much about the act of building a software organization and a culture that enables innovation.

Soon after joining Twilio, Chee introduced a few new ideas. First, he scrapped our old system, in which engineers could only pitch products during the fourth quarter, when we were making budgeting decisions for the following year. That's a pretty traditional way of doing things at most companies. Everybody shows up with their ideas, a few get approved, and management doles out head count and budget for the winners. Most people leave the process disappointed.

The problem is that "good ideas don't come along only during the planning cycle. They hit you at any time of the year," Chee says. He introduced the idea of a rolling pitch season. Instead of forcing people to come in once a year and make a huge budget ask, we've set up a forum where anyone can pitch an idea whenever they want. If the idea gets approved, we fund a very small exploratory team, maybe as small as a fraction of a person's time. The "team" gets just enough money to run a short experiment.

Sometimes, experiments aren't about cracking a new market or growing revenue at all, but rather some other business outcome, such as saving money. Chee recently ran a contest to gather ideas for the "Biggest Efficiency Improvement," and the winning team got permission to use a full two-week sprint to flesh out the idea, plus additional funding assuming their two-week sprint proves their initial hypotheses.

"From there," Chee says, "if you hit your milestones, we'll ramp up just like a startup would ramp up, getting the next round of venture funding. So we explore, build some confidence, and finally fund a small team to get to the first commercial release."

As a result, we're able to run a lot more experiments at the same time, and though many won't succeed, we can at least figure that out faster and move on to the next experiment.

GOING TOO BIG

In 2019, Jeff Immelt joined the Twilio board of directors after a long career at General Electric, where he had served as the successor to CEO Jack Welch from 2001 to 2017. Under Immelt's leadership, GE had attempted a digital transformation at epic scale. With over 330,000 employees, turning the helm of the ship of the more than 125-year-old company turned out to be a herculean feat. One of his bets was GE Digital: building a software business that would help customers get more efficiency out of their investments in GE industrial equipment, such as wind turbines, jet engines, and locomotive engines. Using the data captured in these machines, he posited that GE could predict failures before they happened, tune the equipment in real time using AI to increase performance, and ultimately help customers run more efficient machines that needed less service and repair. Unfortunately, much of GE's revenue and profit came from parts and repairs, so the digital initiative was met with initial skepticism by other GE business leaders. However, Jeff knew that becoming a software business was the only way to protect and grow services. He had the right instincts, and thus he launched GE Digital to bolster these service businesses with big data, Internet of Things (IoT), and machine learning talent—and beat the variety of digital native companies to the punch. Launching the initiative, he committed hundreds of millions of dollars behind a big idea: a platform for industrial IoT applications.

The commitment was impressive and, as he noted, necessary to let the company know he was serious. He was quoted as saying: "For us to be a successful industrial company, we have to be this successful digitally. I don't really have a Plan B." Despite the investment of hundreds of millions of dollars, after five years, GE Digital was only taking in $15 million in customer revenue—far short of their goals. Subsequent to Jeff's departure, much of GE Digital was dismantled, letting competitor Honeywell build a successful industrial IoT product in their vacuum.

Where did GE go wrong? If you phrase the problem as "We need to turn the wheel of this $100 billion company with one big idea," the pressure is on and there's not a lot of room for failure. As Jeff says, "I had to let people know I was serious, and this wasn't just a passing fad. One way you do that in a company of our size was with the pocketbook." However, this approach was quite the opposite of an experimental mindset. They had a plan on the drawing board, hundreds of millions in funding, a shiny new office in Silicon Valley, and an experienced executive team assembled to execute. By my logic, GE would have been much better off committing not $200 million, but $20 million divided by five to ten different teams, each with a hypothesis to prove about the future of digital at GE. Every several months, leadership would evaluate their progress, granting more funding to the teams whose work was proving their hypotheses about what customers needed from GE in their digital future. Some teams would get cut, or pivot to new hypotheses.

Jeff also notes that the talent he hired was probably inappropriate for the transformation. "I hired *big tech* pedigree leaders—from Cisco, SAP, IBM, and Oracle—but not true entrepreneurs. They thought about scale, not experimentation. I would have done that differently."

It's counterintuitive for big company leaders, but sometimes overcommitting is the issue. When you fund an initiative with hundreds of millions of dollars and big fanfare, the pressure for a big outcome in an unrealistically short time hangs over the team. With fewer dollars and a more iterative, experimental approach, I suspect that by spending far less, they could have achieved far more. In retrospect, today Jeff agrees: "I had a team and a process that was set up for scale, not for experimentation. I wish I'd started small, with an entrepreneurial team, and got it started under the radar. And after they found early success, then I could apply the scale that GE was so good at."

HUGE SUCCESS, MISERABLE FAILURE, AND EVERYTHING IN BETWEEN

Okay—so you run an experiment and one of three things can happen. You strike gold; you strike out; or you find yourself somewhere in the fuzzy middle. We've made mistakes in all three scenarios.

Let's talk first about the big success case: everybody's dream case, where initial assumptions are validated and customers are loving the idea. But running experiments doesn't work unless you're able to follow up with the winners in a meaningful way. At Twilio we've made this mistake before. We've started an experiment and seen it succeed, only to keep considering it an experiment for too long, and not give it the funding to explode like the market wanted it to. We didn't properly water the sapling.

What we learned is that when you conduct experiments, you should remember to hold back resources to give needed rocket boosters to the winning experiments. Amazon does this well. Alexa, its AI-based virtual assistant, was an experiment. When Alexa started to take off, Amazon realized it was something special and needed to be fed.

The small Alexa team suddenly needed to scale up by hiring new members. There were so many open requisitions that the team could have spent all their time recruiting and interviewing prospective hires, instead of building and operating Alexa. They were in danger of being overwhelmed by their own success! So Amazon implemented a rule: anybody who accepted a job anywhere at Amazon had the option of going to work at Alexa instead if they wanted to. Think about that. The Alexa team could poach any new hire from anywhere in the company. That's an extreme version of feeding the experiment.

Now let's look at what happens if the business hypothesis proves to be false. We've talked a lot about hypothesis generation and testing. But the thing that kills an entrepreneurial, experimental culture is when people get punished for running an experiment that proves a hypothesis false. (Note that I don't call this "failing.")

It's easy for the boss to say, "Well, we gave you a bunch of money and we didn't get a hit product, so you must have failed." That's a guaranteed way of ensuring that nobody will ever take the opportunity to run an experiment or take a risk again.

Instead, think about it this way: "We had a hypothesis, which ended up being wrong. To our credit, we figured that out in only three months and for only $50,000 invested. Now we can focus our energy elsewhere."

An alternative would be where the company put a team of hundreds on the idea, took five years to build the "perfect" thing, took out a Super Bowl ad, and spent $25 million on a big ad campaign—all to find out that customers don't care, or there aren't enough customers who do care, to make the investment meaningful.

Wouldn't you rather figure that out in months for thousands of dollars, instead of years and millions of dollars? Instead of thinking about how that small team wasted $50,000, consider that they saved you $25 million! You should give them a ticker-tape parade and hand them their next assignment as quickly as possible.

Finally, let's look at the trickiest situation, the fuzzy middle, where the hypothesis remains in an unproven state, neither true nor false, and your metrics are all over the place. Those are the hardest calls. This is the one actual kind of failure story for a team running an experiment. If your goal is to prove or disprove a hypothesis, and you can't do either given a reasonable amount of time, then the experiment may actually be failing. This is why clarity of metrics is so important at the onset of an experiment.

What to do next? First, make sure you have given the experiment enough time. Sometimes patience is a virtue. Change your tactics. If the tests you're running aren't giving you answers, try testing in a different way. Maybe your hypothesis was untestable, so try changing your hypothesis into a more testable form. Perhaps the problem is your team. It's certainly possible, as in any endeavor, for a team to be poorly executing. In an experiment, the failure mode is extended periods of time with no answer to the question of whether the hypothesis is true. During the rapid iteration phase of an experiment, it's useful to check in with the team on a weekly, or perhaps biweekly, basis to help guide the experiment based on the rapid pace of learning. But if the team is continuing for six months or a year with no learnings, it may be time to make some changes.

WHEN TO PULL THE PLUG? ASK YOUR DEVELOPERS

One way to break through the problem of the fuzzy middle and find out if you should scrap an experiment is—once again, as with so many things—to Ask Your Developers. It may be that nobody is making a decision because nobody wants to tell the business leader the honest truth. It's just human nature; a lot of human beings do not like to be the bearer of bad news. But one thing you might have gleaned from reading about Patrick McKenzie, Ryan Leslie, Leah Culver, and Chad Etzel is that the engineering mindset is often predisposed to (a) having strong opinions and (b) not keeping those opinions to themselves. To engineers, facts matter. I just think of it this way: engineers hate bullshit. So if you need someone who will tell you the truth, even if it's ugly—go find a frontline engineer.

Jeff Immelt faced a situation like this when he was CEO of GE, doing a product review with a group of executives about a problem with the design of the brand-new engine that GE had developed for the Boeing 787 Dreamliner. Engineers had narrowed the cause down to a critical flaw in the low-pressure turbine design. Now GE was facing a potential crisis. The company had spent five years and over $1 billion developing the engine. The market for this engine was worth $50 billion.

Jeff watched and listened as people debated how to proceed—and then something dramatic happened. One of the frontline engineers who worked on the turbine stood up. He was not a manager, not an executive. He was just an individual contributor. He said something that most people probably did not want to hear: "This is wrong," he said. "We designed it wrong. It's not working the way it's supposed to be working, and this is going to cost us hundreds of millions of dollars, but we have to do it over."

As Jeff recalls, "This was a master technologist, a guy who would not even think about being politically correct. He said this with such conviction. He knew the consequences of this decision were going to cost the company probably $400 million to fix."

Jeff took that engineer's advice. It was a costly but correct decision. This story shows why it helps to have engineers who are building the experiments to give their point of view, as they're deep in the details. Sadly, experiments in jet engine design are a lot more expensive than most decisions we make in software.

I made this mistake once. Early in Twilio, we struck a deal with a major phone carrier to build several communications apps for their small business customers. It was pretty outside of our core business, and the developers I asked to build them really questioned the wisdom. I heard their concerns, but I asked them to build the apps anyway because it could open a broader relationship with the carrier. "Strategery," I told them. Over the greater part of a year, they dutifully built the apps even while they continued to question the decision. Literally the day before launch, a senior executive at the carrier changed his mind and pulled the plug. Our developers' work never saw the light of day. Nobody said it, but "I told you so" was clearly on their minds.

From this experience I learned two things. One, this wasn't an experiment. Due to the contract, we were all in, building blindly without any customer validation. The developers building it knew this. Second, I should have listened to the frontline engineers, who thought the apps were worthless and the business judgment unsound. We wasted over a million dollars of our precious startup cash on this misadventure. We could have avoided that if I'd paid attention to my frontline developers.

DON'T LOVE FAILURE, BUT TOLERATE THE PROCESS

Few words are more polarizing in the world of business than *failure*. In Silicon Valley, there's this strange fetishization of failure. People talk openly about celebrating failure. Investors talk about rewarding a founder who fails by funding their next company. There's a zealotry toward failure that's baked so deep into the DNA of Silicon Valley that you'd almost imagine highly successful entrepreneurs walking around sulking, with dreams of eventual failure dancing in their heads.

But it's not the failure that's celebrated, it's the deep learnings that advance the mission. Failure is merely accepted as a natural consequence of the learning. When people talk about accepting failure, they're talking about accepting the journey of discovery.

Notice above, when I talked about running experiments, it's not about success or failure, it's about accelerated learning. When you disprove a hypothesis, that's a valuable learning that many would call a failure. But I would call it a success: when you reach a dead end quickly and cheaply, that's valuable to the business. That's the whole point of thinking of the process as a series of experiments that lead to eventual innovation. Innovation is not something you can just will into existence. It's a slog. And if you don't celebrate the journey and get value from your mistakes, most people would quit along the way. That's why Silicon Valley goes so overboard in addressing failure head-on.

Let's be honest, though: nobody likes to fail. True failure is not pleasant, and any normal person hates it. Failure in isolation is not actually celebrated, and no entrepreneur whose company is failing is actually happy or celebratory as the myths would have you believe. The fetishization of failure risks getting out of control, but it's the stigma of failure that innovators over-rotate to avoid.

HOW TO FAIL WITHOUT FAILING YOUR CUSTOMERS

The biggest concern people have about experiments is how to avoid harming customers in the process. Because in the process of invention, when you do find a great product, you still need customers to sell it to. If you burned all your relationships along the way of discovery, that doesn't bode well. Luckily you can experiment while also bringing your customers along on the journey if you structure it well from the get-go.

Large tech companies like Facebook, Amazon, and Google have sophisticated tiered deployment systems that can light up a new feature for a subset of customers. Maybe a random 1 percent of all users see an experiment to test the response. Maybe it's a more targeted approach—like only users in a certain country or a demographic. Since it's just a fraction of people, it's a great way to learn without making a big commitment to your customer base. Shutting down a 1 percent experiment is easy, and also cheap. It's much more difficult and costly (in dollars and reputational damage) to shut down an experiment that has been rolled out to a large number of subscribers. Of course, this works well when you have hundreds of millions or billions of users, so it doesn't work for every type of company. Luckily, many ways of testing ideas are decidedly less sophisticated and work just as well.

The easiest way is just to talk to customers. "Would you buy a thing that . . ." is a very easy way to test the waters. If you remember when we started Twilio, I asked many developers if they could use a service that could enable communications in their apps. That was a very low-cost, low-risk experiment. I actually ran the same process for multiple other ideas at the same time—one idea was a distributed data backup system similar to Dropbox. The other was an idea to use the Internet and BitTorrent to enable cheap or free cable TV. All I did was interview potential customers to see whether my idea would solve a problem they had in life. Since you're not making any promises, there's little chance you'll disappoint a customer. Mostly, they're just happy somebody is asking them and thinking about their problems.

Another way to test ideas online is called the "painted door" test. If you hypothesize the world needs some technology product, you can test that hypothesis easily by building a quick website and buying ads on Google—seeing if you can get people to bite. You don't have to actually build the product, just the marketing website to see if the value proposition resonates. Given the efficiency of online advertising, you can target your hypothesized buyers pretty well and test whether they hit the "buy button" on the website or not. Here's where you might let people down: the buy button doesn't actually work if you haven't built the product. Usually the button leads to a page that says, "Thank you for your interest. The product isn't ready yet, but we appreciate your input." You can always use a fictional company name if you don't want to risk some brand harm.

I did this in 2007 when I was brainstorming ideas prior to starting Twilio. In building Nine Star, I'd had difficulty getting emails from our point-of-sale system delivered successfully to customer inboxes. They seemed to get stuck in spam folders periodically. I hypothesized that other developers were having the same issue, so I ran a quick "painted door" test. I bought the domain name MailSpade.com, and spent about an hour building a simple website explaining the value proposition to prospective customers. Then I spent about fifty dollars in Google ads to drive some traffic to the site. The site included a "Get Started Now" button, but after clicking it, the site merely said "Coming Soon." I was just testing whether the value proposition was strong enough for potential customers to want to buy the product. By watching the patterns of these early window shoppers, I could learn a lot, all for about five hours of work and fifty dollars. Not bad. Ultimately I decided to pursue the Twilio idea, but in 2009, three developers, Isaac Saldana, Jose Lopez, and Tim Jenkins, started a company called SendGrid to solve the email problem. Ten years later, Twilio acquired SendGrid for more than $2 billion, proving that it too was a great idea!

In reality, it's quite easy to run experiments without hurting your customers. However, one mistake to avoid is treating an experiment like it's not an experiment. If you aren't sure the world needs your idea, do the work to test it experimentally, as I've advocated in this chapter. But if you jump straight to a huge investment and a big splashy launch, that's when you're more likely to hurt your reputation with customers. If, with big fanfare, you launch a big dud—that's a brand and PR issue. (New Coke, anybody?) If you do a big launch, you're likely to get *some* nonzero number of customers. But if that number doesn't meet the big investment you put in, you're more likely to want to kill the project. And that's where you will likely now disappoint customers. So I believe that experimentation is not likely to hurt customer relationships. Rather, it's the lack of experimentation that is likely to do more lasting harm.

SWING FOR THE FENCES

Successful innovators know that the path to success may be lined with failed attempts. Thomas Edison once said, "I have not failed. I've just found 10,000 ways that won't work." Winston Churchill noted, "Success is stumbling from failure to failure with no loss of enthusiasm." But my favorite take on experimentation comes from Jeff Bezos. In his 2015 letter to Amazon shareholders, Bezos reminded investors that three of Amazon's biggest successes—Marketplace, Prime, and Amazon Web Services—began as experiments, and that, when they were conceived, nobody knew whether they would work or not. After all, most of the company's experiments fail. Bezos used a baseball analogy to explain why he pushes his developers to keep running as many experiments as possible: "If you swing for the fences, you're going to strike out a lot, but you're also going to hit some home runs." He went on to note that in baseball, the very best outcome from swinging the bat is a grand slam, scoring four runs. However, "in business, every once in a while, when you step up to the plate, you can score 1,000 runs."

Therefore, why not take as many swings as you can? Especially when the cost of running experiments is so cheap. You're talking about three to five people to get started, and the potential outcome is so huge! Because of the inherent scale of the Internet, that experiment could net an app with hundreds of millions of users. The risk-versus-reward calculation is incredibly good, so keep swinging that bat!

In baseball, a batting average of .300 is amazing, and .400 is pretty much unattainable. That means the majority of the time in baseball, a player doesn't achieve anything with the at bat. So in business, if the potential outcome of an at bat is 250x greater, a .0012 batting average would be equally sufficient for the major leagues of business! Of course this is all made-up math, but you get the point. In business, there's often an expectation of a 100 percent success rate—and therein lies the fear for people to experiment. Breaking through that fear is key to successful innovation.

Next time you experience resistance to trying a new idea, ask your leaders what's the worst that can happen. If the answer is "It'll take a long time," then ask how to shorten the time to learn. Can you learn something in a day or two with a painted door test or some customer interviews? If the answer is "It might fail," then violently agree with them, and ask again why they shouldn't try it anyway! If the answer is "We might let down customers and damage the brand," then scale back to test the idea with a small group of customers. Ask your leaders (probably one-on-one) if they fear their career will suffer if they fail. If the answer is yes, then consider how to celebrate the process of experimentation versus just the outcomes. Ask your developers how they measure intermediate progress of experiments they're running—ahead of building a $100 million business, how will they know if they're on the right track? Ask them what hypothesis they're trying to prove with the experiment, and if needed, help them fine-tune the hypothesis so it's testable with reasonable investment. These questions will help you build a culture that recognizes and celebrates the process of experimentation, and ultimately a culture of innovation.

CHAPTER 6
RECRUITING AND HIRING DEVELOPERS

It doesn't make sense to hire smart people and tell them what to do. We hire smart people so they can tell us what to do.
—Steve Jobs

Over the past few chapters, I've talked about why it's so important, and easier, for companies to become software builders. To do that, you need talent. In the coming decade, the winners will be companies that build the best software—which really means, the companies with the best software developers. If you've struggled to hire or keep great technical talent, then this chapter might help you understand how you can attract and retain developers by appealing to what matters to them. If you chronically have more open technical roles than you can fill, maybe you can change your pitch to developers to make your company into the place where developers know they'll be able to do their best work. If you've lost talent to companies like Apple, Google, and Facebook, I actually think it's not that hard to make the compelling case that your company is a superior career choice. We've hired our share of technical talent from those companies, or convinced candidates to accept our offer over one from the tech giants. In this chapter, I'll share some observations I've had through the years, both as a developer and as an employer, on how to recruit, retain, motivate, and compensate great technical talent.

There's a shortage of developers in the world. In 2019, there were four times as many open software jobs as there were new computer science graduates. So it's a tremendously competitive market for talent, but the good news is you don't have to get ridiculous providing tricycles, free haircuts, and fifty styles of IPA to win here.

Mostly, you just have to treat software developers like people. Not ornery nerds to be hidden in the server closet. Nor delicate unicorn flowers to be coddled. Developers are just people, replete with ambitions to learn and grow, motivations to do their best work, and a full range of skills they want to exercise. In companies where this is understood and respected, and where developers are given a seat at the table, they'll be engaged, active company builders with you.

Your early hires are especially important. Bringing in the right leader at the start can be key to success because that leader will attract a cadre of lieutenants who can in turn recruit great managers and individual contributors. But recruiting talent is only the first step. Managing to retain them might be even more challenging. If your organization is dysfunctional, developers won't sit around hoping that things will get better. They'll bounce. Unfortunately, I learned this through experience, as I will explain in Chapter 11.

RECRUIT A GREATER LEADER—AND THE REST WILL FOLLOW

When Patrick Doyle took over as CEO of Domino's in 2010, his first goal was to improve the quality of Domino's product—simply put, to produce a better pizza. His next goal was to expand the company's technology capabilities. It might seem counterintuitive for a company in a commodity business to make huge investments in technology. But as Patrick saw it, there were only so many ways to differentiate Domino's based on its product offerings. A pizza is a pizza is a pizza. Patrick reckoned there were even bigger opportunities to differentiate Domino's from its rivals by using technology to improve the customer experience.

The company's existing IT department would need to change from more internal-facing functions, to becoming builders of software that customers would experience. Like many IT departments of the time, Domino's technology team was primarily focused on things like racking hardware, installing updates and patches, and keeping the servers running. But Domino's needed to build a creative software organization that could build new apps and create user experiences. To build that organization, Patrick began by hunting for the right leader. In 2012, he scouted Kevin Vasconi, a veteran technologist who admits that at first he wasn't particularly interested in working for a pizza company.

When Kevin joined in 2012, his mission was to build a completely new technology organization. At the time, Domino's had 150 workers in IT globally. Eight years later that number has grown to 650, of whom only 50 were part of the group Kevin inherited. He began by turning to his professional network and hiring a strong core team. This wasn't just executives. A good technical leadership team consists of senior architects, principal engineers, and line managers. The main thing is to make sure your early hires have strong technical chops. The first hires might also be the toughest. But over time it gets easier. Kevin's advice to others—don't rush and don't settle.

In the past eight years, Domino's has radically changed the pizza business by building a world-class software organization and turning developers free to create innovative and even eccentric software experiences. These include using voice recognition or tapping an emoji to place an order. Some ideas begin almost with a whim. One day Patrick asked his developers: "How could I order a pizza while I'm sitting at a stoplight?" That was the entire question—stemming from an observation the CEO had on the way home himself. "Ordering at a stoplight" might seem like a bit of a weird request, but in fact it's a real use case—the busy mom or dad who doesn't want to cook dinner and can order a pizza on the commute home. But the simple question opened up the door for years of innovations that make ordering and tracking an order easier and faster. None of it would have happened without the team that was customer-facing and ready to execute.

AUTONOMY, MASTERY, AND PURPOSE

In his book *Drive: The Surprising Truth About What Motivates Us*, Daniel Pink argues that compensation isn't necessarily what motivates people. Or it does, but only up to a point. Companies need only compensate employees to the point where they feel they are paid fairly. (I'll talk more about that toward the end of this chapter.) Once you meet the bar of fairness, employees focus on the real reasons for work: autonomy, mastery, and purpose. I believe this is especially true for developers.

Autonomy means the ability to work independently and not be told what to do. Mastery means the ability to get better at your craft over time. Purpose involves the feeling that the work you do actually matters. Let's inspect each of these a little more closely, especially through the lens of developers.

Autonomy

Every human wants to feel empowered, and developers are no different. But even more so, as professionals they bring technology domain expertise that's valuable to the companies they work for—but is often overlooked. The essence of autonomy is feeling trusted to make decisions. If someone else can just veto whatever decisions you make, then you're not really all that autonomous. Of course, if you pull rank in a company, you can always make the decisions. But wise leaders who want their teams to feel trusted resist the temptation to overrule their teams' decisions, instead erring on the side of autonomy. That's how I think about it.

But full autonomy can become counterproductive in a world where teams have lots of dependencies, and it's tough to wrangle thousands of people off in their own land. By empowering developers, you are trusting them to do their jobs and giving them tools, but you also instate some guardrails and rules. This is more realistic than full autonomy, especially for an organization at scale. Especially when we do need a full R&D org to focus on things like incident reduction, security, stability, and more.

So instead of letting developers just run around and do whatever they want, autonomy actually has its basis in rules. Without guardrails, people won't know how to make decisions, and leaders will tend to second-guess them constantly. By creating rules, you paradoxically set people free—in the space between guardrails.

One of my favorite examples of this was from my high school. I was a member of my high school's radio station, WBFH, known colloquially as "The Biff." Broadcasting at 360 watts, we were proudly metro Detroit's most powerful high school radio station. Being on radio station staff meant we all had jobs, like those at a real radio station, and we each had a weekly two-hour show to host. My senior year of high school, I had the job of music director, and my two-hour weekly show was called the *Seven Hour Prison Experiment.* Pete Bowers, the blond, lanky Tom Petty–esque teacher who ran WBFH, had only three rules for us: everything we did had to be "safe, fun, and legal." Outside of that, it was our station to run! For example, when we wanted to promote the launch of the new Smashing Pumpkins album by broadcasting an on-air pumpkin smashing competition on the sidewalk outside the school—Mr. Bowers heard the plan and replied, "Well, it sounds fun, and legal. Just make sure it's safe." Not only are my WBFH memories some of the best from high school, but it was an amazing learning environment. Mr. Bowers let us make mistakes (as long as we were keeping things safe, fun, and legal) and learn from them. I've used Mr. Bowers as inspiration to guide my thinking about how to create an environment where the ground rules are known, and then everybody feels empowered to sprint forward.

What's also implied, though, is that you should pare the rules down to the minimum needed to create a system that works. As leaders, you do need to create a system where teams can successfully collaborate, where talent will be successful, and where your customers can trust you. A lot of what we've outlined in this book—small teams, platforms, microservices, and so on—are parts of such a system.

Another facet of autonomy is influence—inviting developers to key decisions shows you trust them and value their input, which I think you should!

When my friend (and Twilio cofounder) Evan Cooke worked at the U.S. Digital Service, autonomy was the biggest thing they demanded. They were not going to be relegated to sitting in some back room taking orders like a bunch of code monkeys. They wanted, and were granted, the ability to build systems without interference from product managers, management consultants, or various other nontechnology constituents.

They also advocated strongly for being included in big decisions. The White House technologists came up with a concept called technical quotient (TQ), akin to the notion of IQ or EQ, to explain to executive leadership across departments and agencies—whether at the Pentagon, the White House, the Small Business Administration, the Department of Education, the Department of Health and Human Services, the General Services Administration, or the Department of Homeland Security—the importance of having "TQ at the table." "We are at a point in history that technologists need to be part of the decision-making process for nearly every important decision," Evan says.

Evan and other software engineers sat in meetings alongside cabinet members, department secretaries, and four-star generals in full dress uniform. At first it seemed weird, but people adjusted. After all, as Evan points out, "When it comes to public policy, the entire delivery mechanism is mediated by or driven entirely by technology." Crafting public policy without involving technologists "is like trying to solve a legal problem without having a lawyer in the room."

Creating a system of rules also means eliminating rules that aren't needed. How do you convey to developers that they have autonomy? This involves a lot of things, and some of them may seem small or trivial—but they matter. One recent story comes to mind from Twilio. We have a team of developer educators who often run hackathons inside large enterprises undergoing digital transformation. At one such event, they arrived at the particular enterprise to set up for the two-day event, and in the assigned break room where the hackathon was to take place, there was a TV in the back with a sign telling employees they were not allowed to change the channel. That's a way to let people know they don't have autonomy. Some people might think, "Who cares? That's not such a big deal." I can only tell you that when our folks came back from that hackathon they were all talking about that sign. To them, it was a huge deal. They all noticed it. "How are you going to give developers autonomy to create software when you don't even trust them to change the channel on a TV?" was how one person put it.

Here's another issue you might think is silly that actually rankles developers in a big way: clothing. Dress codes. Making people wear "business attire," or whatever. Like the TV sign, it's small but sends a big (and wrong) message, which is: "We don't even trust you to pick out your own pants."

The dress code issue famously became a huge problem when the White House organized the U.S. Digital Service. My friend Evan and the others who went to Washington were told that women at the White House were to wear pantsuits, and men at the White House were expected to wear suits and neckties. In Silicon Valley that's just plain nuts. Nobody wears a suit and tie—ever.

The developers tried to explain this but were told that this was not Silicon Valley. This was the White House, and at the White House suits and ties were required. Most developers went along with it, perhaps grudgingly. But one important guy put up a stink—Mikey Dickerson, a brilliant engineer from Google who was recruited to help salvage the HealthCare.gov website.

Mikey happens to be a curmudgeon—and a defiantly terrible dresser. He told the White House that he would come to Washington and fix their websites, but he wouldn't wear a suit and tie, and hey, it's your call, guys. For a while the White House insisted, but Dickerson wouldn't budge. In the end they struck a compromise.

Mikey didn't have to wear a suit, but he did agree to wear shirts with buttons and collars, albeit wrinkled ones.

You might think Mike was being petty or arrogant, but he was actually doing something important. This was Mikey's way of assessing if he would be able to make developers successful in this environment. If they couldn't get some autonomy to decide what to wear, it was a bad sign for their influence over other, far more important decisions.

The gesture wasn't really about clothes; it was about testing the waters of autonomy.

What happens if you don't provide real autonomy? Developers are unlikely to do their best work, and you'll be less likely to retain great talent. "The moment someone says, 'Here are these three things you need to do, don't worry about the rest of it, don't look at the big picture,' that's really, really demotivating and frustrating to me," says "Jazzy" Chad Etzel.

Chad says his best experience as a developer was when he built his own company—simply because he had autonomy. "I had basically full autonomy and control over the product and the direction and the pieces that needed to be built. I could just do all of that," he says. He talked to customers, they told him what features they wanted, and he just went and built them. "That ability to just forge something from nothing is where I get my greatest fire and energy," he says.

He's had a hard time finding autonomy in regular jobs. In six years, from 2009 to 2015, Chad went through six companies. "I've worked at a lot of places. It's been very hard for me to find the type of company that actually allows the sort of autonomy and freedom where I feel like I fit in and I can give them my full self," he says.

Since 2015, Chad has worked at Apple, which gives him enough autonomy and freedom that it feels close enough to running his own company.

Apple is famous for not having product managers who throw product specs over the wall. Developers are given problems and can solve them however they think is best—the essence of the Ask Your Developer methodology. The result of that trust in developers is that Apple produces beautiful software, which in turn has led to its incredible success in the market.

Mastery

In 2016, Kaya Thomas, an undergraduate computer science major at Dartmouth College, published a heartfelt essay that shook up Silicon Valley. Kaya wrote about how frustrating it is for black and Latinx computer science majors to get hired in the tech industry. She also wrote about the culture that has evolved in some tech companies that she and many others find so off-putting,

"I'm not interested in ping-pong, beer, or whatever other gimmick is used to attract new grads. The fact that I don't like those things shouldn't mean I'm not a 'culture fit.' I don't want to work in tech to fool around, *I want to create amazing things and learn from other smart people*. That is the culture fit you should be looking for," Kaya wrote (italics mine).

The statement I've italicized is probably the best distillation I've ever read of what young developers are looking for in an employer. Those two factors—create amazing things and learn from other smart people—are basically what all of us look for from our work.

Kaya was seeking mastery. The very best developers, young or otherwise, are always hoping to be pushed, to learn, and to grow. They want to get better at what they do, and to find mentors who will help them develop.

After graduation Kaya had a bunch of offers. She chose to work at the company Slack, in large part because she believed she would learn there. "I definitely had mentorship. I worked with incredibly smart people from all types of backgrounds, people who had worked at lots of other companies. I was able to learn and grow a lot," Kaya says.

Computer science majors leave university with a degree but still have a lot to learn about how to ship production-level commercial code. "I had staff engineers who taught me about building mobile systems and mobile frameworks, and people teaching me about larger architectural design and principles for developing software. That was incredible," Kaya says.

Equally important were skills Kaya developed that were not related to programming—things like communication, writing, making presentations. You might think of them as "soft" skills, but Kaya learned they're actually a huge part of an engineer's job and a big factor in how well an engineer succeeds inside an organization.

"There's a common misconception that you get hired as an engineer just to write code," she explains. "But communication is a huge aspect of the job. How do you take very technical ideas and make it possible for people who aren't engineers to understand them? You need to learn about code reviews, how to give a code review and how to receive one, and how to learn from that information. You need writing skills, to create technical documents. You need public speaking, to be able to speak at conferences, or just to get up and disseminate information to other teams."

Everybody wants to feel like they're progressing, not just in their title or salary, but in the mastery of their chosen profession. That's why the best employees often pick an environment that will foster their professional growth over all else—including salary or perks. As leaders, there are things we do formally and informally to create a learning environment—Chapter 7 is all about how to create such an environment.

Purpose

Like anybody, developers want their work to matter. They want to develop systems that generate revenue, or save money for the company, or enable the company to deliver new experiences that delight customers. They want to invent new lines of business. Show them that in your organization, developers are considered key to the company's future, solving problems that have impact on millions of people.

Ali Niknam, CEO of Bunq, the mobile bank based in Amsterdam, says his startup has been recruiting great developers in the Netherlands, even though there is a huge shortage of developer talent there. What's more, Bunq even manages to lure developers out of bigger tech companies like Uber, Google, and Microsoft—even though Bunq pays less than those big tech giants. "They are all taking pay cuts," he says.

How has he done that? One reason is the mission. "We're changing the course of the financial industry. You can be a part of 130 people who are shifting an entire industry on its end," Ali says.

When computer scientist Tom Bilske moved from his native Australia to Amsterdam, he leapt at the chance to join Bunq. He was attracted by "cool people building a product they really liked and solving problems for people," he says. He also wanted the challenge. "I was stunned when I got here by how fast it is. It's ridiculous. We release code every week. We develop features in no time at all. I was very impressed by the engineering organization. The developers here are very good. I've worked for a few other organizations and they were really good—but this is night and day." That's purposeful because Bilske both believes in the mission and believes he can influence the company's ability to fulfill it.

As leaders, it's our job to connect the company's greater mission to the work our technical teams are doing. Everybody has parts of their job they love, and parts they loathe, and developers are no different. So when a developer is in the drudgery of debugging legacy code or writing tests or waking up when the pager goes off—purpose is what makes these moments tolerable and even sometimes interesting. Knowing that customers and your coworkers depend on you, and that you're changing the direction of your organization and those around you, is a powerful motivator. In fact, the more people who are touched by your work, oftentimes the greater the purpose. And the amazing thing about software is the scale. Writing code that will be used by millions or even billions of people is powerful. Very few professions share the same sense of scale or impact. That's why developers are particularly motivated by purpose.

Remember my story from Chapter 4 where President Barack Obama flew to San Francisco on Marine One to personally recruit the first few developers to the U.S. Digital Service? This was the most amazing recruiting pitch I've ever heard about. It was all about purpose. The developers were given a mission, with high stakes and high impact. They were asked to solve problems that even the world's most accomplished technologists would find challenging.

Including Obama was a stroke of genius. Why was Obama there? Why did he bother to fly all the way up to San Francisco from an event down on the peninsula—just to stick his head in the room for ten minutes? Obama knew his presence conveyed to the developers that they would have support from the very top of the organization, that this digital transformation was one of his highest priorities. That's why he made the extra effort.

RECRUITING

That's all well and good, I can imagine you saying, but what if you're not recruiting for the U.S. Digital Service and can't get Barack Obama to swoop in as your closer? What if you're not hiring computer scientists to build top-secret world-changing new divisions at Amazon? How do you make your company sound sexy? How do you convince a new computer science grad to work for your company instead of going to Google or that cool startup down the road?

First of all, you might not have Obama, but you do have a CEO and other executives (you may be one yourself), and when you're recruiting top technology talent, they should be involved. Ideally your CEO already knows why technology is important to the company, intends to work closely with your top technologists, and therefore already intends to be part of the recruiting process. If the top brass don't show up, smart technologists will realize that their work isn't central to the company—and they probably won't come to work for you. It's easy for executives to exclaim "we're on a path to digital transformation" because it sounds good, but to really embark on this journey, leadership has to be invested in the process and, more important, the people who will make it a reality.

When Jeff Immelt set out to transform GE, with its 330,000 employees, he asked endless questions of tech experts because he truly wanted to understand what they knew. He wasn't afraid to admit when he didn't understand, and he gave technologists a seat at the table. That's the kind of dedication from the top that shows that digital transformation isn't just a buzzword.

Engineers sometimes need help to realize that nontechnology companies are filled with important, challenging, and difficult technology problems that would be really cool to work on. "I'm finding there are a lot of very interesting challenges in every large corporation," Werner Vogels says. Werner spends most of his time traveling the world and meeting with companies that use Amazon Web Services. That includes pretty much every cool new startup in the world as well as thousands of huge incumbents from nontechnology industries. Traditional companies are doing lots of work with the Internet of Things (IoT) and other new technologies. "These companies are operating at such tremendous scale, and they have these very interesting, very meaty problems to solve," Vogels says.

The challenge is how to make engineers aware of these problems and get them excited about solving them. Again this all comes back to explaining the mission—and making it seem compelling. That's why in every spy movie there's a scene early on where the hero gets called to a meeting and told about the next mission. You'll notice that the mission isn't usually something like "We want you to come in every day for the next thirty years and sit at a desk and do something boring that you don't really care about. And if you fail, it's no big deal because nothing bad will happen." No! The bad guys have a nuke! The clock is ticking! If you fail, the world will be destroyed! Storytellers call this the "Hero's Journey." It begins when main characters receive the "call to action" and embark on adventures that challenge their abilities and force them to overcome obstacles. Rocky Balboa's call to action happens when he gets offered a fight with Apollo Creed.

To be a good recruiter you need to present your version of the Hero's Journey. What do we do here? What challenges are we facing? Why is our work important? Why should you care about your job? What's at stake? Why will you be excited to come to work every day? "You have to tell them the story about how your team functions," says Josh Hoium, former longtime director of voice engineering at Target in Minneapolis and currently the director of network engineering at Liberty Mutual. "I think a lot of what's happening right now, especially in the tech spaces, it's believing in the boss that's going to hire you. So telling them about what you're going to do, telling them about your vision—that has been the key to hiring people. It takes some convincing. A lot of people didn't really think of Target as a tech company. But I've hired three people in the last twelve months and a couple of them had some pretty different opportunities to go somewhere else. It's being able to walk through how you want to change things, and how you want them to be the focus of the work as part of an engineering-led organization."

Sure, Josh says, he's lost a few, too. Three developers who did internships at Target later went to Facebook, Google, and Zynga after graduation. But even candidates who are entertaining offers from tier-one tech shops can be won over, he says. There's the appeal of being a big fish in a small pond versus going to a giant tech company, where there are thousands of others just like you. "That story is like, 'Hey, if you come into Target, we want you to learn and grow and to be able to drive technical decisions. I don't want to dictate what those decisions are. I'm going to look for you to make those choices.' And for a lot of young engineers that resonates quite a bit," Josh says.

For midcareer developers you can offer a chance to grow and develop new skills—just at a time when some might start to feel stagnant or stuck with skills that are becoming less relevant. In other words—mastery. Show them that they can expand their skills and learn new languages, design and write new apps and put them into production.

At Twilio, I know we've recruited many developers who had offers at Google, Facebook and the like. For us, the compelling pitch was our small-teams approach, which enables all three facets of autonomy, mastery, and purpose; I talk about this more in Chapter 8. When you can be yet another cog in the machine, or a key member of a small but important team—many developers find the latter is a pretty compelling opportunity.

COMPENSATION

Earlier in this chapter I mentioned Daniel Pink and his theory that compensation isn't really what motivates people, that the point is only to make employees feel that they are paid fairly. Yet many employers focus on bonus structures. They end up conveying a message to employees that management sees them as coin-operated machines, which misses the point on why most employees want to work. Once their basic needs are met, most employees want intrinsic motivation, like autonomy, mastery, and purpose.

That's why at Twilio, we don't have bonuses for anybody in the company. We've operated the company this way for about six years, and I think it's far better.

Most companies, even in our backyard, pay a bonus tied to weird corporate objectives. One kind is tied to company-wide objectives like revenue or profitability, the idea being that the whole company bands together to achieve these goals. The problem is that in reality no individual employee has the kind of impact to make or break these goals. So their compensation, which they will focus on a lot, is not tied to their job. It's essentially random. Another problem is that you might have done a great job, but those idiots over in that other department didn't do theirs and now nobody gets their bonus. What a rip-off!

Management By Objectives (MBO) is another method of assigning bonuses, tied to goals that are set at an individual or team level for the employee. On paper this sounds better because you articulate what the team needs to do, and then the team members or individual get paid more if they do it. Yet I've seen companies burn so many calories trying to figure out what these MBOs should be! Sometimes it takes so long to set the MBOs that by the time they're set, they're irrelevant or wrong. Then employees are focused on achieving the goals versus doing what's right. You also get into a negotiation between setting lofty goals, which is great but often means you're setting employees up to miss their bonus; or setting goals that are easy layups and so that everyone gets their bonus and thus will be motivated. Either way, each one of these compensation levers is another vector for employees to feel their compensation is not fair. And, back to Daniel Pink, the best compensation plans are those where employees feel they're compensated fairly, allowing them to move their attention from comp to the work.

You don't want employees focused on bonuses. You want them focused on customers. You want creative energy. Daniel Pink references a study where people were asked to do a simple task that required creative thinking. They're given a challenge of figuring out how to attach a candle to the wall, and they're given a box full of pushpins and few other odd items. There are two groups given this challenge. One team is just asked to figure out a hard problem, and the other team is told if they figure it out, they'll get some financial compensation, something like twenty dollars. It turns out, the best way to solve the problem requires some creative thinking. Most people try to use the pins to tack the candle to the wall, which doesn't work out. But with some creativity, teams notice that the box itself can be used, and can make an excellent candle holder, which they can tack to the wall. Guess what? On average, the team with no financial motivation solved this creative puzzle three and a half minutes faster than the financially motivated team.

According to that study and others, bonuses and variable pay structures can actually inhibit creative thinking rather than enabling it. This makes sense to me, because I've seen this firsthand. For the first few years of Twilio, we had a management team bonus. When things are ambiguous, as they often are when you're building something, it's hard to set goals. At the start of every year we had the same big arguments about setting the goals. Are they too hard? Too easy? At the end of each year we argued about whether the goals had been set well at the beginning and whether the bonuses were merited or not. In some years, we blew away the goals and the board was concerned we'd sandbagged them. In other years, we missed the goals, and the team felt that the goals were unfair to begin with. In every case, we ended up paying out the money. That's when I decided this wasn't worth the effort.

We pay higher than most similar companies in base pay, which is guaranteed and not subject to some management fad or poorly set goals. And we tend to give a little more stock equity as well, to compensate employees for the lack of bonus—with the side benefit of focusing employees on long-term versus short-term objectives. My belief has always been to pay people well, so they feel it's fair, but don't cloud things by believing that compensation is the great motivator, especially for creative roles. (I recognize that for sales, it's different. In sales, commissions are part of the game.)

For what it's worth, Ali Niknam, the founder and CEO of Bunq, believes that paying people less than top-of-the-range actually becomes a way to attract the best talent. "When you work at Bunq, you don't work at Bunq for the money. You work at Bunq because you really believe in what we're trying to do. We pay an average salary, and that's what we say to everyone. It's not high, it's not low. It's average. Traditional banks pay above that average salary, because frankly nobody wants to work there," Ali says. "I think for me and for Bunq it's important to have people who are not just here for the money, but also for all the other reasons—because those are the best people."

I feel similarly about perks. Of course, we offer competitive health care, dental, vision, 401(k), and other benefits to our employees, and we have some reasonable snack and drink options in the office. But we don't go overboard on perks like tricycles, haircuts, or a dozen beers on tap. While those things are attractive to prospective employees, I think you risk employees taking the job for the wrong reasons. I'd certainly prefer employees join Twilio because they love the work, they enjoy their teammates, and they want to serve our customers—those are the durable motivators. I once visited a Silicon Valley company that had twelve locally brewed beers on tap. That's great. But what happens when the company next door installs thirteen beer taps?

All of those forms of compensation I believe are superfluous at best and, more likely, major distractions from intrinsic motivations of autonomy, mastery, purpose.

The best way to find out why talent is or isn't attracted to your company is to . . . Ask Your Developers. Seriously. Ask your existing talent what's working at the company, and what's not. Ask developers who've been around what they love and what they hate about the company. How often do they think about looking for new roles, and what are they feeling when they think that? Last time they turned down a recruiter, what was going through their head? When you're interviewing prospects, ask what they're looking to accomplish and learn in their next role. Ask if they have ambitions to be more of an owner—and commit to helping them achieve that. When developers decide to leave your company, what do the exit interviews say about their motivations to leave? Sometimes exit interviews are simple multiple choice surveys, so don't accept vague, inactionable answers like "better opportunity." Of course, if it was a worse opportunity, they wouldn't have taken it! Find out *why* they believe some other company is offering a better opportunity. Is it something simple like pay? An ineffective manager? Or something more cultural: Are developers given opportunities to shine and grow? Ability to contribute, or build mastery, autonomy, or purpose, is often the true root cause of somebody's decision to move on.

PART III

MAKING YOUR DEVELOPERS SUCCESSFUL

So now you've got a sense for what makes developers tick, and perhaps on a one-to-one level how to engage with developers to motivate them. But creating a world-class engineering culture is about building a system in which a large number of developers, product managers, and executives can have repeated successes building software. This final section is about how to craft a system of mechanisms and practices that enable large teams of developers to focus on building great products, honing their craft, and serving your customers. It's not too in the weeds—that's for your engineering leaders to implement. But it is important that executives and managers know the fundamentals of what creates a successful culture of innovation, because you play an important part.

CHAPTER 7

CREATING AN OPEN, LEARNING ENVIRONMENT

When you stop learning, stop listening, stop looking and asking questions, always new questions, then it is time to die.

—Lillian Smith

In most companies, "learning and development" is an HR function that means training—typically in a classroom, maybe online, where people learn skills. That's all valuable, but the kind of learning I'm talking about here is embedded in the very construction of the company and its culture, not just extracurricular activities that the most ambitious employees voluntarily undertake. It's on-the-job learning, taken to an extreme. The goal, always, is to find the truth. That must be our north star, the destination toward which we navigate.

In Chapter 5, we talked about experimentation, which is a method of making progress toward a business innovation—but it's really a process of learning. The faster you can learn, the better you'll be. That mentality isn't just about the things you need to learn—for example, what do our customers need?—but it also involves learning how to learn.

This should come naturally to us, since it's what each of us experienced in school. When kids give a wrong answer, they're not kicked out of school. They're helped. School isn't so much about learning content; it's about learning how to learn.

That process of learning to learn is one that every child goes through, starting in kindergarten. Yet once we graduate and enter the workforce, we seem to forget about all that. The process of "learning to learn" gets lost. We create rigid, unforgiving cultures that punish people who make mistakes. That approach might have worked in some bygone era—though I have my doubts. But it certainly does not work in today's economy, where companies are locked in a Darwinian battle for survival in a world where the rules keep changing. Survival means being lean, nimble, fast, and constantly able to adapt.

As a leader, deep down what do you really want? Do you want people to just blindly accept what you say, or do you want them to think for themselves and come up with the best solution to the problems at hand? In the moment of a discussion or a meeting, it sometimes feels like we wish people would just do what we told them because it's easy to fall in love with our own ideas. And look, if you're the highest-paid person in the room, people will do that if that's what you really want. But deep down, you probably know that in order to win, you need the best answer, not the one shouted most loudly or by the highest-ranking person. You want knowledge and truth to win, not politics. You need your teams to be constantly learning, you want your future leaders to be better than you are, and you need your frontline customer-facing teams to be the wisest of all. If deep down you share those beliefs with me, then what I describe as an open, learning environment will help you get there.

An *open, learning environment* is one where the organization is receptive to not having all of the answers, is comfortable with uncertainty, and strives to get better every day. It means being flexible instead of rigid, and having a culture where people *continually seek the truth*.

Companies are full of people with opinions. It's very common for the person who gets paid the most to have their opinion matter the most. Sometimes that is merited—a high-level leader may have purview or wisdom that the team can and should learn from. But sometimes it's the young people, the folks just out of school, who are closest to the technology trends and have their hands on the new stuff, who have the best ideas.

I've always liked what Andy Grove, the legendary CEO of Intel, wrote in *High Output Management*:

> When someone graduates from college with a technical education, at that time and for the next several years, that young person will be fully up-to-date in the technology of the time. Hence, he possesses a good deal of knowledge-based power in the organization that hired him. If he does well, he will be promoted to higher and higher positions, and as the years pass, his position power will grow but his intimate familiarity with current technology will fade. Put another way, even if today's veteran manager was once an outstanding engineer, he is not now the technical expert he was when he joined the company. At Intel, anyway, we managers get a little more obsolete every day.

As technical leaders, the more we progress in our careers we tend to exchange up-to-date technical competency for managerial competency. Two valuable but different knowledge sets that we bring to the table. Whose opinion is right—the one with more experience, or the one with more knowledge of the technologies?

Well, business decisions shouldn't be about anybody's opinion.

People have hunches and instincts. Just theories, really. But those theories need to be tested. And that's where you need an openness to learning—and learning quickly.

If you think about it, most hierarchical companies (which means most companies) are structured such that the person or people at the top supposedly know all the answers (even though we all know they don't) and therefore make the decisions. That's not open. That's fearful. People become afraid to make decisions, for fear of doing something wrong. So they freeze up. Or leaders are afraid to give others any decision-making ability, because they fear those folks will make the wrong decisions. After all, leaders are the ones who are on the hook for results, so they're unwilling to trust their fate to others. Fair enough. But the result is that nobody shares problems and instead they delegate tasks. But I see *Ask Your Developer* as a better way of getting what you want—results—rather than command and control.

An open environment is one where you give people autonomy by sharing problems, but it's not just a matter of throwing out big problems and letting folks sink or swim. As a leader, you're still on the hook for results, so sinking doesn't sound so awesome. Rather, an open environment provides (a) guardrails and (b) support. Instead of "sink or swim," we give people swim lessons—and even let them wear floaties if they need them.

A big difference between an open, learning environment at work and the one we experienced in elementary school is that in school, the teacher knows the answers but shows students how to do the work to arrive at the answer on their own. In business, especially when you're working on the cutting edge of technology, you're not looking for an answer that someone else already knows. The business and its employees must find answers to questions that have not been asked before. But an open, learning environment provides the way to find those elusive answers.

OPEN PROJECT REVIEWS

Chee Chew, our chief product officer at Twilio, has introduced a lot of smart ideas since he joined the company in 2019. One of his most important innovations is a concept he calls Open Project Reviews (OPRs).

It means that every time Chee meets with a team to discuss a project, anyone is welcome to observe. This might be a first meeting where an engineer pitches a new product idea, or a meeting where a team of developers are explaining what progress they've made on a project that has been up and running for years.

The meetings are published on a public calendar to which anyone can subscribe. Two days before the meeting, participants must publish a document about what they're presenting. Everyone participating is required to read the document before the meeting.

To keep the meeting from devolving into chaos, only a few essential people are given permission to speak, which Chee (being a Software Person) calls "read/write" status. Everyone else is considered "read only," and can just observe. Once in a while, a "read only" attendee might ask for "read/write" permission to ask a question or contribute an idea. But for the most part the "read only" people are there to observe. All of these meetings are recorded, so people can watch later, and the documents become artifacts that can also be referenced later. The "read only" policy represents a big part of the open, learning environment, a way for everyone in the company to learn from others but still have a functioning meeting.

The goal is to address one of the shortcomings of the "two-pizza team" approach, which is that when you have a large number of small teams (our product side alone has 150 teams) they all start to run in a thousand different directions and it can be difficult for any single team to know what all the others are doing. But some initiatives require multiple small teams to contribute code. Each team often has dependencies with other teams. So they all need to keep tabs on each other. The OPR approach lets teams get a quick check-in on other teams and stay up to date with what they're doing.

A side benefit is that OPR meetings become a kind of classroom. The "read/write" folks are learning because their business is getting inspected by Chee, who can be kind of intense. He knows so much about software that he's actually kind of scary, especially to teams that are missing their metrics or to people who show up less than well prepared. These meetings can be tough, but that's how people learn. Constructive criticism isn't about tearing people down; it's about helping them get better. It's actually a form of respect. And it's how people learn.

Making meetings open to the whole company means that sometimes an engineer gets skewered in front of an audience. That might make the experience even more unpleasant, but on the other hand, knowing that a lot of people might see your performance does create an added incentive to get your act together before you show up. It also sends a message to all of the "read only" people who are watching about what they should expect when it's their turn in the box. The ultimate goal is to help everyone learn faster. The same lesson that the "read/write" people are learning now gets shared with everyone else who watches.

Another benefit is that OPRs hold people accountable. Decisions are made out in the open, in front of everyone—not in secret meetings in closed rooms, where others only learn about things secondhand, through the grapevine, and messages can get muddled. Everyone in the company knows exactly what the people in that meeting are expected to deliver. There's no going back and changing things later.

Finally, let me acknowledge that it can be difficult for an organization to embrace the OPR approach. At Twilio it's now a normal part of business, but it took a lot of effort and internal communication to get everyone on board. If or when you adopt this policy, know that you will need to have support from the very top of the organization. That support needs to be highly visible and persistent to bring that change about.

THE SOCRATIC METHOD

Our OPR format and strategy is adapted from a practice that Amazon has long employed, called the Weekly Business Review. Andy Jassy, who leads Amazon Web Services, did this even in the early days when AWS was just getting started, and I believe it's a big part of their success to this day.

This was a weekly meeting where the general managers (GMs) of all the services assembled. In my day there were about ten people in the meeting; today there are probably hundreds. Andy looks through the metrics of each team. When he finds something that's off, for example something that's trending in the wrong direction, he stops and asks the leader why their metrics are off and what they're doing to fix it.

Here's the key part—sometimes the leader has a great answer for the issue and what they're doing, and obviously the leader feels good and looks good in front of many other leaders. But more important is that every other leader in the room just learned what excellence looks like. Metrics will inevitably go off-kilter, but what's important is the owner is on top of it.

Of course there are the opposite scenarios, too—the times when the leader doesn't know or can't explain why the metric is off course. That's bad. You have to know your business. Or maybe the leader knows what's wrong but has insufficient plans to correct it. That's bad, too.

Andy will spend time leaning into the situation, coaching the leaders (sometimes forcefully, to be honest) in how they could run their business better. These meetings are pretty legendary in Amazon Web Services, because you'd better be prepared, which drives each team to run a tight ship, but also because it's a master class in being an owner. That's the kind of open, learning environment that drives innovation and success.

The hard part is to balance that open environment for feedback without creating an environment of fear. That's where the "open" part comes in. Leaders should expect the best from their teams, and when a GM is unprepared, it should be apparent to that person, but also to the room, that this is not acceptable. That said, the leader should not humiliate that person. It's easy to do, but it just causes everyone to shut down and is not productive. It's obviously better to set the expectation of excellence and show the GM and everybody else how to solve a problem in a forceful but supportive way.

Chee acknowledges this tension all the time with one of his favorite sayings: "Our goal every day is to suck less than we did yesterday." Sounds like a downer—but it's actually quite an effective way of saying: "We're not perfect, but as long as we're learning and improving, we're doing good work."

If the same person comes in the next week with the same problem and the same crappy answer—now you have a problem. That person isn't learning. They suck as much as they did yesterday. Repeated failure is certainly a problem and needs to become a personal performance conversation. But that part isn't open; that's the private part.

Those big meetings with Andy Jassy grilling us provided a great (and fast) education. His approach was similar to one that professors in graduate programs, especially in law school, have been using for more than a century—and which in fact dates back to the fifth century BC. It's the Socratic method, named after the Greek philosopher Socrates.

In this mode of teaching, students arrive to class having read the material (hopefully) and then the professor singles people out and peppers them in a rapid-fire exchange. The Socratic method is intended to teach students how to think critically and make arguments on their feet. My law school friends called this "getting pimped" in front of the class. It was nerve-racking—but asking tough questions and coaching the right answers in front of the group helped everybody learn. Why has the Socratic method remained in use for 2,500 years? In *The Paper Chase*, the great actor John Houseman, in the role of Harvard Law School professor Charles Kingsfield, explains: "We use the Socratic method here. I call on you, ask you a question, and you answer it. Why don't I just give you a lecture? Because through my questions, you learn to teach yourselves."

That's what we're looking for in our companies. We want to teach employees how to teach themselves. That's the essence of a learning environment. We're building a mindset, a way of analyzing and solving problems. The Socratic method is as effective with business problems as it is with complex legal cases.

I should note that these programs at graduate schools are sometimes famous for making students cry—or worse. In *The Paper*

Chase, a first-year student who has taken an intellectual beating from Kingsfield in front of his peers races to the men's room to get sick. To be clear: I definitely do not advocate going that far. But the same approach that's used in complex graduate education can be applied to the task of training business leaders. It's much more effective than sitting through a seminar or reading a book.

THE BLAMELESS POSTMORTEM

We often talk about learning to make decisions in the context of business planning, but what about when things go wrong? You've been there—in a technical organization, it might be when the servers fail and the product suffers an outage. Outages aren't the only kinds of failures, though: maybe it's an M&A integration that went south, or a financial model that didn't remotely pan out, or the mis-hire of an important leader. There are countless varieties of mistakes we constantly make as individuals, teams, and organizations. How we as leaders, and the company as a whole, handle these situations makes a big difference to how employees treat mistakes, and whether the company actually gets better and better at these things. Or, as Chee would say, "suck less."

When things go wrong, it's either a time to blame, or a time to learn. I believe each failure is an opportunity to uncover deep learnings about how the organization operates, and what could strengthen it systematically, and then take action. We, and many other software companies, do this via a ritual called the "blameless postmortem." The purpose of the blameless postmort is to dig below the surface of some kind of bad outcome to the true root cause, and address that as an organization. Here's how it works:

Let's take a common type of issue. A software developer introduces a bug into the code, which makes its way to the production servers and takes down the website. First, your teams will need to identify the bad code and revert to an earlier version, thus restoring service. Obviously that's the top priority. But after that's done, it's time to figure out what went wrong that led to a customer-facing outage.

It's natural to blame the engineer for writing bad code. Doing so is a common instinct, but nothing is really gained by it. As human beings, even the best engineers will make mistakes and, trust me, they feel horrible about taking down the website. So blaming them won't accomplish much, other than pointing out that they're human, and making them less likely to want to write code—at least for your company. The bug they introduced is the obvious cause of the outage, but it's not the true root cause. Rather, the true issue is somewhere deeper in the way the organization operates. So rather than blaming the person, the real question is this: Knowing that people inevitably make mistakes, why did "the system" allow that mistake to impact customers? Answering that question will get you to the true root cause, or, more realistically, true root causes.

The way you get there is repeatedly asking "Why?" We usually start by asking a simple first question: "Why was there a customer-facing outage?" The answer is the obvious cause: "An engineer introduced buggy code into production." Okay, next you ask: "Why did the buggy code in production result in an outage?" Maybe the answer is that the software wasn't written defensively enough—really robust software might have detected the issue and been able to survive in some degraded way. Or maybe there was no way that the software, even if it was robustly written, could have survived and therefore the question is: "Why did the buggy code make it out to production?" A likely answer might be: "Because there wasn't good enough testing of the code in question." This would be an easy place to stop and unfurl the "Mission Accomplished" banner atop the aircraft carrier—but doing so would be stopping short. Why? It's just a thinly veiled version of blaming the software developer. If only they, or perhaps a quality assurance engineer, had only written better tests, then the problem would have been avoided. So you keep going: "Why did code go into production knowing there wasn't good test coverage over a critical piece of code?"

Ah, now we're getting somewhere. The true root cause is rarely technical in nature—it's organizational. How did our organization fail this human being so that they could harm our customer and our business? Imagine a nuclear power plant with a big "meltdown" button sitting in the middle of the console. A technician puts his lunch down on the button, and boom. Would you blame the technician? It's more likely you would ask why that button existed in the first place! It's the same thing here. Why did "the system" allow poorly tested code to go into production? Perhaps it's because the testing infrastructure is so poor that the path to proper testing is too difficult, so engineers regularly bypass writing good tests in the interest of progress. If so, building great infrastructure will make the correct path easy, enabling engineers to meet customer feature requests and do it with well-tested code. Or perhaps the organization hasn't invested in training engineers to write good tests, or taught them why well-tested code is important? Eventually, you'll get to the systemic true root cause, and you can address that one.

This is important because if you only address the surface-level cause of the incident, you may indeed fix that particular cause. Maybe by some draconian mechanism, you can be damn sure that particular developer won't introduce a bug again. However, other engineers will have learned nothing. It would be like removing one "meltdown" button, but leaving hundreds of others scattered around the reactor. You're likely to have another meltdown. By addressing the true root cause, you're going to not just fix the cause of your last outage but also likely address the cause of your next outage. If you repeat this process long enough, you'll systematically build a stronger and stronger organization.

I used a technical example, because the practice of blameless postmortems is more common in technical organizations. However, I've seen this method applied to every part of our business and it works the same way.

In 2010, a fledgling ten-person startup called Uber (actually UberCab at the time) became a Twilio customer. Over the years, they experienced meteoric growth and by the time we went public in 2016 they represented more than 10 percent of our revenue and were a prominent part of our IPO road show. Throughout 2016, they continued to grow at a meteoric pace, reaching nearly $60 million of annualized spend, which was in retrospect unsustainable, especially as they started focusing their attention on cost savings instead of "growth at all costs." Under the new cost savings priority, we were a juicy target. At the beginning of 2017, they indicated that they would start reducing their spend with us. On our Q1 2017 earnings call, we disclosed to investors that our highly visible largest customer, one that had been an anchor of our IPO prospectus, would be reducing their spend with us. It was bad. Our stock dropped more than 30 percent in one day. Our employees were shell-shocked. Now, obviously, this was a short-term blip, as a company is more than just one customer, and through Q1 2020 we've grown our revenue more than 400 percent, while reducing the concentration of our top customers from 30 percent in 2016 to 14 percent in 2019. But nonetheless, it was a clear misstep for our newly public company and a mistake we didn't want to make again.

I asked our CFO at the time, Lee Kirkpatrick, to run a blameless postmortem. The finance team had never run one before, so we tapped Jason Hudak, our head of technical infrastructure, whom you'll meet in Chapter 11, to lead the cross-functional process. Instead of starting with "Why did we have a customer-facing outage?" the question this time was "Why did we have such a big investor-facing misstep?" It would have been easy to blame the sales rep covering the Uber account, but as you can see, that wouldn't have been the true root cause. "Because our largest customer is going to start spending less and we disclosed that to investors." "Why?" Eventually, it came down to two true root causes. First, we had a small handful of customers who, because of our usage-based pricing model, had grown too large and therefore represented risk to us. We needed to manage our "customer concentration" better, even if it meant proactively lowering prices. But more important, the other true root cause was that we didn't have enough salespeople covering all of our accounts. At the time, we had only about fifteen quota-carrying sales reps covering more than 36,000 accounts and prospects. As you can imagine, our sales reps were stretched incredibly thin, including at our largest customer, spending more than $60 million per year. Our second true root cause was that we needed more account coverage. Since then, we've gone from fifteen to many hundreds of reps and grown our revenue from $277 million in 2016 to more than $1.1 billion in 2019, all while cutting the contribution of our largest ten customers in half.

INTO THE DEEP END

An open, learning environment is also one where you are training your next generation of leaders. Sure, there's training in the traditional sense, going to seminars or classes. But then there's real learning, the kind where people learn by doing. You can't learn to swim by watching videos and listening to lectures. You learn by getting into the pool.

At Amazon, most initiatives are run by a general manager. There are GMs who run big businesses, like the entire Amazon Retail business or Amazon Web Services, both of which generate tens of billions of dollars. Those GMs are wise, and experienced. But Amazon takes this to an extreme. Most companies only have a few GMs at the very highest levels. The people underneath them play a functional role, but the GM owns the P&L outcome. Amazon, in contrast, has GMs running things at every level. GMs report to other GMs. Some GMs are Level 7 on the pay scale and others are at Level 3. In addition to being "single-threaded leaders" who drive urgency and focus for each line of business, these GM roles represent thousands of learning opportunities for future leaders around Amazon.

I often imagine the (maybe real, maybe fictional) person at Amazon who runs the "Amazon Tire Store." (It's true, Amazon actually sells tires.) Somewhere there's probably a young talented person who was given the GM job of running the tire store. It's a tiny fraction of Amazon's total business, so it's a low-risk role for leaders to hand to a young leader. Yet for that young leader, it's the opportunity of a lifetime. I mean, how likely are they to be hired out of an MBA program and given the CEO role at Pep Boys or some other company? Yet at Amazon they can take a risk and provide a training ground. If the tire store flounders, well okay, for a short period of time, it's good training. If it goes on for an extended period of time, then maybe a new leader is needed. But what better way to train your army of future leaders than to give them the reins of a part of your business? And all it takes is a recognition that it's okay to give up that leadership and decision-making.

For a time at Amazon, I was the GM of the Simple Queueing Service (SQS), which was actually the first publicly available product from Amazon Web Services. Before we launched, SQS had zero revenue (of course) and at some point after launch the service was doing thousands of dollars a month in revenue. That's not huge, but still—it needed an owner at the wheel if it was going to succeed. But succeed or fail, that really didn't matter to Amazon—what's a few thousand dollars to a company that big? Even if SQS blew up in size, it still wouldn't have been a huge needle mover for Amazon.

So why bother anointing a twenty-seven-year-old general manager and giving me the reins? Well, it was a training ground. I learned how to be a GM, and be an owner, when the stakes were low. If I succeeded and learned, I would get to move on and own something bigger. I don't know, but I suspect there are probably thousands of GMs inside Amazon today. This is a deep bench they're training to be GMs and owners of the next wave of Amazon ideas. I believe this is a big reason for their continued successes. As new ideas spring up, there's an army of business leaders who can run with them.

In most environments, employees who excel at a functional job, like engineering, sales, or finance, get promoted until one day, they're a GM of some large business unit. In this system, there's an assumption that competence in one field (engineering, sales, finance, etc.) transfers to competence in another field: being a GM. Sometimes that's right, but too often it's not. There's even a term for it: the Peter Principle. It's the idea that people rise to the level of their incompetence. It's pretty obvious when you think about it: being an owner takes a unique skill set; it's not just an uber-salesperson or uber-engineer. It's a unique skill set that you should be training people for.

An open, learning environment is key to both building successful products in the fog of ambiguity and to developing future leadership talent that you will need to succeed. When you hand the reins to employees, you're teaching them how to take ownership of their work.

LEARNING BY DOING

Lots of companies help employees learn by holding events like brown-bag lunch sessions, off-site leadership courses, or online training videos. But I believe that the most valuable form of learning is by doing, and that's up to leaders to let their people run things. Look for projects where the stakes are low, where a leader-in-training can screw up a few noncritical things without doing much harm and become a better leader in the process. Remember the Tire Store GM at Amazon? It is unrealistic to expect that a leader-in-training will magically get everything perfect. That's okay. You don't want to have an environment where people get shunned or punished for mistakes. Imagine what that does to the next person you ask to take a lead on an assignment. They will long remember how the last person was treated when they made a mistake.

These assignments are sometimes more about learning than they are about short-term output. When we work with companies that are trying to become builders, we encourage them to start small. Choose a modest project that isn't mission critical—something that would be nice to have and will deliver a payoff and will not take long to complete. Most important, choose a project where your team can fail, or fall short, and it won't interfere with regular operations.

A good example is a project at Target that Josh Hoium and his team in the voice engineering department tackled. In the fall of 2018, Target's HR department had a problem. Mudslides in Southern California were forcing Target to close some stores. But managers didn't have a good way to reach employees and tell them to stay home. Employees would make the sometimes dangerous journey to work, only to find out the store was closed. HR wanted to send alerts to employees. But HR also wanted employees to be able to communicate back. During an emergency, Target could check on employees to make sure they were safe, and employees could send back requests for help if they needed it. It was critical that the communication was received immediately, which meant email wasn't a reliable channel for this use case.

Target did have a system in place, but it wasn't very effective. Employees could find out if the store was open by calling into a voice-mail system and then tapping through a menu system to get a recorded status message. The drawback was that employees often didn't bother to call in. Instead, HR wanted to be proactive and send alerts via SMS to every employee's mobile phone.

The HR department had sized up a software package from a commercial vendor and assumed the best path was for Hoium to just buy it. But the software was expensive, and didn't really do exactly what Target wanted. Hoium told HR that a better approach would be for his team to write an emergency alert application from scratch.

This was a great project for Josh to use as a learning exercise with his engineers. It was relatively small, and the stakes were low. If Josh's developers couldn't develop the app, Target still had the old system as a fallback. And they could still go buy the commercial solution. It would only take a few weeks to find out whether Target's in-house engineers were up to the job.

The learning aspect of the project was that the application had to be written in Python, and none of the four engineers assigned to the project knew that language. They weren't really software developers. Their background involved managing commercial systems made by Cisco, Avaya, and other vendors. Those skills used to be in high demand but are becoming less valuable over time.

The alert system project gave these four engineers the chance to learn a new language that would make them more valuable in the marketplace. The tricky part is that the engineers wouldn't first take a course in Python and then write the app. They would just dive in and start writing code, learning Python as they went—a pure example of the "learn by doing" approach. As Josh tells it, the HR people were skeptical that in-house engineers could actually build an app. Indeed, the engineers were skeptical, too! "It took some selling on my part to convince them that this was really something that we absolutely should do," Josh recalls. "If nothing else, it would be a good experiment."

Incredibly enough, it worked. In six weeks these four newbie Python developers produced a working prototype. A week later the software was put into production across all of Target's 1,800 stores in the United States. That little app has made a big difference. In the fall of 2019, when wildfires broke loose in California, the software became a lifesaver as it enabled store managers to check on employees and notify them about store closures, saving employees from making potentially perilous journeys. But it also had a big impact on the careers of those four engineers, and "gave them some confidence to write more code," Josh says.

Target has made a big commitment to training and education. Every member of the IT staff spends fifty days a year on learning—which is a lot! Some of the learning comes through reading books or taking classes and seminars, but most of it is learning by doing. Josh learned about AI by building a couple of neural networks that

Target now uses in some applications. "A lot of our learning happens because we're able to take risks—like hey, is there a way I can try something out and see what happens at a small scale where I don't have to bet the farm," Josh says.

HATCH-TEACHING AS HIRING ADVANTAGE

At Twilio, we've found that investing in people is an advantage in the highly competitive market for technical talent. In particular, there are hordes of talented, high-potential developers emerging from bootcamps every year, and many companies aren't willing to invest in hiring and continuing their training, so they miss out on this rich source of talent. Bootcamps are short programs—from three months to a year—that train mid-career professionals to become developers. People join bootcamps often because they see a more promising career in coding, or merely because it piques their interest and they're interested in pursuing a more technical career. As opposed to four-year undergraduate degrees, bootcamp grads get a crash course in coding and quickly learn job-relevant skills needed to build a variety of websites and apps. Another benefit is that these bootcamps bring underrepresented people into the tech industry.

I'm always in awe of bootcamp grads because they took an incredibly difficult path to coding, building up the activation energy to change careers, often taking a leave from their paying jobs to retrain and re-skill. When we look at resumes, it's common to measure a candidate's position in their career: did they attend a top-notch school, did they work at prestigious companies prior, and so on. These are measures of position, but they don't measure distance traveled. I think it speaks volumes about grit and capability when a candidate, for example, was the first person in their family to attend college versus people like me, whose parents and grandparents also attended college. This is called "distance traveled," and when you account for how far a candidate has come in life as a measure of future potential, bootcamp grads rank highly on my list.

Many companies hesitate to hire bootcamp grads because they only have three, or six, or twelve months of coding experience but they will happily hire twenty-one-year-old four-year-college grads in droves. Some companies do hire bootcamp grads but throw them into the deep end hoping they can swim with the other, more experienced engineers on the team. It's not surprising that many fail, and are quickly let go, which is a double loss. It's a loss for the company that won't benefit from the talent, but more important, it's a loss for the employee who certainly suffers a confidence hit in their new career.

So we created an apprenticeship program called Hatch, where we offer six months of paid training for bootcamp grads as a transition period from learning to doing. Participants spend the first three months doing hands-on building with the fellow members of the Hatch cohort, under the leadership of a manager whose job is to educate and help them foster their skills. They build a combination of internal projects, which are lower risk than some customer-facing products, and products for nonprofit customers. For many, this is their first "real world" coding, and they learn incredibly fast, especially with a manager whose sole job is their successful graduation.

Then the apprentices spend the next three months embedded with a sponsoring product team at Twilio. They are a full engineer on the team, but like an intern, their manager knows they're still riding the learning curve, so they invest time to help them succeed. And the managers are incentivized to invest in their success—their budget is paying the full six-month salary for the apprentice. At the end of the apprenticeship, the manager has the option to offer the apprentice a full-time job. More than 90 percent of Hatch graduates have become full-time Twilio developers. I suspect one of the reasons they're successful is that by signing up for the Hatch program they have already self-identified themselves as risk-takers and independent thinkers—exactly the kind of people who make great developers.

The best measure of somebody's future travels are their past travels. We want people who want to learn, and bootcamp grads who've changed professions mid-career demonstrate exactly that willingness. That's why we invest in Hatch and other learning programs.

IMAGINE THE ALTERNATIVE

I believe the goal of our culture is to build an army of empowered, truth-seeking, good-decision-making leaders. The more we enable our frontline teams to ask the right questions, put aside politics and titles, and come to the best answers, the greater chance we have of solving hard problems and serving our customers. Consider the alternative. Government has historically been the bastion of big projects, big politics, and big blame. Whether you're in favor of small government or big government, we can probably all agree that most governments aren't exactly known as innovators. Why? What happens when something goes wrong in government? Instead of quickly learning and iterating, or using it as a learning opportunity, the participants are hauled before Congress and grilled on national television. It's the World Series of grandstanding. What do you think that does to organizational morale and risk-taking? Naturally, nobody wants to be hauled in front of Congress, so they will be sure to never stick their necks out. That leads to actors always making the safest possible decisions, and passing off accountability.

Most executives envision a company culture more like Google, Apple, or Facebook than like the U.S. federal government. But ask yourself: When people make mistakes, are there blameless post-mortems, or are your people hauled in front of Congress (aka the executive team)? Are people encouraged to learn quickly, even at the risk of making mistakes? Do you provide venues for learning from each other, and even take risks by giving younger leaders the reins to parts of the business? We've made the mistake of "hauling teams in front of Congress"—it's human nature to get frustrated, and become inquisitive. Some of my quarterly business reviews have even been called "the Inquisition" in the past. But that's not the goal, that's a failing. It's my job as a leader to build an environment where our leaders feel constant, gentle pressure to perform, and support for their continued, urgent exploration of their problem domain—but not an inquisition.

What kind of environment do you have? You can find out: ask your leaders what happens after there's an outage. Not the "get it back online" part of the answer, but what happens after that? Is a person to blame, or is a process to blame? Ask your leaders if there are parts of the business that you could entrust to a set of upcoming general managers? If you get pushback on giving up the reins, ask "What's the worst thing that could happen?" If you've got a part of the business that is small and troubled, chances are you'll want to kill it. But what if next time you give it a dedicated GM and see what happens over six months? Ask your technical leaders if they'd be willing to do their project reviews in the open, as Chee has done. What's the downside to sharing these sessions with a broader group, as long as it's not disruptive? Consider asking your teams, maybe in your next big company survey, if they're more motivated by chances of success, versus avoidance of failure. These are some questions that might help you understand if your culture is oriented toward learning and truth seeking.

The open, learning environment I describe here is designed to train our leaders in these skills. We're not perfect, but we're continually iterating our way toward a more and more open, more educational environment. Or as Chee would say, every day we "suck less." I can live with that.

CHAPTER 8
SMALL TEAMS AND SINGLE-THREADED LEADERS

It's very difficult to solve a lot of problems from the top down.
—Megan Smith, CTO of the United States

In 1998, my friend Dave Schappell (no, not comedian Dave Chappelle) joined fledgling Amazon.com as (roughly) employee 100. He helped launch Amazon Marketplace, Amazon Associates, Amazon Auctions, and some of their other platforms. He was also the person who recruited me to join AWS in 2004. By that time, the company had grown to approximately 5,000 employees, and Dave left Amazon to found a startup called TeachStreet. Eight years later, in 2012, Amazon acquired that startup and Dave again found himself employed by Amazon, which by that time employed more than 75,000 people.

Shortly after he rejoined Amazon in 2012, I called him up with a simple question: How would you compare and contrast those three companies—Amazon at 100 people, 5,000 people, and now 75,000 people? He thought for a few moments, and then said this: "You know, it's the same company. The same sense of urgency. The same bounce in people's step. The same intelligence. It's awesome." In 1998, there was a single floor full of employees in its Seattle office, full of startup hustle and drive. In 2012, it was the same picture, only there were nearly a thousand such floors full of Amazon startups scattered all around the world. It's truly amazing to think about how Amazon scaled its culture so many times over.

As a leader, we're constantly trying to instill a sense of importance and urgency to the work our teams undertake. Yet as a company gets larger, it seems almost like an unwritten rule that things will slow down, people will lose a connection to the work, politics take over, and urgency will diminish—short of some existential threat. However, at least according to my friend Dave, Amazon didn't suffer that fate. Whether you're a big company looking to bring back agility or a small company with aspirations of growing while keeping your edge, what can we learn from the successful scaling that Dave described? At the heart of Amazon's scale are small teams with empowered, mission-driven leaders. In essence, a collection of startups.

Think about it this way: a startup moves fast and moves boldly because it has to by necessity and design. Its small size means that there's not much overhead and that lines of communication are clear. The presence of a founder, a CEO, or at most a small group of cofounders and execs who can make decisions fast and feel singularly accountable for the outcome makes the results personal. If the company wins, they win. If the company fails, they fail.

It's exactly the same for small teams within a large company, which is why they're crucial. Amazon's structure built on teams of no more than ten people is a testament to how to scale up a company without losing the urgency, focus, and quality of talent that characterizes a startup by building a large company out of what are essentially many startups. Among other things, it eliminates complexity of collaboration, which grows rapidly with the size of a company. That means it's (almost) exponentially more difficult to coordinate a company as it grows. If you've experienced this in your company, it's not just you, it's math. Coordinating a 10-person team requires 45 relations between people, but coordinating a 100-person team results in nearly 5,000 relationships, and coordinating a 1,000-person company requires nearly 500,000 relationships to work. Amazon at 75,000 people in 2012 could have necessitated 2.8 billion relationships, making it 500,000 times as confusing and soul-crushing to navigate as the 100-person company it was at the start. Yet that wasn't the case. It felt like the same company—a modern miracle built on small teams.

TWO-PIZZA ORIGINS

Around the turn of the millennium, Amazon was a fast-growing startup, yet innovation was starting to slow. According to then Amazon CIO (and now Twilio board member) Rick Dalzell, the codebase was a monolithic hairball and the product development was organized into a few big divisions, like browse and search, fulfillment, and shopping cart. It was getting slower, and harder for people to ship code because so many people had their hands on the same code. Aside from code, there were too many decision makers poking into everybody's work, because everybody's work was so utterly intertwined. As you can imagine, it was frustrating for engineers and product managers who struggled to build their ideas, and it was especially frustrating for CEO Jeff Bezos.

Most years, Jeff would spend a week offline, devoted to deep thought on the business. These annual "brain-benders" gave him time to rethink first principles and write down these ideas, usually resulting in a series of one-page documents with new ideas he brought back to his leadership team. Rick recounts how in 2001, Jeff went on his retreat with the slowing pace of innovation on his mind. So he came back with a simple idea: if teams were organized into startup-like sizes, if they owned their road maps and they owned their code so they could move quickly, they could act like startups again, just as they had in the early days of Amazon, when Jeff remembered they could feed the whole team with two pizzas. But in order to work together, they'd need to build a bunch of APIs so they could interface with each other. This would enable them to move independently, with the relationship between teams formalized in technology. With this one-pager, the "two-pizza team" was born. Rick went back to his leaders and within a week turned Jeff's initial idea into a six-page workable plan that Amazon quickly adopted.

DOZEN-BAGEL TEAMS

At Twilio, we had already started organizing ourselves into small teams. But that 2012 conversation with Dave Schappell confirmed for me that this was the best way to scale the company while keeping our edge.

At the beginning of Twilio, it was just Evan, John, and I—three developer-founders. At that size, we could hold the entire business in our heads. On any given day, we might generate some new idea, write some code, support customers on email or phone, pay the bills, and even make a Costco run to stock the office. We were constantly building demo applications on top of our APIs, so we knew the kind of experience our customers were having. When we did customer support, we gained an instinctual understanding of what customers were trying to accomplish, where we were falling short, and where we needed to keep investing.

In one instance, I remember that a customer reported a bug on

Twitter and I wrote the fix within five minutes—but actually held off deploying it for a day because I didn't want us to look like such a small company. That was just a bug fix, but I recall times when we took customer insights and turned them into whole products in a matter of days. One such product is our "sub-account" system, which enables developers to segment their usage of Twilio into multiple buckets—it's useful for software companies building on Twilio who themselves have many customers using their apps. We had a realization that such a feature would be useful, and I built it one night and deployed it the next day.

When Evan, John, and I needed to make a decision, we could usually do it pretty quickly. Every day, we were all deep in customer conversations, the architecture of our software, and how all the pieces fit together. We could imagine how our decisions would play out over time. Even though we each had our areas of expertise (Evan wrote a lot of the infrastructure, John wrote a lot of the core product services, I wrote a lot of the API, web, and billing layers), we all knew enough to act as one brain. When you hold the whole picture in your heads and you work together every day, you can make progress incredibly fast. That's the power of a small team—there are no proxies; you're just directly solving customer problems with your code.

That's the magic that makes startups so special and so productive. There's so little overhead to manage, the coordination energy is negligible, and people tend to have a tremendous intrinsic drive because they're so close to the customers and, therefore, the mission. Startups can succeed or fail based on many factors, but motivation and speed are not usually the fatal flaw. Who wouldn't want that kind of energy in their business? I've never met a business leader who doesn't want employees to feel that kind of intrinsic motivation and drive to succeed, yet the way we usually structure our companies deprives employees of the raw ingredients. Our organizational charts separate employees from customers, our decision-making processes leave employees feeling unempowered, and success becomes navigating the organization as opposed to serving customers. Nearly all companies succumb to varying degrees of this fate as they scale.

In those early days, the three of us met every Monday mid-morning to start the week, and somewhere along the way I began stopping on my commute to pick up bagels—three bagels to be exact. As the company grew, so did our Monday mid-morning meeting, and so did my bagel order. I soon was buying a half-dozen bagels. Then a dozen bagels. Then two dozen bagels. Then three dozen. And as the bagel orders grew, I found it was getting harder and harder to hold the whole business in our heads. (It was also harder and harder to carry the bagels.) In particular, I also noticed that the way we'd been running the company wasn't working well anymore. People couldn't see the whole picture, so they didn't intuit the plan the way we had done as a small team. Employees started to silo. Engineers didn't talk to customers; only the support team did. Some people were working on our first product, Twilio Voice, while others had started building our second product, Twilio SMS, and others were working on building infrastructure. Each knew what they were working on, but didn't have the whole picture. I also realized that new employees weren't having the same experience we had—many of the new engineers weren't handling support requests, and our new support people hadn't built an app on Twilio to understand the product inside and out.

With about thirty people on the team, I was growing frustrated and so was everybody else. It wasn't clear why people couldn't see the whole picture the way Evan, John, and I could back in the early days. One day I was at a meeting of CEOs that one of my early investors, Albert Wenger of Union Square Ventures (USV), had organized. Asked how things were going, I replied honestly (as I tend to do): "Well things feel pretty shitty, nothing is working on the team anymore." Fred Wilson, a cofounder of USV, asked me to draw the org chart, something I'd actually never done before.

I picked up a marker and drew this:

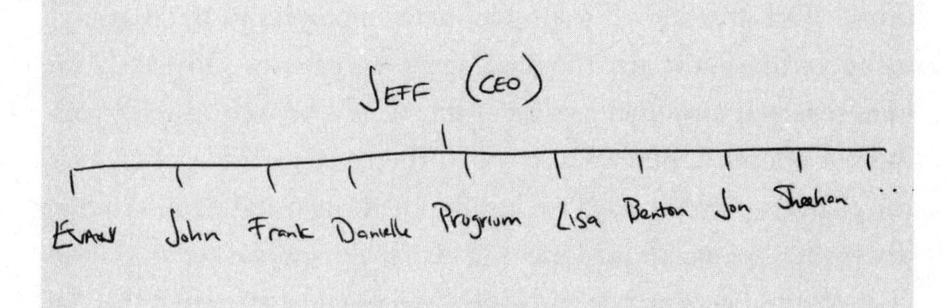

It went on for a while. A big straight line with thirty-some people, all of whom reported to me!

"There's your problem," Albert declared, correctly. I had never thought about the org chart before. We'd just kept hiring people and, as with all people before them, they reported to me. Once we'd crossed about ten people, the straight-line org chart became the source of our dysfunction—so obvious once I wrote it down. The problem was that we'd outgrown the capacity for the team to internalize the entirety of what we were doing. So I came back with a plan to break the company into smaller teams, but how to divide things up?

One obvious solution is to divide things functionally—the support people work together, the engineers work together, the product managers work together, and so on. Thinking back to the days when Evan, John, and I all did customer support, designed products, and wrote code, I wanted to figure out how to replicate that experience for the entire team as we grew.

First, we instituted an idea that all employees would do some amount of customer support—not as their full-time job, but enough to maintain a customer connection. We asked all new employees to handle fifty support tickets in their first couple of weeks to get to know our customers, our product, and our customer service approach. We also started asking all new employees to build an app using Twilio—not just the developers, everybody. Obviously the sales reps and customer service agents would be well served by using our product. But we also asked the lawyers, the accountants, the analysts—everybody—to build something using Twilio so they knew what we enable customers to do. The point was to build more connections between our employees and our customers. To this day every new Twilion, no matter their role, learns the basics of coding and builds an app on our platform. When they complete their app they earn a red Twilio track jacket—a true badge of honor!

The most meaningful change was the beginning of our small-teams approach to team structure. We went from a group of thirty-some people and divided nearly everybody into three teams: Twilio Voice (our existing product), Twilio SMS (our upcoming product), and Twilio Infrastructure (our internal platforms)—each small enough to be fed by a dozen bagels (to continue with Twilio's food item of choice).

On the surface, this seems like an obvious way to structure the company at that moment, but as those teams grew, we repeated the process, continually dividing the teams back into small startups. When you have two products and some infrastructure, it's easy. But dividing the team up repeatedly over the years is harder than it sounds because there are a thousand ways to execute on this idea.

Here's what we've learned over the last ten years, expanding from those three initial teams to now over 150 small teams within R&D.

CUSTOMER, MISSION, AND METRICS

For a team to develop the intrinsic drive of a startup, they need organizing principles that articulate their purpose. I typically start by defining the customer they're serving. This could be an external customer in the traditional sense, or it could be an internal customer they're serving. For a product-facing team, identifying the customer segment or persona can be useful. For example, this team is building for small businesses or that team is building for consumers. That's a fairly obvious part of establishing a new initiative. But it's less obvious for an internal team, which actually makes it more important to articulate and document. For example, the Twilio Infrastructure team I mentioned earlier explicitly stated that their "customers" were the other internal developers at Twilio. That helps clarify why they wake up every day. If they need direction, they need to ask their customers about their biggest problems. Lacking a customer, the loudest voice or the highest pay grade decides what people should work on. But having a customer grounds the team's work in discoverable truths that customers can express.

Once you have a customer defined, then you define a mission. This isn't a marketing exercise, as company mission statements might become. Rather, this is a core purpose that the team themselves can agree upon and align around. For an infrastructure team, that might be "to maximize the productivity of our engineers to build, test, release and operate high-quality Internet-scale products." The mission statement should be accessible, easy to remember and articulate, and devoid of jargon so the team members actually believe it.

Last, to measure progress against this mission, and to know if customers are being served by the team's existence, they need measures of success. Many companies would consider these objectives, as in a Management By Objectives (MBO) system or an Objectives and Key Results (OKR) system. Call it what you will, but I believe these should be relatively long-lived measurements that tell the story of progress toward the stated mission, versus objectives that change quarterly. For example, when Twilio Infrastructure got started, our build system, which packages our code for deployment to servers, was horribly broken. It could take half a day to build and deploy our software, and half of the time the build would fail for unknown reasons. It was killing developer productivity. So the Infrastructure team took on a measure of "time from code check-in to deployment." In the short term, it was clear they had some cleanup to do, but over the long term, this is a clear measure of engineering productivity that the Infrastructure team could impact. Note, it wasn't "fix the build system" or "reduce errors from 50 percent to 5 percent," because those represent short-term projects rather than long-term measures of progress toward achieving the mission.

For a customer-facing product team, these are all a bit easier. For example, the Twilio SMS product team knew their customer was other software developers and the companies they worked for. So their mission was to be "the leading global, omnichannel messaging API trusted by developers and enterprises globally," and their primary measures of success were revenue, customer count, API uptime and latency, and customer net promoter score (NPS).

With a strong customer, a clear mission, and metrics of success, the team is well set up to execute, driven by an intrinsic motivation. These three things are not invented by executives in the boardroom—they are created by the team themselves. That helps keep it personal.

The other benefit of a small, driven team: nobody can hide. If you're a cog in a machine, or one of dozens or hundreds of people on a project, it's easy to feel like your contribution doesn't matter, which is bad for morale and does not make the most of every employee's skills and talents. It also makes it easy for a low performer, or somebody who's checked out, to coast along. But on a small team of five to ten people, neither of those things is possible. Everybody has an important role, and there's little room for somebody who isn't giving it their all (and trust me—this becomes very apparent).

Defining customer, mission, and metrics is the foundation of the small team.

MITOSIS

As business grows, so will your team. So how do you keep your teams small while you scale the business? When you have a net new initiative, or a 1:1 ratio of products to teams, the answer is easy: fund a small team to tackle a new problem. But when you have a product, for example, that's growing in team size and scope, how do you do it? For example, our Twilio SMS team started as a single small team back in 2010 but now consists of hundreds of engineers. How did we scale it with small teams? The answer is mitosis.

A team starts small, say five people. As they grow and near the ten-person mark, we start to plan for how the team might soon be divided into two teams. The big question is typically how to divide the teams. How you do it is situationally dependent. Sometimes it's by function of the product, sometimes it's by layers of functionality, sometimes it's by customer segment—but the most important thing is that you keep the customer, mission, metrics, and codebase together with that team. That last bit—the codebase—is the hard part because you have to plan ahead. Likely the system was built as one large codebase, and in order to split your teams, you must refactor the system into two codebases that two teams can independently own. This takes time; you usually plan these team splits at least six months ahead of time. But one upside is that you're continually investing in your codebase, refactoring it into microservices, and fixing prior debt in the process. It's like a regular spring clean, which is good hygiene when a team and product are growing quickly. This keeps your codebase constantly aligned with your teams, who are in turn aligned with your customer needs.

Here's an example: Twilio Voice started out as one team. But as they approached fifteen people, we knew the team had grown too large, so it was time to divide it up. That product had two major aspects: connectivity into the phone networks of the world, and the APIs that sit on top of those connections that allow customers to build dynamic interactions like saying text, playing back audio, and conferencing people together. In the connectivity layer, customers care about global reach and cost-effectiveness. In the API layer, customers care about features, such as conference bridges that scale to hundreds of people, or more realistic-sounding text-to-speech voices. This was a natural way to split the product into two teams. We called them Voice Connectivity and Programmable Voice. As a result, we had to detangle the code between these two parts of the Twilio Voice product, and doing so ended up allowing us to onboard and test new carriers much more quickly, and scale out our data centers around the world much faster. Speed of developing features accelerated, too, because those teams no longer had to also worry about carrier interconnections. And then with a team to focus exclusively on the customer needs for Voice Connectivity, they realized that connectivity itself could be an independent product. In 2014, that team launched their newly broken-out product as Twilio Elastic SIP Trunking, which now serves over six thousand customers independent of our Programmable Voice product. So the team split not only forced a very healthy architecture rethink but also enabled our teams to focus on respective customer needs independently, and even resulted in a new revenue stream for the company.

SINGLE-THREADED LEADERS AND STREAMLINED DECISION-MAKING

The last and arguably most important part of scaling small teams is, unsurprisingly, leadership. If you want a small team whose members are focused on a mission, empowered to make hard decisions, and dedicated to running fast in service of your customers, then a leader is critical. We call such leaders "single-threaded" because they wake up in the morning with only one thing on their mind—how their team can win. (*Threads* are units of execution in a computer program—a multi-threaded program is doing a lot at once, but a single-threaded program is focused on doing just one thing.) This may seem obvious, but most corporate structures don't provide this. Most common is an executive higher up in the company, maybe a VP, to whom all of product and engineering reports. That executive ultimately makes key decisions that impact the teams on the front line, then teams on the front lines have to "cascade" their objectives into their plans. The other common approach to running a small team is to have "two in a box" leading the team—typically a product manager and an engineering manager. This is very common. It's how Google runs, for example. However, in this world, it's not clear who's accountable, and nobody can break ties to unblock progress. In a startup, there may be multiple founders and team members, but there's only one CEO who's ultimately accountable.

Lots of companies talk about empowerment but are ultimately too risk-averse to give their leaders enough freedom. Executives are too worried about their own success to actually let the people who report to them have any real agency. We talk about empowerment, but then we second-guess our teams. As a leader you may be asking: How can I empower small teams, and trust them to execute when my neck is on the line? How can I *not* overturn a bad decision my team is making? How can I step back and let teams work without being in the details?

We had this problem at Twilio when we hired VPs of engineering and product. They either stepped in too much, overruling their teams' decisions and in essence removing their autonomy, or did the opposite, sitting back and not doing anything because, hey, their teams are empowered and can do whatever they want. Obviously, neither is ideal.

The way I've coached them is to say: "Look, I'm the CEO of the company and we're public, so I'm accountable to the board and to investors." If we have a good quarter, I share that news, and if we have a bad quarter, I don't say: "Well, a director of product made a bad decision, you should go talk to them." Obviously, the results the company posts are my responsibility. So I'm accountable for our results, and the way I'm going to get good results is by hiring and empowering single-threaded leaders, and leading small teams who are close to problems. The best thing you can do is train people to listen to customers and make good decisions. I believe that's how I'll achieve my goal, but of course I'm still on the hook.

Maybe there are some less-than-optimal decisions—but you weigh the cost of unwinding them, and unwinding the trust in your leaders versus letting those decisions move forward. If the decision will sink the company, or do lasting harm to customers, then yes, you should probably step in. The problem is that many times leaders step in on unimportant and inconsequential decisions. It's called "bikeshedding."

Bikeshedding is one of the accidental behaviors that executives and managers engage in that annoys our teams—and it's such a great term. Here's the background: Imagine you're part of a government committee responsible for building a nuclear reactor. The engineers come to the committee soliciting a decision on what kind of reactor to build: a pressurized water reactor, a boiling water reactor, or a light-water graphite reactor. They're likely to offer expert advice and a recommendation to the committee. Because you're not an expert in nuclear reactor design, you're probably not going to probe deeply into the details, and you're likely to accept the recommendations of the expert engineers. Yet if they were to ask you what color they should paint the bike shed outside the nuclear reactor, a large discussion would ensue, with each committee member attempting to add value and express their opinion. Bikeshedding, therefore, is the tendency for nonexperts in charge to expend a lot of calories on unimportant details, because they lack the context to make the most important decisions.

That said, it's natural for leaders to want to delegate upward. It's a sanity check on the decisions, but for hard decisions, it's usually easier to ask your boss to make the call. But doing so is escaping accountability, which isn't good for building a culture of empowered leaders. As a leader, I tend to ask more questions than answer them. My goal is to make the single-threaded leaders accountable, but help them answer their own questions. I'm not perfect, and too often I fall for the trap of making the call when asked, but my goal is to help them clarify their own decision-making instead.

Without single-threaded leaders who are empowered to make decisions, companies end up with other decision-making frameworks that I believe are less effective. Maybe you've heard of the

RAPID® framework for decision-making—it's one of many such systems that help organizations understand "Who has the D"—or decision. RAPID® was created by Bain as a tool to clarify decision accountability, assigning roles to the five key roles in any decision (Recommend, Agree, Perform, Input, Decide).

At Twilio, we've experimented with RAPID® in parts of the company, but we realized the efficacy breaks down when there's this other, silent role in it—V (Veto). You can agree to this whole RAPID® process, but if there's always a manager who can just veto the whole thing, the person who in theory has the decision really doesn't. That's the opposite of empowering a single-threaded leader. You *say* they have the authority to make decisions, but if you second-guess or, worse, veto those decisions, you're actually just giving them agency in name, not in actions. They'll be afraid to make decisions, and will delegate most things upward to you. I think of this as the great destroyer of intrinsic motivation.

So what's the solution? People feel empowered and "in the know" as a function of how close they are to the decision maker, which breaks down like this:

- If you're the decision maker, you have complete autonomy.
- If your manager has the decision, you're likely to understand their process by which the decision is made, you're in conversations that inform the decision, and you're likely to go along with the decision.
- If somebody far away, whom you interact with rarely or don't even know, makes a decision that impacts you, you take on a victim mindset. These are things being done *to* you, not *with* you. You start to believe you're a passive part of the process, as opposed to an empowered and trusted actor.

Small teams and single-threaded leaders who run them help minimize the chances that people find themselves in that third position—disempowered and victimized by decisions they disagree with.

THE FALLACY OF BETTER COLLABORATION

One problem you soon encounter scaling up a bunch of small, autonomous teams is how they coordinate their work. The more teams you have, and the more autonomous they are, the less they are likely to collaborate, which many leaders will bemoan. In fact, when things in a company aren't humming along, it's common for leaders to exclaim "We need better collaboration" as the answer. And while that sounds nice, it's not realistic to say that people just need to manage their thousands of relationships with other people and other teams better. The whole system, and agility, would collapse under the weight. It's no surprise that meetings proliferate and most employees just check out.

That's what I call "the fallacy of better collaboration."

Small teams have the potential to require less collaboration, because like a startup, they ideally get to focus their time and attention on their customer and the small number of people around them on the mission. But of course teams will have to interact with each other to get anything meaningful done.

Therefore, it's important to formalize the relationships between teams as "service contracts." Imagine each team was a literal different startup—and if you did business with them, their product was well defined and their pricing well understood. Imagine the other team's website, describing their products, with a "Contact Us" or "Get Started" button if you wanted some of their product. When crossing corporate boundaries, these kinds of formalized contracts are a necessity—the product must have definition, the pricing must be agreed upon. But inside a company, it's all loosey goosey. If each team exposes to other teams a formalized notion of "Here's what we do, and here's how to engage with us," then the cost of coordination is reduced. It's a way of standardizing those types of interactions, making them into a well-understood and scalable process. You can even put a "price tag" on the services, to aid with internal accounting and resource planning.

In technology teams, these interfaces are usually APIs and good documentation. When the Programmable Voice team needs to place a call to a telephone somewhere in the world, they make an API request to the Voice Connectivity layer to initiate the phone call. This well-defined service contract between teams provides a stable, predictable, and documented way for teams to interact with each other, and even accounts for billing of the underlying services. But this practice isn't limited to just technology teams. In other parts of the organization, you can deploy similar organizing principles. For example, your legal team probably spends lots of time negotiating customer contracts in partnership with your sales team, but is there a clear "API" for how to engage with them? How does a new contract get submitted? How is progress tracked? What does it "cost" to engage an in-house attorney, and is that cost factored into the cost of sales? You can imagine a legal team providing a self-service platform where salespeople can pull preapproved boilerplate language off the shelf, which doesn't require an attorney to engage. That would be a great product! Many salespeople would love that, as it would speed their deal cycles, and it would require less "collaboration" with the legal team.

Here's another creative example: A few years ago, a vending machine popped up in our offices, chock-full of keyboards, mice, laptop power adaptors, and the like. Instead of cash, you scan your employee badge to get the gear you need (which is tracked for accounting and frugality purposes). This is our IT team's way of building a new service contract with employees. Instead of having countless employees walk up to the IT service desk each day to get help with a dongle or keyboard, they made a well-defined interface (the vending machine), a clear process (swipe your badge, mouse drops out the front), and even a price tag. That's a new way of interacting between the two teams that offers a standard interface to how to work together.

Taken to its logical conclusion, teams can choose the "product" of an internal team, or even choose to pick a vendor outside the company who provides the same service, perhaps at a better price, or with a better set of features or better service. When everybody has great interfaces, it allows teams to pick the best tool for the job and forces teams to up their game to "win" the business of internal customers. Certain conditions need to be met for a team to pick an external option, such as minimum thresholds for security or reliability being met. But assuming that's true, it allows each team more autonomy to service their customer. That's why including economics in the interface is important. Without an internal price tag, it has the appearance of being "free" when in actuality, there is of course a cost. When you want a small team to act like a startup, having "revenue" as a measure of success is pretty clarifying. Otherwise, more teams depending on you is actually just more work, not winning.

This is really just allowing every team to think about their output as a product, designed to serve customers in the same way we serve people outside of the company. If you're a commercial legal team, your product is getting legal contracts done that protect the company but allow it to grow, and your customers are your sales team and your end buyers. If you can design a way to serve those customers, and iterate rapidly on how to better serve them, that's a software/product way of thinking about the problem versus throwing more bodies at the problem—and of course with more bodies comes more complexity (recall the exponential growth of complexity when people are added).

I believe the goal isn't better collaboration; it's actually *less* collaboration. Great companies don't say: "I need better customer support." They say: "We should reduce the need for customers to contact customer support." In the same way, great companies reduce the need for teams, and individuals, to collaborate by standardizing or productizing the interactions between the groups. This frees up teams to spend more time innovating, and less time in internal coordination meetings. The key is treating other parts of the company as customers rather than collaborators.

STRIPE ATLAS: BUILD A TEAM THAT'S LIKE ONE BRAIN

Remember Patio11, whom you met in Chapter 4? He has a great analogy for what building a successful small team is like: building a single brain made up of all the necessary functions. Creating teams this way helps avert what he thinks is a major issue at many companies, even though it's standard practice: siloing developers away from the business processes. As he puts it, "This is an organizational design problem in a lot of ways. The typical thing is for companies to say, 'Okay, we have a business unit here, and then we have an engineering team in the company here, and they have an interface.'" The "interface" he's skeptical of refers to Product Requirements Documents (PRDs), Kanban tasks, or other systems of throwing work over the wall. In fact, it often tends to create an adversarial relationship because the software people write their schedule and do their work, but then—as always happens—the requirements change. That's when the accusations start flying. In Patio11's words, "The folks who have been working on the software say, 'You're changing the rules of the game on me, I've got to throw out work. I'm now behind on what I want to do. Those blankity-blankers in the business unit don't understand how software is written.' Then the business folks say, 'Oh, those blankity-blank developers promised us the system would be ready by March. It's February and we're nowhere close to getting the system done.'"

To sum it up, he concludes, "Developers are from Mars, requirements analysts are from Venus, and never the twain shall meet." This structure and its predictable outcome are baked into every company where somebody decided to put the people who build the thing in a separate unit, with separate incentives, from the people who understand what the thing is to be built.

It doesn't have to be, though. This is where small *multidisciplinary* teams come in.

Stripe, where Patio11 now works, has long been good at putting developers and businesspeople on the same team to build projects. But in creating the team to develop Atlas, the product that enables entrepreneurs to spin up a Delaware corporation with just a few clicks, they took things even further in terms of combining functions. For that project, they literally moved not just developers and businesspeople onto the same team, but added customer service, legal, and marketing. Not only that, they literally had them sitting together.

This has enormous benefits in terms of efficiency alone. As Patio11 describes just one outcome, "Legal for Atlas was sitting next to the engineering team. It was a heavily legal inflected product. When someone would come up at 11 a.m. with a question like, 'I'm not sure if this bit of copy that I'm writing onto this screen is okay,' they could literally turn to the lawyer and say, 'Hey, quick question for you with regard to this legal thing. I want to say blah, blah, blah. Am I allowed to say that?' And the lawyer would say, 'Well, step back for a minute, there. Why are we even saying that at all? Could we address that in another way?'" And then they'd spend five minutes coming up with the optimal approach.

Compare that to the usual process, in which a developer works for about twelve weeks, and only then does the project get reviewed. At that point, "it's infeasible to change the assumptions that have gone into the number of screens and the flow between them," Patio11 explains. "You're locked in on that and all you can do is attempt to address poor understanding of the legal environment with the best possible words on those screens." That's why getting everyone together on one team, and even eliminating the physical and organizational distance between them, is such a powerful tool. It catches wrong assumptions and bad decisions early in the process.

It also does amazing things for morale. Everybody on the Atlas team at Stripe identifies first and foremost as a member of the team, rather than a member of a function. Instead of saying, "My name is Susan. I work on the User Ops team, and I'm assigned to the Atlas project," she would say, "My name is Susan, I work on Atlas doing User Ops work." (User Ops is how Stripe describes support.) Simply put, her tribe isn't Stripe, or the User Ops team, it's Atlas. User Ops (support) is a great case where companies often inject social distance between the frontline agents and the team building the product. That creates situations where people think of themselves as cogs in the machine. "People feel like, 'My job here is tickets in, tickets out.' That gets draining after a while, and turnover in that role is typically pretty high," Patio11 says.

The opposite is true for the Atlas team. People feel so connected to Atlas that some turn down transfers, even ones that include career advancement opportunities, because they want to stay with their tribe. Better yet, they feel the same connection to their customers, creating a feedback loop that is "probably the best of any team I've ever been on," Patio11 says.

That tight feedback loop and cross-functional ownership of Atlas's outcomes means their engineers can deliver what customers want—and do so almost immediately. Here's one example. At first, the Atlas service was intended solely to help startups incorporate, usually in the state of Delaware. That was great, but as you can imagine, the act of initial incorporation is just the first in a number of byzantine government interactions that entrepreneurs need to navigate while building a company. So customers started turning to Atlas for other areas where they were struggling dealing with government bureaucracy, which is almost always a distraction for an entrepreneur.

It was November 2017, about a year after Atlas launched, and in a regular team meeting the User Ops group raised the question of why they were suddenly getting an influx of questions about "taxes" from their customers. Patio11 was intrigued and asked what kind of taxes they were asking about—of course, companies pay sales tax, income tax, payroll tax, and so on—and the User Ops representative replied, "something called franchise tax?"

As an experienced serial entrepreneur, Patio11 immediately recalled the pain of the annual Delaware franchise tax calculations and payments that every company has to submit to. And it made sense that they'd get a bunch of questions from customers, as the Delaware Franchise Tax Board (the dreaded FTB) had just sent their start-of-the-year reminders to every company that they owed sometimes large, and often miscalculated, tax bills. Users were turning to Atlas, which had incorporated them with the promise of taking care of all the complexity, for help.

The team first built a quick-and-dirty answer to help their

customers, and prevent them from having to write in for help. "We built a thing within the dashboard to help people pay the Delaware state franchise tax, but one would have had to calculate it using the instructions from the state of Delaware, which are not straightforward to follow for many Internet entrepreneurs."

You can imagine the allure of solving the next problem for their customers—actually filing the taxes for them, preventing them from having to navigate the confusing Delaware website. At first, the engineers in the room instinctively replied, "Taxes are out of scope." Patio11, though, as the leader, brought an insight: there was a great opportunity here. If a million companies each spend two hours annually figuring out how to file their Delaware franchise taxes, but the Atlas team could spend a few weeks building it in software, they'd save millions of hours of work every year for businesses, and they would essentially make humanity more efficient.

Having filed those taxes several times, Patio11 was a domain expert, so he could describe the software needed that would streamline the process for their customers. But they had a problem. Filling out the forms for customers semiautomatically could be problematic. There are two ways to calculate the tax, Method A and Method B. Basically, startups should always use Method B. The Atlas developers wondered if they could just tell users to go to Method B, but lawyers on the team thought this skated too close to giving legal advice. Engineers proposed a compromise, in which the software automatically defaults customers into Method B, but also says that if an attorney has advised them to use Method A, they should go deal with the state of Delaware directly. That one passed muster with the legal team.

And like that, they'd taken a customer need they hadn't originally anticipated, turned it into a legally complex solution that saved customers lots of time, and had sign-off from the legal team to go build it. You can imagine if legal hadn't been on the team and in the room, how they might have responded with a much more firm "No, what are you thinking? We can't give legal advice to our customers." Instead, they understood the problem and were along on the problem-solving journey. With that, they could start building the software, which built in ample time for the upcoming tax season.

The engineers developed the tax feature—quickly enough to ship it in the next version of Atlas, in time for tax season. The program sends customers reminders to pay taxes on time, and helps them figure out how much tax they need to pay. A process that used to take two to three hours now takes less than a minute. "We have a great experience. And it wouldn't have happened unless the User Op had said in the room, 'Taxes are six months out and people are already asking about our plans,'" Patio11 says.

This would not have happened if engineers on the Atlas team were isolated from everyone else. It happened because the whole team sits together, and they're all part of every decision. The engineers don't have their own engineering meetings while marketing people have their own marketing meetings and customer service folks have a customer service meeting and the legal folks have their own legal team meeting. When the Atlas team meets, everyone attends. Thus everybody stays close to the customers and can give them what they want. They're one brain, serving customers.

Teams do their best work when each member of the team feels accountable to the customer, and a deep sense of purpose to serve the customer. Small teams enable that kind of connection and purpose, with a mission that comes from inside the team, driven by a primary interaction with the customer and their problems, not from executives.

What you want is for members of the team, and the team as a whole, to believe what they're doing is important. That intrinsic motivation doesn't come from inspirational speeches or a big paycheck. It arises from the knowledge that your work has real impact on the lives of fellow human beings.

In most companies, the directives flow down the organizational chart. But at Twilio, Stripe, and many other companies that believe in small teams, it's the reverse. People, often investors, ask me why we give so much autonomy to small teams to own their priorities and road maps. I reply: "Who knows best how to serve customers? I'm sitting here right now, talking to investors, while my teams are busy talking to customers. Who do you think knows more about what we need to do for our customers today?"

To me, the greatest purpose of small, multidisciplinary teams and single-threaded leaders is to keep teams feeling close to customers, accountable for decisions, and knowing that their work directly translates into progress. To see how your teams feel, you might inquire about how decisions are made. For example, ask your developers who made some recent decision, and whether or not they were involved in the decision. When the decision was made, even if they disagreed, did they commit and move forward as a team? You might ask whether decisions are informed more by customer need than by the org chart. To understand if the team feels accountable for progress, ask what metrics they're measured by, and whether they feel they can reasonably control them. Ask how many people outside of their team decide what they can or can't do. Ultimately, what you're getting at is a feeling of accountability and intrinsic drive. Ask your leaders if they succeed or fail in a given undertaking, do they feel it was largely within their control? If not, you might think about how to organize your teams so everybody feels like they're accountable for decisions and outcomes. Otherwise, people have a tendency to check out.

CHAPTER 9
WEARING THE CUSTOMERS' SHOES

People will forget what you said, forget what you did, but people will never forget how you made them feel.
—Maya Angelou

Once you've organized the company into small teams, defined by a customer, a mission, and metrics of success, it's time for them to get to work sprinting in service of your customers. But how to do that? Nearly every company claims to be "customer-focused" or "customer-centric," yet why is it that in practice, we as customers so rarely feel "focused on" or "centric-ed"? It turns out, being "customer-centric" is very subjective and hard to implement. Most of the time when companies fail to serve customers, they do so inadvertently. Very few employees wake up in the morning saying, "I can't wait to screw with a customer today!" Hopefully your interview and talent review processes can identify and reject any such misanthropes quickly. The vast majority of the time, this begins with leadership needing to be more prescriptive in how to be customer-centric, and building mechanisms to reinforce their prescription. You have to put some meat on the bone because it's harder to truly serve your customers than just saying it implies.

Every leader likes to think that their company "gets it," that their teams don't make head-slapping mistakes that negatively impact customers. Yet as companies grow, we build systems of abstraction so deep that as leaders, we're often removed from knowing what our customers are really experiencing. Sure, we've got NPS surveys to tell us the cumulative effect of our actions on customers. But let's be honest, customers who take the time to participate in a survey are mostly those who've developed strong feelings one way or the other about us, not representative of the typical customer. And surveys are strongly influenced by a customer's last interaction, good or bad. It's a point in time, but it really doesn't tell us if we've created an organization that routinely internalizes and prioritizes customer problems to be solved over politics and organizational charts. Sadly, as executives and managers, our primary window into viscerally understanding how well we're serving customers is the quantity and content of the many LinkedIn InMails, tweets, and emails we receive unprompted from customers.

Customer centricity, as the name implies, is creating an organization that constantly self-corrects to put customers at the center of our decisions. Like a gyroscope that resists being moved off-center, a customer-centric organization resists the many forces that attempt to deprioritize customers. But it's incredibly hard to do, and that's where it's helpful to learn from the masters.

One of my heroes is the restaurateur Danny Meyer, the CEO of Union Square Hospitality Group in New York. For more than thirty years, Danny has operated some of New York's most loved restaurants, including Union Square Cafe, Blue Smoke, and Gramercy Tavern. He also founded and serves on the board of Shake Shack, the wildly popular fast-food chain that started out as a Madison Square Park hot dog cart. I don't live in New York, and I'm not much of a foodie—so why is Danny one of my heroes? In his book *Setting the Table*, Danny explains how the concepts of hospitality and service apply to every business. His ideas were incredibly influential to me in the early days of Twilio, and they have guided many of our ways of structuring our company. He believes hospitality doesn't belong just in the hospitality industry—restaurants, hotels, cruise lines, tourism—but in every industry, in every company, in every transaction.

Notably, Danny believes hospitality is not the same as service. Companies often talk about a culture of great service, but to Danny, that's not the point:

> Hospitality is the foundation of my business philosophy. Virtually nothing else is as important as how one is made to feel in any business transaction. Hospitality exists when you believe the other person is on your side. The converse is just as true. Hospitality is present when something happens for you. It is absent when something happens to you. Those two simple prepositions—*for* and *to*—express it all.

I loved Danny's book so much that I invited him to speak to our employees at Twilio and share his ideas about hospitality, a phrase not often uttered in software companies. To him, it means making your customers feel you're on their side. That's a universal truth, not limited to restaurants or traditional hospitality businesses. But does that mean service isn't important? No, good service is necessary, but insufficient to be a great customer-centric organization:

> Service is the technical delivery of a product. Hospitality is how the delivery of that product makes its recipient *feel*. Service is a *monologue*—we decide how we want to do things and set our own standards for service. Hospitality, on the other hand, is a *dialogue*. To be on a guest's side requires listening

to that person with every sense, and following up with a thoughtful, gracious, appropriate response. It takes both great service and great hospitality to rise to the top.

These two ideas were instrumental in how we thought about our small-teams approach at Twilio. Because if you believe, as Danny and I do, that you need to have a dialogue with customers, then you need your teams close enough to customers to engage. You need to listen. But how do you create a structure where your small teams are in a position to listen effectively?

In a restaurant, that's pretty easy—you have a server standing at your table. But in a technology organization, serving perhaps millions of customers, and where success looks like customers *not* actually having to talk to you—how do the builders of those technologically mediated experiences get the proximity to customers so they can truly provide hospitality in every interaction?

In the early days of a startup, it's common for all of the employees to remain close to customers—it's hard not to. But as companies grow, people tend to take on specialized roles that separate "customer-facing" roles from those that aren't. Support and sales and product managers talk to customers, but engineers are heads-down. While there's a certain practicality to that, it also creates a culture of gatekeeping that does a disservice to both the developers and the customers they're building for. As Danny Meyer writes:

> In every business, there are employees who are the first point of contact with the customers (attendants at airport gates, receptionists at doctors' offices, bank tellers, executive assistants). Those people can come across either as agents or as gatekeepers. An agent makes things happen *for* others. A gatekeeper sets up barriers to keep people out. We're looking for

agents, and our staff members are responsible for monitoring their own performance: *In that transaction, did I present myself as an agent or a gatekeeper?* In the world of hospitality, there's rarely anything between.

In a software team, those customer-facing roles can serve as two-way gatekeepers. They're both preventing customers from engaging with developers, but also preventing developers from engaging with customers. Product managers often see themselves as "gatekeepers," describing their role as "protecting" engineers from customers. To some extent this makes sense. You don't want your engineers getting bogged down handling every customer and every complaint. Engineers need big chunks of uninterrupted time to go off and work in solitude. But it's a mistake to wall them off from customers.

The biggest risk companies face, especially as they grow, is that they become inward-facing. Employees compete internally with each other rather than with rivals in the marketplace. People spend more time navigating internal politics, or simply figuring out how to get things done, rather than serving customers. Turning your small teams outward, giving them mechanisms to focus on customers instead of politics, is the message of this chapter. It's easier said than done, but if you do it right, the speed and intuition your teams gain will become a real source of competitive advantage. What company doesn't want their customers to love them?

WEARING OUR CUSTOMERS' SHOES

In around 2012, we began the process of articulating our company's values. In my experience, values can be empty words on the wall, or they can be guiding principles used daily by employees to make countless decisions. What takes them off the wall and into practices is two things: memorability and mechanisms. If they're memorable, then employees are more likely to remember them, refer back to them, and want to use them in daily interactions.

"Customer-centric" is not very memorable because it's bland and commonplace. Every company says it, so it becomes part of the wallpaper. Customer-centric doesn't express any opinion about how one should go about serving customers, it just *says* that you do, which honestly is pretty obvious. I imagine most governments' motor vehicle departments include some variant of "customer-centric" in their values, but clearly the *how* is often lacking—as anyone who has ever stood in line to get their license renewed will attest.

We decided that the prerequisite of customer focus was empathy, and the best way to build empathy for somebody is, as the saying goes, to walk a mile in their shoes. So we decided to articulate one of our core values as "Wear the Customer's Shoes." Then we took it one step further: we commissioned a run of Twilio-red Chuck Taylor Converse shoes, with the Twilio logo (which is round) opposite the Converse logo on the side of the shoes. We called them the TwilioCons, and we made a deal with customers. If they gave us a pair of their shoes, we'd give them a pair of ours. Quickly we amassed hundreds of pairs of customers' actual shoes, which we hung all around our offices (yes, we did spray them with disinfectant, thank you for asking) along with a small sign with the customer's name. From worn-in trainers to leather loafers, there's a constant reminder in every conference room to wear our customers' shoes. We don't literally wear them, but I can't tell you how many times people, especially new employees, interviewees, or prospective customers, ask, "What's with the shoes?" The question is the perfect lead-in to discuss our approach to customer-centricity, which keeps the value alive and a part of daily conversation. Yes, it's cheesy, but it works.

But having a memorable company value around customers that's discussed frequently still doesn't magically enable the company to serve customers well. Over the years, I've discussed this problem with many other leaders, and I've observed a variety of customer-centric companies develop mechanisms, or repeatable, measurable practices, to keep their development teams close to customers.

The first step is ensuring proximity to customers. Keeping the people who build the product close to customers makes so much sense, it almost seems unnecessary to explain how and why companies should do it. But in many, maybe most, software organizations, developers never talk to customers at all. They operate in a kind of bubble, developing software that someone on the business side has specced out and handed to them. One way to do it is the public "idea forum." This is the approach Bunq used.

BUNQ

Remember Bunq, the Dutch mobile banking app I told you about in Chapter 1? It created a customer feedback loop with a guy named Leroy Filon, who never imagined he could fall in love with a bank. Filon is a thirty-two-year-old videographer who runs a small creative agency in Apeldoorn, a small city about an hour east of Amsterdam. Leroy liked Bunq so much that he started telling everyone he knew about it. But he kept running into a specific problem—he couldn't walk them through the app without also exposing his bank account balance. So he posted a suggestion on Bunq's online user forum, which is built right into the app: Wouldn't it be cool if I could show my friends the app without letting them in on the details of my finances? Soon enough, other users started chiming in, and before long, Leroy had received seventy-seven "high fives" for his suggestion.

A forum for customers is fine, but too often nobody is listening to what customers are saying. But not at Bunq: the company requires developers to participate on the forum, and a developer there soon spotted Leroy's idea and saw other customers up-voting it. He liked it, and Bunq began developing the feature. Soon thereafter, at a theater in Amsterdam, Bunq introduced an updated version of the app, which included the ability to demonstrate the app without disclosing personal information. They put Leroy's photo up on the screen during the presentation, and Ali Niknam, Bunq's founder and CEO, personally thanked Leroy for his contribution. As you can imagine, Leroy was thrilled to get a shout-out from his bank's CEO. But more important, Bunq showed its other customers that it listens, and that it's a company worth engaging with.

To me, though, the most interesting part of this story is the efficiency these forums achieved. The actual work for the software developers to hide the account balance is probably quite small. But the amount of work required for customer support teams to filter ideas in that forum and present their findings to product managers—who in turn sort through the list, decide what's in and what's out, and develop sprint plans and User Stories for the engineers—is enormous and could easily take months. In such a process, at each step there's a loss of information from the original customer's intent. At some point, an engineer gets a spec to "hide the account balance," but probably the developer now lacks the original context. What if the developers can imagine a better way to enable what the customer wants, which is to show off the app? But chances are more likely, somewhere along the way, that this particular idea would be deprioritized for something that "moves the needle" more. That's where customers' needs are often ignored. Any individual feature is too small to merit the organizational effort to prioritize it. Yet when you remove all that activation energy, and let a developer see a cool customer problem and spend a few hours solving it—almost as a passion project because they can—your customers see you as a responsive, customer-focused organization.

As I've noted before, most things in code aren't actually all that hard to build. Most of the work often goes into the overhead of planning. But by putting engineers directly into the flow of customer feedback, you achieve two things.

First, you humanize your customers. Instead of being a requirements document, the developers get to hear straight from customers not just what they need, but *why* they need it. Customers likely express this with a depth or eloquence that would get lost in the translation process to a specification. And when you interface directly with the customer's words, the need becomes more real—more human—and the work becomes more meaningful. Leroy's experience made him an even bigger fan of Bunq. In fact, it turned him into an evangelist. He goes around telling his friends and colleagues how great Bunq is. Imagine what happens to the developer who created that feature and saw how that small bit of work had such a big impact—it's such a rush! Trust me, I've had this experience as a developer myself; it's an incredible feeling. Once you've felt it, you want to feel it again. That developer at Bunq will get fired up and go try to find more customers and turn them into rabid fans, too.

Second, you let the developers make instinctive decisions about work-versus-reward trade-offs. A product manager might deprioritize the "balance hiding" feature because, in the grand scheme of things, it doesn't seem very important. Frankly, that might be true. But would their conclusion change if they knew it would take only ninety minutes to build the feature versus ninety days? I imagine it would. Developers can often make these quick estimations, so their instincts serve them well in picking ideas that give the most bang for the buck.

By removing layers of overhead, engineers who are close to customers can make low-risk decisions that benefit customers. Customers become human beings, not database entries or masses acting statistically. Those stereotypes about developers being antisocial types who are detached from humanity—that's rubbish. Developers, like most creative professionals, want to see people use and love the results of their work. And these "tight feedback loops" don't just make developers and customers feel warm and fuzzy—they drive growth.

Bunq opened for business in 2016, grew 800 percent in 2017, and then doubled in size in 2018, finishing that year with €211 million in customer deposits. In 2019, Bunq doubled again, to €433 million in receipts. This tiny company in Amsterdam has built the kind of extreme engagement and passion with customers that every company in the world dreams about. Not only that, they've done it without ever employing a single storefront or salesperson. Instead they depend on happy customers like Leroy Filon to sell the product to people they know.

I love stories about developers learning directly from customers what to build. However, I don't ascribe to the idea that every customer idea should be built. Nor do customers even always know what they want. However, customers are very good at expressing their problems. Danny Meyer, the biggest advocate for customers, even acknowledged that in his book: "One of the oldest sayings in business is 'The customer is always right.' I think that's become a bit outdated. I want to go on the offensive to create opportunities for our customers to feel that they are being heard even when they're not right. To do so, I always actively encourage them—when I'm on my rounds, in our comment cards, and in letters or emails to us—to let us know if they feel something's not right. When they do, I thank them."

More important than having access to the raw customer idea stream, developers are well served by being in the flow of customer problems. When developers are kept close to customer problems, they can help vet the problems with an instinctual understanding of the problem and its possible solutions.

GET YOUR FACE IN THE PLACE

Helping developers build empathy for customers is somewhat easy when they themselves are also customers, which is the case at Bunq and even Twilio. But what do you do when you create a product that your developers don't personally use? It's clearly harder to viscerally understand a problem domain when you're observing it from the outside. That's when it's even more important to build deep connections to customers and their needs.

But in a cruel irony, these are the types of companies that are often *most* likely to separate customers from the people building the product. Business-to-business companies, for example, typically employ armies of salespeople, customer success advocates, customer support agents, and domain-expert product managers as buffers between customers and the development team. The thinking goes that each of those roles has an expertise in serving customers, which obviously benefits customers, but also benefits developers by acting as a buffer. And while from day to day you do want developers to be able to focus without constant customer escalations, it's unwise to accept that developers should be buffered all the time. Yet it's easy to fall into that way of thinking based on assumed efficiency gains.

Our sales team at Twilio follows the mantra "You gotta get your face in the place," inspired by former Salesforce executive David Rudnitsky's sales playbook. That means that sales reps have to get out of the office and visit customers. That's pretty obvious for a sales team, but less obvious for a development team. But that's exactly what's needed to periodically create the human connection with customers.

One of the best stories I've ever heard about the value of customer connection comes from Ben Stein, a senior leader at Twilio who oversees our developer experience group—meaning he and his team focus on developers who use Twilio and try to make sure they are delighted with the product.

Ben studied electrical engineering at Cornell, then took a job as a software developer at Bloomberg, the financial technology and media company. He was writing code for the company's terminals, which are a fixture on every trading floor on Wall Street.

"I got the job because they were hiring any smart developers and engineers, and even though I knew nothing about finance, they were like, 'Don't worry, we'll teach you what you need to know,'" Ben recalls. "I told them, 'I don't even know what a trading floor is. Like, I saw the movie *Wall Street*, and that's about it. I don't know what I'm doing here.'"

Shortly after he joined, Ben asked his manager if he could go visit a trading floor and meet an actual trader. After all, if he was going to be writing programs used by traders, it might make sense to go talk to them and see how they used the Bloomberg terminal.

"My manager was like, 'Wow, that's a great idea. I would love to do that one day,'" Ben says. "I was like, 'Oh my God, you've never met a trader either.' This was so weird. No one in this entire team had ever been to a trading floor. It had never occurred to anyone to just ask. But we were building trading software."

Ben befriended a sales rep who worked on the Merrill Lynch account. He took Ben to visit the traders there. "I was the first person on this team who had ever done this," Ben says. "We met traders and chatted with them, and just walked around."

One big revelation struck him right away. Back in the software shop, Ben and the others were writing programs with the assumption that their applications would fill the entire screen on a trader's terminal. But in fact "our application was in this little teeny corner of the window and they had nine other things going. They're viewing my stuff on this tiny little window, so everything looks terrible and they can't read it. I realized that things like font size mattered, and contrast mattered. It made me realize that the choices I was making as a developer were wrong. It was really enlightening."

The epiphany changed the way he thought about writing software. Ben brought that customer-centric worldview with him when he joined Twilio in 2015 and has been pushing it out throughout our organization.

Engineers on his team are required to speak to at least one customer a quarter. Getting that done isn't as easy as you'd think. One way is to attend a hackathon or meet-up that Twilio hosts for customers. Another is for an engineer to listen in on a call where an account manager is checking in with a customer. The best might be when a sales rep brings a developer along on a sales call, in addition to the sales engineer. "They can bring along the person who actually builds the product," Ben says. "Sure, the developer won't be as polished as the sales rep, but a smart rep will play that to their strength."

Sometimes developers are reluctant to meet with customers, usually out of social awkwardness. "They're out of their element. It's hard. Maybe you've never done this before. It's strange. It's uncomfortable. You don't know how to act," Ben says.

Even so, most developers come back from a meeting feeling jazzed up. "The one thing that gets my team most excited is knowing that what they're doing matters. We don't always tell them why it matters. Or if we do, it's filtered. It's never direct. But understanding how the work you do impacts somebody is important."

This doesn't have to happen every day. Developers don't need to field every call from someone who is angry and wants to yell about it. They don't have to be part of every sales deal. "But once a month, or once a quarter, to find out that you built something cool and it saves this person thirty hours a week of manual labor, that's pretty neat, right?" Ben says.

Developers don't even have to come back with an idea for a new feature. "Sometimes the outcome is just that you come back to your desk feeling good. We're not always trying to get something out of it. It's just about feeling that emotional connection," Ben says. "Get them out of the basement, right? They're not troglodytes. Get them talking to people."

START WITH THE PRESS RELEASE

At many companies, product ideas or reviews will center on strategy documents, competitive analysis, or maybe wireframes. At Twilio, the first step in defining a new product or feature is writing the press release. This may sound counterintuitive, as the press release is usually the last step before launching a product. But this practice is part of a process of "working backward" from the customer need that has roots at Amazon. The press release is a great artifact on which to base product conversations, but it's easily misunderstood. The goal isn't to actually send the press release out on the wire. Rather, the format of a press release, if written correctly, relays in order of importance why customers will care about the product you're building—which is a great basis around which to build a product from the get-go.

Budding journalists learn about the format of a new article: the headline captures interest, the lead does the heavy lifting, and the rest of the article, in descending order of importance, lays out the details. That's pretty much how every news story you've ever read is structured. Press releases work the same way. Think about the format of a news story or press release: they're written to relay the most important piece of information in the headline. Effective headlines hook the reader by tapping into something they care about. For a customer, it's a problem they need solved. The subheadline puts a little more meat on the bone. The opening paragraph, more detail, and so forth, until the closing sentence relays the least important detail.

If you imagine the reader as your customer, then the press release format forces you to start with what's most important to your customer, and explain why what you're doing is relevant to them; otherwise they'd stop reading. Forcing this kind of clarity is good, because it puts the customer at the center of the artifact.

Even though we write press releases as our key early-stage artifact, it's very common for newcomers to do the assignment—write a press release—but still miss the point. It's easy to write a press release whose reader isn't the customer. The author can write a press release for their manager or the CEO as the reader. Or they can imagine a journalist as the reader, and position the product vis-à-vis the competition. Often products are depicted not from the customers' point of view, but from the perspective of strategy, or the company's other products, or the company's vision, which the leaders have been advocating for. Managers often believe if they articulate their plans in the context of the CEO's vision, then they'll get approval. Yet in customer-centric organizations, not strategy-centric or CEO-centric organizations, discussions start with the customer. Great product development press releases start with the understanding that the customer is the reader, and the words have to hook the customer into caring about the product.

As I mentioned, we adapted this practice from Amazon. Jeff Bezos calls this "working backward from the customer." It means developers don't just go off and build stuff that they think is cool. Instead, they start with what customers want, which isn't always the same thing. There's typically many interactions on the press release to ensure early alignment around the customer problem. The process seems time-consuming, but overall it saves time because developers don't spend weeks, months, or even years working on products for which it turns out there is no customer demand. Many never make it past the early stages.

"You build products for your customers. It's not like, 'Let's go build some technology in the wild and see what happens with it,'" Werner Vogels says. "You need a very strong mechanism to make sure that you know exactly what you're going to build for your customers." The press release is such a mechanism, ensuring customers are at the center of your product plans from the earliest stages.

DOORS NOT WALLS

The structures of so many companies create walls between customers, and the people we want to serve them. Instead of building walls, think of building mechanisms that are doors—ones that you can crack open, allowing customers and developers to communicate.

When you do, magic happens. For Bunq, one version of opening the door involves making developers participate in the customer forum, and celebrating customer contributions to the software. The payoff has been incredible customer loyalty and rapid growth as Bunq continues stealing customers from stodgy old banks whose developers probably never talk to customers and may not even understand how customers use the software they develop.

You can tell I'm a bit wary of the word *strategy* because it can be mistaken for marching orders from executives, versus listening to customers. At Twilio, I often say "our strategy is simple: build things our customers want for which they'll pay us." Obviously we have long-term plans for the business, but I don't want teams to confuse our company's goals for serving our customers. The only way we can bring our corporate plans to life is by serving customers. My favorite way of understanding if teams are wearing the customers' shoes is to walk around and ask developers what customer problem they're working on. If they tell me a feature, then I ask what customer problem it's solving. If they can't answer it, then that's a sign that the team might not be building enough connection with customers. You can do this, too—it's easy. Another thing to ask your developers: during product reviews, start the conversation with the customer problem. Don't jump right into talk of strategy or features, but start with why the customer will care. Ask your leaders about which customers demonstrated the problem, and how they validated that the customer problem represents a broad market need. The answer doesn't matter as much as the process does. Does the team have the right mechanisms in place to truly understand customers? By asking these questions, you'll start to understand how your teams think. Once they know these questions are coming, I bet it'll set them on the path to wearing your customers' shoes.

CHAPTER 10
DEMYSTIFYING AGILE

We are uncovering better ways of developing software by doing it and helping others do it.
—Agile Manifesto, 2001

In business and in software (and in this book) we talk a lot about agility—the ability to react quickly to changing environments. The process of building software implements agility as the aptly named Agile Software Development methodology. It's hard to lead today without at least hearing about Agile, and chances are, your software team practices some forms of Agile in how you build software. Yet many business leaders don't know how Agile works, why it's better than any other known system of building software, or how to avoid its pitfalls.

You have probably felt some of the impacts of Agile as you work with your technical teams and wondered what's going on over there in developer-land. For example, maybe developers have told you it's impossible to know when a product will ship, or what features it will have when it does. Pretty frustrating, right? You might have suggested throwing money and head count at a product to accelerate development, only to be told that the pace is the pace, regardless of head count, and no amount of money can change the timing.

If you've ever wondered what the hell the developers are doing, and why things are the way they are, and why you sometimes get these incredibly frustrating answers—then it's helpful to understand a bit more about how Agile works. But it's also important to see how it has been abused and taken to extremes that aren't necessarily helping. At some companies, Agile can become a huge source of frustration—for executives, managers, and developers alike. Creating a company that's *agile* is important, but to achieve it, executives should understand the benefits and drawbacks of the *Agile* methodology before blindly accepting it as the answer.

WHY AGILE?

In the 1980s and '90s, software development products were wrought with failure. Even at great software companies, the spiraling complexity, changing requirements, and large time scales of these projects doomed them. These challenges plagued organizations big and small, from startups to large enterprises. For example, accomplished software entrepreneur Mitch Kapor, who founded Lotus Development Corporation, which created Lotus 1-2-3 and Lotus Notes in the 1980s, funded an ambitious project in 2002, to build a next-generation collaboration software called Project Chandler. Six years later, after failing to deliver a product that remotely addressed the initial goals, the project was finally shut down. Even Microsoft, the preeminent software company of the era, has struggled to deliver these kinds of gargantuan software projects. In 2001, Microsoft embarked on its most ambitious upgrade to its dominant Windows operating system with a project code-named Longhorn. The software took five years to complete, with a major reset halfway through, and finally launched in 2006 as Windows Vista. By the time Vista reached the market, its developers had cut many of its features and failed to deliver the innovation that Bill Gates and Steve Ballmer had envisioned half a decade earlier when the project began. The bizarre thing is that these examples weren't exceptions—they were the norm.

The core problem was that most software projects started with meticulous requirements gathering, and then planning out months or years of work, with hard dependencies between myriad teams to deliver a final, working product in the end. The ubiquitous, and loathed, Gantt chart showed how all the pieces would flow together over time to finally deliver value to the customer at the end. Owing to the shape of the Gantt chart, this process became known as "Waterfall" development.

Jeff Sutherland is one of the computer scientists who began the Agile software movement. He's one of the prominent critics of the old Waterfall development method. Since the 1960s, this was the standard way to build software, but Sutherland calls the Waterfall method "a colossal blunder" that "has cost hundreds of billions of dollars of failed projects in the United States alone." Sutherland claims Waterfall fails 85 percent of the time in projects that cost over $5 million. In 2004 a study of 250 large software projects found that 70 percent had major delays and cost overruns or were shut down without being completed.

Australian airline Qantas wasted $200 million on a development project led by IBM and canceled the contract after four years of a ten-year deal. But that was only its first fiasco. In 2008, Qantas shut down its "Jetsmart" parts management software system, which cost $40 million and was so awful that aircraft engineers called it "Dumbjet."

In his book *Scrum: The Art of Doing Twice the Work in Half the Time*, Sutherland tells the story of a massive government project that was rescued by Scrum and Agile. In 2000, the FBI commissioned a five-year project, Virtual Case File, to replace the bureau's antiquated paper record-keeping system with digital files. Contract developers used the old-fashioned Waterfall approach, and by 2005, after spending $170 million, the FBI had to scrap the project and start over. The next attempt, called Sentinel, was outsourced to Lockheed Martin, with a budget of $451 million. Lockheed also used Waterfall methods and after five years of work, in 2010, had spent $405 million—and was only half done. The company estimated it would need $350 million more and could finish the job in six to eight years. Instead, a pair of innovative tech executives brought the project in-house, slashed the development team from hundreds of developers to fifty, stuck them in the basement of the FBI building, and got the job done in twenty months for $12 million. How? They used Agile methodologies instead of Waterfall.

The Agile movement began to solve an important problem—software development lacked a working process like so many other engineering disciplines. When you build a skyscraper, the surveyor surveys the land, the architect designs it on paper, the client checks off on the design, and then the architect hands it off to the general contractor. The contractor subdivides construction into specialized disciplines, and coordinates their work. We've honed this model over the last couple hundred years, and it tends to work.

Yet in software, it was common for requirements to change constantly throughout the building process. Imagine you're just completing the fiftieth floor on a new skyscraper when the customer asks for a completely new foundation. That used to happen to software engineers constantly. But while it's easy for anybody to understand how expensive it is to tear down a skyscraper and start over, it was often not as clear in the world of software. A relatively small change, late in the game, might have profound implications for some underpinnings. Thus it was common for software projects to be thrown way off track by changing requirements. The main problem was that in software, requirements were often not truly knowable at the get-go of a project, so all of the meticulously crafted dependencies and assumptions were often wrong, and the business needs would change faster than the software project could keep up.

Additionally, due to the hard dependencies between teams, when one team slipped, often the whole project slipped. When you consider changing requirements, slippage was the norm, not the exception. Thus, even when talented, best-intentioned project managers included a buffer in these plans, unpredictable cascading slippage became unmanageable. As such, billions of dollars were wasted, developers and business execs alike were incredibly frustrated—and it made sense that most companies believed they couldn't successfully build software.

One way of solving the problem was to get even *more* meticulous in planning, or to forbid all changes once the project commences. However, smart folks realized that those goals sound good but are just unrealistic.

That's the backdrop in which Sutherland and a group of top software development gurus met for three days in 2001 to find an alternative. They hammered out a one-page document called the "Manifesto for Agile Software Development," which strove to create a better, more efficient, reality-based way of building software that would increase organizations' chances of successfully delivering business value on time and within budget. It's short, so here it is:

Manifesto for Agile Software Development

We are uncovering better ways of developing software by doing it and helping others do it.
Through this work we have come to value:

Individuals and interactÚns over processes and tools
Working software over comprehensive documentation
Customer collaboratÚn over contract negotiation
Responding to change over following a plan

That is, while there is value in the items on the right, we value the items on the left more.

Kent Beck
Mike Beedle
Arie van Bennekum
Alistair Cockburn
Ward Cunningham
Martin Fowler
James Grenning
Jim Highsmith
Andrew Hunt
Ron Jeffries
Jon Kern
Brian Marick
Robert C. Martin
Steve Mellor
Ken Schwaber
Jeff Sutherland
Dave Thomas

The Agile Manifesto authors built upon the four tenets with twelve principles, which put meat on the bone and are really the founding principles of every one of the many Agile practices in existence. It's likely that your company practices some sort of Agile, but there is no single definition of Agile. Many practices have emerged, all under the umbrella of Agile, that constitute a spectrum of improved software development practices. You might have heard of some of the more popular ones, like Scrum, Kanban, or Extreme Programming (XP). And even within these practices, there are a wide variety of sects, and various degrees of adherence to the "rules." Over the past twenty years, Agile Software Development has swept the world. In a 2019 "State of Agile" survey, 97 percent of respondents said their development organizations practice Agile methods. Regardless of particular implementation, they all share the same purpose: to build effective software. It's likely that your company practices some sort of Agile, so let's dig in a bit.

AGILE ESSENTIALS

At the core of Agile is agility (duh)—the ability to move quickly and easily, change direction quickly, and respond to changing inputs. The problem stated by the Agile Manifesto authors is the reliance on pre-planning around incorrect assumptions, and the lack of coordination between business owners and developers. By fixing those two core problems, Agile Software Development aims to make the act of building software more agile. While there are many ways to implement Agile development, they all revolve around three main ideas: anticipating change, chunking up work, and maintaining close collaboration between the business and developers. Let me walk through these three critical ideas.

Anticipating Change

The first concept is anticipating that there will be changes to the requirements, so instead of being surprised and upset by changes, creating a system that expects them. Agile does this in a few ways. First is by limiting work in progress. If you have one hundred things that are 10 percent done, the chance that changes will come along and interrupt at least one of those workstreams is great. But if you focus on getting one thing 100 percent complete, then you're less likely to have to unwind completed work. Agile limits work in progress by breaking work into short sprints, often only two weeks long, with the goal of delivering a working product at the end of each cycle. It doesn't mean the project is done in two weeks, but some small portion of it is in working order at the end of each sprint, as opposed to hanging in an unfinished state for long periods of time.

These short cycle times create great adaptability. When changes enter the picture, they can be accounted for in a future sprint because the team isn't wed to anything beyond the current sprint. Even within a sprint, changes to the work in progress are accommodated. Most sprint teams hold daily stand-up meetings, which can be a venue for changes to be discussed and the day's plans adjusted. This very tight collaboration, as a single small team including the product manager, facilitates changes. Instead of "throwing it over the wall" and getting defensive about changing requirements, it's quite the opposite. The team operates with a shared understanding of the work, and as such, they're more often supportive of change, not resistive. It's a whole process designed around agility, aka making changes.

Chunking Up the Work as You Go

The second concept is chunking up work *as you go*, into units that are manageable, predictable, and implementable. Unlike Waterfall, where the work was divided into rows on a Gantt chart (sometimes years) ahead of time with an imperfect set of assumptions, Agile focused on creating manageable work units that are implementable quickly, and only as far out as the current sprint. This process is designed to make each work item predictable in scope and time to implement, giving a high degree of confidence to the work. In and of itself this doesn't necessarily provide a confidence level in a large, multiyear project, but it allows you to build a big project on the back of many small, high-confidence intervals. That may not sound good, but it's better than the alternative—building a big risky project atop many smaller risky projects.

If you need to run a mile, make sure each stride is well executed. It's important to deliver working software with every sprint. That's why many teams implement "sprint demos" on the last day of the sprint to show off the results of their work, creating cultural reinforcement of this key tenet of Agile. The demos allow them to celebrate their skill at chunking up work and getting it done in a sprint. Conversely, if they don't have a working piece of software, they can't demo it—creating more cultural pressure to improve in the following sprints.

As you might imagine, accurately estimating the amount of work required to implement functionality in software is an art, which we attempt to turn into a science with Agile practices. And it's a team effort. When teams first form, they're often not very good at accurately predicting their productivity. Their knowledge of the codebase (if it's an existing project) or of the problem domain (if it's a new project) is often imperfect, so the estimate of work needed to implement a capability will be subject to error. But over time, as codebase expertise and domain knowledge grow, the estimation accuracy improves.

Teams often use a fictional metric, such as "story points," to measure and constantly improve predictability and productivity of their sprints. The metric describes the amount of work to implement a given piece of functionality, as well as how much capacity for work the team can accomplish in a sprint. As they get more and more accurate in predicting the story point cost of work, and their productivity in terms of story points, then the predictability of the team's work grows. Once they establish a baseline, they can focus on getting more story points done in a sprint, as a way of growing efficiency and productivity. Note that story points are a fictional metric—they're not based on any hard metric, like lines of code written—so they're not transferable between companies or teams. (As an aside, lines of code written is a horrible metric that you should never care about—less is more when it comes to good code.) All you care about, as an outsider, is whether a story points metric gives the team an increasing degree of predictability and productivity. Don't bother asking why one team accomplished one hundred story points, and another only did fifty. Unless they've calibrated their definition of story points—which is rare—they're apples and oranges. But you should look at whether over time, each team becomes more productive in terms of their story points. If they averaged 100 story points per sprint a year ago, and now they average 150, they've become 50 percent more efficient, which is a good sign of a performing team. Better teams produce more predictable and more quality work, and story points give leaders a way of assessing their teams' progression.

Another benefit of chunking up work and delivering a finished piece of code in every sprint is that you get to deliver incremental value to customers along the way. Imagine finishing 10 percent of a project, but only shipping it at the end. You're holding the 10 percent of features hostage until the other 90 percent are done. But by chunking up the work, and shipping frequently, you can actually get those 10 percent of features out in front of customers immediately.

Agile teams typically chunk up complex tasks by creating a backlog of work to be done. While the engineers implement the current sprint's backlog of tasks, the product manager's job is to get the next sprint's backlog ready by resolving ambiguities and removing uncertainties as best as possible. Beyond the next sprint, there's probably a sea of tasks in various stages of definition, but only as the sprints progress do they get to a finer and finer resolution. But that's not a failing of Agile, that's the point. Push out decisions until just before they're implemented, so that the most information can be known. This limits wasted work.

Close Collaboration Between Business and Developers

In most Agile teams, there are two roles: the Product Owner and the Development Team. In Scrum, there's a third role as well: the Scrum Master. The Product Owner's job is to understand and advocate for the customer, writing "User Stories" that depict what the user needs the software to do. These User Stories are how the Product Owner and the Development Team interface. This may sound like a "throw it over the wall" system, but in a well-functioning Agile team, there's tremendous collaboration between the Product Owner and the developers on crafting and iterating on the User Stories.

Think of the User Stories as an artifact that describes the work to be done, all from the customer's point of view. This differs from the Product Requirements Docs (PRDs) of yesteryear, which focused more on what the software needed to do than on what the customer needed. The difference may seem subtle, but it's important. In a well-functioning Agile team, the creation of the artifact and the discussion that produces it are focused more on the customer than they are on the software itself.

A bad User Story describes a large complex system, while a good one is limited in scope. This increases predictability and limits surface area for misinterpretations or big open questions. A good User Story, though, does describe end-to-end what the customer needs to accomplish, so that the developer can internalize and understand the customer problem. This allows the developer to make good implementation decisions and use their intuition versus just "doing what they're told."

The Product Owner, as you might expect, is typically the product manager. Their job is not to shield the Development Team from customers, but rather to facilitate an understanding of the customer's needs to the rest of the team. They should act as a bridge, and enable conversations as needed between customers and the rest of the team. But a good Product Owner is skilled at correctly abstracting the customer problem to be solved, to represent the broadest set of customers.

The Product Owner manages the backlog of work for the team. Backlog sounds like a bad thing, like some kind of blockage or pileup, but it's not. The backlog represents future work, which is constantly re-prioritized by the Product Owner to achieve the goal of adding maximum customer value to each sprint, ensuring the team is working on User Stories for which there is a high degree of confidence in the implementability and utility to the customer. If a given User Story still has a lot of unknowns regarding customer needs or implementation, then the Product Owner should push it out to answer those questions. This is part of a process called "grooming the backlog," which is one of the Product Owner's major responsibilities. In every sprint, while the Development Team is primarily focused on building that sprint's set of User Stories, the Product Owner is primarily focused on finalizing the set of User Stories for the following sprint. While ownership of the backlog lives primarily with the Product Owners, fleshing out the stories with technical details is a tight collaboration, far from a "throw it over the wall" kind of process.

If this all sounds somewhat complex, it is. The Agile coach is there to help the team implement good Agile hygiene, such as story point calculations or backlog grooming. If a team struggles to deliver working software in every sprint, the coach's job is to help the team diagnose whether the scoping was wrong, their productivity is off, the collaboration isn't right, the User Stories were too vague, or all of the above. If it sounds like the Agile coach is a luxury, perhaps it is, but typically an Agile coach can be shared among several teams. I won't go into too much detail on their role, other than to say it's like any coach—when there's learning to be done to help the team, a good coach can be invaluable.

SO MANY QUESTIONS

So if Agile is the best system we've devised yet for building software, why are there still so many unsatisfying outcomes? Let's dig into a few questions that can frustrate executives when dealing with the ambiguity of Agile product teams.

Why can't you know when a product will ship, and with what features?

One thing that regularly frustrates executives and managers is the inability for engineering teams to commit to hard deadlines—at least if they're being honest. The way I think about it, there are four attributes in software development: features, deadlines, quality, and certainty. Generally speaking, you can pick any three, but you can't have all four. You can build a feature set to a deadline with certainty, but quality might suffer severely as corners are cut everywhere to meet the deadline. You can build to a predictable deadline with predictable quality, but you'll have to cut features along the way as reality sets in. You can build a known set of features with great quality and certainty, but you won't know how long it will take. Or you can have all three: features, quality, and a deadline, which sounds great, but probably with a low degree of confidence.

As an executive, if you demand all four, it's up to you to guess which one is a lie. Or you can get realistic reports from your leaders, who will tell you based on facts what they think will happen. If you have a hard deadline—maybe a big user conference or a marketing campaign that's happening hell or high water—then they'll probably tell you that features should be sacrificed. Or they'll tell you a probability of hitting the deadline, which is rarely all that accurate or confidence inspiring. So most likely, they'll commit to features, certainty, and the deadline. On the surface, that seems like what executives are looking for. However, they're most likely sacrificing quality. This may not be apparent on day one, but will certainly come back to bite you later if customers adopt the product. If the precious launch actually succeeds to win adoption in the market, then customers will experience bugs, scaling issues, security issues, and so on. At that point, all progress will stop as the team backtracks to shore up the foundations—which is arguably far more frustrating because now you have angry customers or unfulfilled demand at your door.

That's why many Agile products start as feature poor. Chances are, features aren't as important as getting an idea in front of customers quickly. So deadlines trump features, with quality as an underlying assumption. Build less, but with confidence, is the path of many early product teams. If you're right about the core, you can always iterate and build more features later.

As an executive, the best thing to do is to have a mature conversation about which attributes you're holding to, and which you're willing to sacrifice. At Twilio, we say that quality and trust are job number one, so we draw a line and hold quality as precious, never to be sacrificed. Sure, we've made mistakes, but we try to make it very clear that quality is never the attribute to sacrifice. Like many companies, we have a big annual user conference called SIGNAL, which is our platform to announce products, get press, and wow our customers. So the deadline is usually set when our marketing team books the venue and starts selling tickets. That leaves features and certainty. Generally speaking, uncertainty doesn't help, so features are the variable that we give teams control over to meet the deadline. We are measuring certainty in the months leading up to SIGNAL, but by a month before, certainty should firm up to a yes or no, at which point features are the only variable to meet the deadline. That's a good trade-off. As executives, we often get very fixated on features, but customers rarely buy based on a feature. They're more interested in the big picture, and we can always add features later. It's therefore incumbent upon executives and product leaders to align early on which features are paramount for early customer adoption and market awareness, and which are merely nice to have.

Why can't you throw more developers at a problem?

Usually managers are excited to receive more resources, so when engineering managers are offered more head count or budget to accelerate a project, leaders are often perplexed by a refusal of the offer. Who wouldn't want more budget and head count!? The reason is that throwing more people at the problem, especially if a project is in progress and running behind, is not likely to help. In fact, it'll probably further delay the project. Why the paradoxical outcome, especially in the short term? Well, obviously there's the time commitment associated with hiring for any role, developers included: spending time recruiting takes away from work in progress. There's also the ramp-up time for a new developer. Even if you hire them today, they're not productive until they know the codebase and the working style of the team. This process typically takes months. Those are manageable, and not dissimilar to the act of staffing up any function. Take sales—if you hire a new sales rep, it takes time for them to learn the product set and get deals closing. So if you're going to miss the current quarter's revenue goals, hiring more sales reps today won't help you. It's the same with developers. There's a high up-front cost before productivity sets in. But if developers can be brought in from another team, many of those costs are defrayed. Why not do that? Software has some other, unique challenges.

In 1975, early software pioneer Frederick Brooks Jr. published *The Mythical Man-Month*, a collection of essays on software development. One of the core ideas, which gave the name to the book, is the "mythical man month"—henceforth I'll de-gender it as the "mythical developer month"—which says that the more developers you throw at a project that's late, the more you will only make it later. Why this counterintuitive outcome? Two things: First is the ramp-up time for new developers. But more important is the communication overhead between those developers thrown onto the project. All those new resources need to ask a lot of questions about how things work, and those questions interrupt and disrupt the currently productive developers. Net-net, you'll get less progress than if you just left the currently productive, albeit behind schedule, developers to finish the job. That's the mythical developer month at work.

To be sure, there are times when you can expand the team to accelerate progress, but mid-project, in a pinch before the deadline, is not one of those times. Obviously, much has changed since Brooks published *The Mythical Man Month*, but the concept has largely held true.

This chart approximates what I've anecdotally witnessed. I made up the formula,[*] so this is far from scientific—but ask your developer if they think this approximates truth, and they'll probably agree.

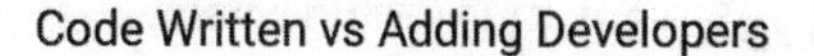

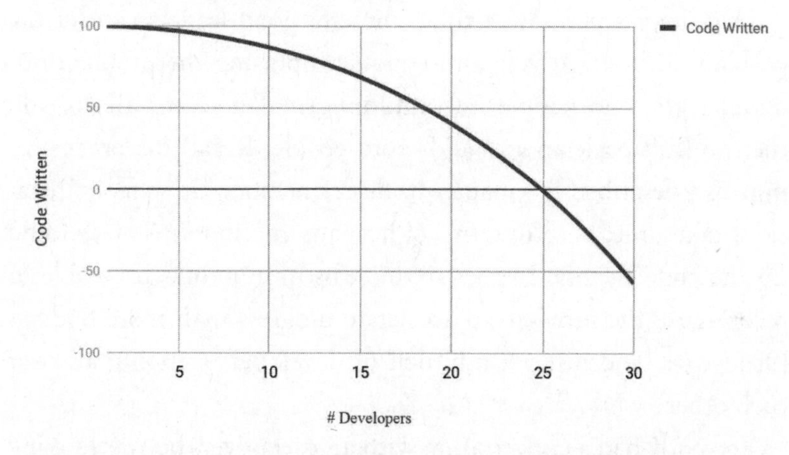

There are not just diminishing returns, but negative returns, to adding developers past about ten people. Thus the focus on small teams. But that also explains why you can't add more people, within

* For those interested, the formula is: 100–(N*0.35)^(2+N*0.005), where N=#developers.

an existing team structure, and expect more output. If you look at the jump from ten to twenty developers, you more than halve the productivity—thus a slowdown of the work, not the desired speed-up. At some point at around twenty-five team members, you get negative quantities of code written. I don't know exactly what that signifies, but I'm sure it's not good. But I do suspect it is accurate, from experience.

If you're upset that you can't throw more bodies at the problem, it's understandable. Budget is what we have to work with as executives. But in the short term, don't aim your frustrations toward the team. That will only demoralize an already (probably) exhausted team, and it's pointless. It's like getting mad at gravity. Sure, if your parachute fails, curse gravity all you want, but it won't help.

Over longer periods of time, though, good leaders can fix the problem to better divide and conquer. Splitting the problem domain, code, and people into multiple smaller teams allows you then to staff back up and add more people. Recall the process of mitosis I described in Chapter 8. Just remember, those reorganizations take time, both in terms of humans and in terms of dividing up the code cleanly. Expect six months, minimum, to be able to reconfigure the problem to accelerate progress with more budget. Otherwise, you just get a bunch of developers stepping all over each other's work.

I recently had a conversation with an executive who was looking at a project slated to take three years to complete. It was an important project, and the executive was frustrated that they couldn't "throw $100 million at the problem" and get it done in one year, despite the fact that the engineering leadership said that right now, they couldn't accelerate the project with more budget. The executive then said, "I bet if you gave [name of big consulting firm] $100 million, they'd get it done." I replied: "I'm sure their salesperson will *say* they'll get it done if you wave $100 million in front of them, but they'll fail, too." That's why these big consulting projects always run over time and over budget. Notably, the executive didn't disagree with me, probably because deep down his experience validated what I had said. Sometimes, hard things take time. But I did suggest that the executive ask the technical leadership what actions they can take today, and over the coming months, that could allow them to increase budget in six months and finish the project in eighteen months instead of three years. That's a reasonable question, and a great engineering leader should be able to answer that question, with good planning and strong architecture.

Even in modern Agile environments, the work is still chunked up a certain way into team structures. In order to accelerate work, managers either need to add more people to a team, which, once the team is fully staffed, accentuates all the problems that Brooks outlined, or they need to redivide the work to spin up new teams and add more parallelism to the project. However, that incurs a tremendous amount of overhead, primarily to find a reasonable division line between the two teams' work—and then to build those divisions into the codebase, missions, and responsibilities. It's the classic "slow down to speed up." Then you need to staff up the team and get productive. All things said and done, within a project, you'd be better just letting the team continue their work in the short term, while engineering leadership devotes a percentage of their time to plotting the redesign of the team structure that will enable an acceleration. There are natural stopping points where it makes tremendous sense to reassess, and redivide the problem domain (as I discussed in Chapter 8 on how mitosis lets you divide and grow teams over time), but that time is not in the heat of the project, especially if it's already running behind.

AGILE PITFALLS

Sounds great, but Agile isn't the panacea that converts sometimes describe. Like any system of organizing, Agile has its upsides and downsides. In a recent conversation I was having with the CEO of a public company, I asked how their Agile transformation was going, and he said: "It's a bunch of pipe smokers telling us how to run the business—and nothing gets done!" I almost fell out of my chair. Where does Agile go wrong?

Instead of unleashing the creativity of developers, sometimes Agile can squelch it. In an attempt to bring discipline and predictability to software development, early practitioners of Agile looked to the world of manufacturing, asking: "How can we bring assembly line predictability to software development?" Thus was born the Kanban workflow methodology, which was literally taken from the Toyota Production System.

In Kanban, the Product Owner breaks the week's work down into small tasks, which get written on sticky notes and hung on a Kanban board. Engineers pull tasks from the board, do the work, move the notes to the "finished" pile, and repeat. When the week ends, they report the number of tasks they've finished. Breaking complex problems into smaller tasks is necessary, but the Kanban method risks treating developers like assembly line workers. You can imagine if you've read this far, I'm not a fan of that way of thinking. In an automotive assembly line, you're not looking for creativity. Each car you manufacture doesn't solve a different problem. Quite the opposite. You want each car coming off the line to be identical. And you don't want assembly line workers using a whole lot of creativity. ("Hey, on this car, let's make the steering wheel a triangle!")

That's fine for assembling cars, but it's not how any creative person wants to work. In fact, Kanban boards remind me of an article I read a few years ago that was interesting but also slightly horrifying. The article was about a village in China called Dafen that produces 60 percent of the world's oil paintings, many of them copies of works by great masters. These are basically fine art factories, with assembly lines cranking out hand-painted copies of paintings by Vincent van Gogh, Leonardo da Vinci, Andy Warhol, and others. The painters work in teams. Each person walks down the aisle of easels and paints a few brushstrokes on each canvas. The next artist adds another element. More than eight thousand artists work in Dafen. They crank out three to five million paintings a year. Turning Monet into money is a pretty ingenious trick. But I was shocked when I read about Dafen. It offended my senses that companies would hire creative artists and then completely remove all the creativity from their jobs.

Source: https://www.instapainting.com/blog/company/2015/10/28/how-to-paint-10000-paintings/

Yet that is exactly what some companies do with developers. They hire creative talent, and then stick them into cubicle farms, where they crank out paint-by-numbers software programs, pulling tickets from the Kanban board. People often complain to me that it's hard to hire great developers, and I tell them it will definitely be difficult to get them if you're going to treat them like assembly line workers.

Daily stand-up meetings are another foundational element of Agile. Every day the team starts with a meeting where everyone lets everyone else know what they did yesterday and what they are going to do today. The problem is that many developers absolutely hate meetings—not because engineers are antisocial, but because meetings occupy valuable time that could be better spent writing code. And like any meeting, daily stand-ups can be well run and efficient, or a boundless and unfocused waste of time.

We as executives are pretty accustomed to days full of meetings, and we often expect that everybody in the company has the same schedule. This is what Paul Graham, cofounder of Y Combinator, calls a "manager schedule," which works really well for people whose primary job is interfacing with other people. Cutting a day into sixty-minute blocks is how you can coordinate a lot of people. Just add it to my calendar.

But making something out of nothing usually isn't accomplished in one-hour blocks—it requires focus and what Graham calls a "maker schedule." You may have heard of flow—that state where we've wrapped our minds around a problem, and our maximum creativity comes out. Authors, artists, musicians, and even chefs talk about flow. It's the state of mind where everything clicks, and flow requires sustained concentration. Even one meeting can destroy the state of flow. Graham says: "Each type of schedule works fine by itself. Problems arise when they meet. Since most powerful people operate on the manager's schedule, they're in a position to make everyone resonate at their frequency if they want to. But the smarter ones restrain themselves, if they know that some of the people working for them need long chunks of time to work in."

It's no surprise then that daily stand-ups can cut into flow. Which balance of flow-state time and meeting time works best for your organization? Why don't you . . . Ask Your Developer?

Many developers want the freedom to understand customers, think deeply about the business, and use their whole brain. But an overly rigid Agile system can encourage developers to believe it's not their job to understand customers or the business—so they constrain themselves by playing the role the system expects. It's important we don't let product managers and developers fall into this trap. If developers do allow themselves to get pigeonholed, it may make life simpler in the short term: "Just tell me what to do." But soon enough, they will feel unfulfilled and they'll seek a job somewhere better. Agile itself is not bad for developers—in fact, it's quite good. But implementers need to take care to ensure that developers stay engaged in the business and treat development as a collaboration, not a task assignment exercise.

ANYTHING IN MODERATION

One of my dad's favorite mantras is "Anything in moderation." Most things are okay, as long as you don't get carried away. Alcohol. TV. Sex. I guess that's how I feel about Agile Software Development. Instead of rolling out a full Agile implementation with trainers and consultants and a bunch of rigid rules and procedures, some companies just grab a few principles that make sense and jettison the rest. "It's been a long time since I used any formal methodology," says Breaker cofounder and CTO Leah Culver (mentioned in Chapter 4), who says her engineers still work in quick sprints but don't bother with other Agile practices like having daily stand-up meetings.

Across Twilio, we are not strict adherents to a particular Agile methodology. We allow teams to pick their own working styles, with some teams adopting more formal elements of Agile, and others less so. But we do strictly enforce a few key ideas. The most religiously adhered-to rule is that small, autonomous teams are the basis of progress. We limit the size of teams to ten or fewer people. Instead of a planning system that imposes work on them, we ask them to draft their own goals each quarter based on what they're hearing from customers. When their ideas of what's needed differ from what leadership considers most important, it's not a blind top-down mandate to take leadership's word, but it sparks a very important discussion to resolve the conflict. These are some of the must-haves across all of our approximately 150 product engineering teams.

Once the structure is in place, we usually let teams choose their working style. Most, if not all, teams operate on two-week sprints, with the goal of having demonstrable progress at the end of each sprint. Some teams are better at this than others. All seek to limit work in progress, which is the goal of both Scrum and Kanban, with varying levels of success. Some teams all sit together, while other teams are distributed across the country or even multiple continents. Keeping teams within four or five time zones of each other seems like best practice, though, to permit enough overlap of working hours. Most teams attempt to assign a measure of productivity, using story points, to their work so they can track whether they are getting more productive over time. Although every team's definition of story points differs, that's okay. This practice is a part of many Agile teams' workflows, and I love it. Just as you'd measure a salesperson's productivity in closed sales, measuring the health of an engineering team is equally important.

Our teams have a varying level of Ask Your Developer going on. In some teams the engineers regularly engage in the customer-facing aspects of what they're building, bringing up the customer's "problem to be solved" in conversation. More often than not, those teams are ones that share customer problems, not just User Stories, with the developers.

Often I get the chance to walk the halls of Twilio and ask engineers what they're working on (politely, and only if they aren't deep in concentration). One of my favorite follow-up questions is to ask about the customer problem they're solving. Often we get into a good conversation about the customer, but sometimes I get a shrug of indifference and an answer along the lines of "I'm not sure, it's what the PM told me to do." That's when I can see teams may have taken Agile's division of labor too far, and I know a follow-up conversation with the team might be a good idea—both for the leaders, who could be getting more out of their team, but also for the developers who are content with not knowing. I believe that's ultimately career limiting.

If you're wondering how Agile works, and whether or not it's contributing to your agility, I'd suggest talking to your developers and to your product managers. You'll get a sense for how they work, and how agile and customer-centric their process is. In particular, you might be interested to understand how the relationships are working between your product managers and engineering talent. Ask your developers whether they want product managers to be gatekeepers or facilitators of customer interaction. Ask the product managers whether they view their role similarly. You can ask your teams whether they collaborate to groom road maps, coming from a shared customer understanding, or whether they "divide and conquer," with PMs knowing the customers and engineers knowing the code. I believe teams where PMs know quite a bit of code, and developers know quite a bit about customers, produce better products. How well are sprints working to create shippable value during every sprint? Do teams regularly have progress to demonstrate? There's no right way to implement Agile, but there are ways to implement it poorly and remove customers from the process. Understanding the value of Agile, as well as how your teams have implemented it, will help make sense of the sometimes counterintuitive, and often frustrating answers you get when you seek certainty from your product teams.

CHAPTER 11
INVEST IN INFRASTRUCTURE

Move fast and break things.

—Mark Zuckerberg, 2009

Move fast with stable infra.

—Mark Zuckerberg, 2014

Mark Zuckerberg's famous tagline "Move fast and break things" was brilliant, but ultimately insincere. So it was unsurprising that he ended up changing it in 2014 to the far less memorable "Move fast with stable infra[structure]." The tension between those two statements is what this chapter is about.

At most companies, executives want their teams to innovate, they want products shipped yesterday, and they want their teams to think outside the box. Wonderful! Great! Innovate all the things!

But they also want a mistake-free environment. If there are bugs or outages or security lapses, there are accountability meetings to discover who messed up. If the press or customers respond negatively to a new product, it's likely to be canned and the team suffers negative career consequences.

These two ideas are in complete opposition to each other. Executives say they want innovation, but then unwittingly punish people for its natural consequences. And because human beings are good at pain avoidance, the desire to avoid punishment pretty quickly overrides the innovation directive. The result is an organization that moves slowly, is risk averse, and lacks accountability.

That's the brilliance of Zuckerberg's original motto: "Move fast and break things." He acknowledges that moving fast incurs a cost—things won't be perfect—and he's okay with that. If you break something, I have your back as long as you were pushing the envelope to invent something for our customers. By doing this, he ensures that the innovation directive will prevail.

But here's the thing: he wasn't actually sincere. If you're the developer who willy-nilly broke the machine that makes billions of dollars, they won't actually celebrate you. But luckily, the trade-off between speed and quality is a false dichotomy, and phrasing the choice that way is unsustainable, as Zuck obviously figured out later.

At Facebook, as at many companies, it's common to spend upward of 30 percent, and many times north of 50 percent, of the total development budget on infrastructure and platforms. Given your customers don't actually exactly see the result of this expensive investment, executives often call the large expense into question. This chapter is about understanding the importance of your platform teams, and how they make every other team better and more efficient. At Facebook, it started with a guy named Chuck Rossi.*

Chuck was hired in 2008 as Facebook's first "release engineer." His job was to manage the rollout of software into the production environment and ensure that nothing developers were trying to deploy would break the website. He ran a very tight process that included weekly deployments containing major changes—always

* https://arstechnica.com/information-technology/2012/04/exclusive-a-behind-the-scenes-look-at-facebook-release-engineering/3/.

done during the workday, ensuring engineers were available in case problems arose—and daily minor updates to fix small issues. He kept tabs on which developers wrote code that was problem-free, and he even kept a reputation score on every developer in the company. If you broke Facebook, you got a strike. Three strikes and you were prohibited from shipping code for a while. (Note, not permanently—mistakes were tolerated, assuming you learned from them, despite being in the penalty box.) Acting as a guard dog for the company and its customers, Rossi enforced best practices of testing, code reviews, "canary" deployments, and more.

In short, by providing platforms and processes that helped developers build faster while still having guardrails to ensure that customers and the company were protected from truly bad outcomes, Rossi made sure that when developers moved fast, they didn't break things too much. It turns out, great infrastructure is the foundation of innovation.

This approach isn't all that different from how efficient, innovative companies enable all of their employees to do their best work, while still ensuring some degree of consistency.

If you hire a sales team, you've probably enabled them. You have a group that produces materials to train the sales reps about your products, which makes them more productive because they walk in to see your customers with more knowledge. You buy them sales automation software to help them track their sales deals, and to help them know their pipeline status.

Similarly, you enable your finance team to do their jobs. You have an ERP system that helps the finance team close the books, keep track of expenses, and efficiently and correctly report out your financial status to investors. It's hard to imagine sales, finance, or many other functions existing and being even remotely successful without this critical infrastructure.

Software teams are no different. To make your developers successful, you need to invest in infrastructure. You don't need to do this up front. In fact, these systems tend to evolve organically as your software team gets bigger and more sophisticated, but you do have to actively feed it. There are certain ways of embracing infrastructure that will make your developers feel heard, help them believe that the company is investing in them, and show that the company cares about them as creative professionals.

It's not uncommon for great software companies to invest upward of 50 percent of all R&D funds into infrastructure. But it will be tempting to question these investments. Every budget cycle, you'll see a large expense around these infrastructure teams, and people will wonder if it's really needed. Why are we hiring engineers to manage internal infrastructure instead of assigning more head count to the teams that create products for our customers? It's because the software infrastructure makes all of your other developers more productive and more successful. Kill it, you'll quickly realize how much leverage these infrastructure teams give you. Most companies find a productivity lift far greater than the 20–30 percent you're investing.

Ever wonder why engineers flock to companies like Google? Sure, the pay is good. But the support infrastructure is world-class. It's one thing to coddle developers with free lunch and tricycles, but Google really coddles developers with great infrastructure on which to build. When your tools direct nearly all of your energy toward the task at hand—serving customers and being creative—it's magical. The opposite is also true—when you're fighting your tools, it's a real morale hit.

I learned this the hard way. You'd think this understanding would have come naturally to us, given that Twilio was founded by three software developers. But there was a point early in our life when we didn't invest enough in software infrastructure, and it nearly killed us.

INFRASTRUCTURE GROWING PAINS

In 2013 Twilio was in rapid growth mode. We'd gone from about $1 million in annual revenues in 2010 to more than $30 million in 2012. We'd raised four rounds of venture capital, totaling $103 million, and grown from three founders to more than a hundred employees, more than half of whom were software developers building our products.

But we had a problem. Our "build systems"—the software infrastructure that those roughly fifty developers used to submit their code to our repository, run tests on it, package it up in a deployment, and deploy it to our main production servers—was showing its age. I had built that system in 2008 when we started the company, and it was never designed to support fifty engineers all submitting code all day long and then deploying it to hundreds of servers. When I built it, I could commit my code and have it running on a server in five minutes. By 2013, because of the growth of the codebase and the complexity of the tests and builds, the process was sometimes taking as long as twelve hours! Not only that, but the build would actually fail a substantial number of times—at worst, up to 50 percent of the time—and the developer would have to start over again. We regularly lost days of productivity just getting code out. This was the opposite of moving fast.

Writing the code wasn't the hard part. Wrangling our antiquated systems was. Talk about a self-inflicted wound. As a result, our best engineers started quitting, frustrated at the inability to do their jobs. At first it was a few, and before we knew it, nearly half of our engineers had quit. Half! It was an absolute disaster, and it almost tanked the company.

And so we embarked on a rapid, and painful, plan to rebuild our developer platforms to support our growth. Our first move was to hire a guy named Jason Hudak to head the platform team. Jason had worked at Yahoo for more than a decade, building the infrastructure to support their thousands of engineers. Jason is probably not what you imagine when you think of a software engineer. He's a ruddy-faced Texan and a former Marine. He went to Texas Tech and studied business, not computer science. He's more or less self-taught, having learned to write code after landing a job at a tech company in the 1990s and studying alongside engineers who recognized his potential. Jason spends his free time snorkeling, cycling, and hunting wild boars in Texas. He's also an accomplished abstract painter. He's gifted me two pieces of his art, which hang proudly in my office. He comes to work wearing T-shirts, flip-flops, and trucker caps. But beneath his easygoing manner there's an intensity and discipline that he learned way back in Marine boot camp.

This combination was crucial as we started to embrace a methodology called DevOps in building our developer platform. Even if you don't work directly in technology you might have heard the term DevOps without really understanding what it is.

A cynic might say DevOps has become kind of the "flavor of the month" for software development, the way Agile and Lean Startup did before. Amazon lists more than a thousand books on the topic. You could spend years learning everything about DevOps, but for our purposes I'm going to provide an extremely simplified explanation, which goes like this:

Once upon a time, software development organizations broke

the process of producing a piece of code into multiple roles. Tasks like coding, building, testing, packaging, releasing, configuring, and monitoring were handled by separate people. DEVELOPERS wrote code, then handed it off to QUALITY ENGINEERS, who found the bugs. RELEASE ENGINEERS got the code ready for production. Once people were actually using the program, SITE RELIABILITY ENGINEERS (SREs) were tasked with keeping it running. SREs were the ones who "wore the pager," meaning they were on call at night, or on weekends, and were expected to drop everything and fix the code when a program bonked.

Breaking work into specialized roles had certain advantages, but it also slowed things down. Developers would toss code over the wall to the quality engineers, who would bash away on it and send it back for fixes. That process would go back and forth, and through several different kinds of testing. Then the code would go to the release engineers, who might toss it back, and then to site reliability engineers, who also might toss it back. (You can tell I'm not a fan of throwing things over walls.) At each step there could be delays as a developer waited for a test engineer or release engineer to finish other projects and then get to theirs. Multiply all those potential delays by the number of steps, and you can see how things could get bogged down.

DevOps, first conceived about a decade ago, represents an attempt to speed things up by having one developer handle all of the steps. The concept is reflected in the name itself: instead of having "developers" who write code and "operators" who do everything else, you combine all of the duties in one person. In a DevOps environment, the same developer writes the code, tests the code, packages it, monitors it, and remains responsible for it after it goes into production.

That last sentence conveys one of the most important elements of modern software development and something that we at Twilio consider to be almost a sacred value: the person who writes the code also "wears the pager" for that code after it goes into production.

It's your code. If it crashes, you fix it. We like this idea because it pushes developers to deliver higher-quality code. The dread of taking those middle-of-the-night phone calls provides a little extra incentive to take another pass through your work before you ship.

It's not as though we permit teams to ship code that's constantly crashing, even if they're the ones waking up to fix it. Customers would still be impacted. So Jason and his team created a checklist of best practices called the Operational Maturity Model (OMM). It consists of six categories of excellence: documentation, security, supportability, resiliency, testability, and privacy. In total, there are forty-one steps. And here's the catch: In order for teams to consider their product generally available (GA), meaning it's ready for mission-critical customers, they have to demonstrate excellence in each category. Achieving a perfect score across the board is the highest level of achievement. We call it "Iron Man."

In the traditional model, developers perform only some of those practices. Maybe they write some tests, but not full end-to-end tests. Maybe they document their code, but don't enable the support team. Maybe they have good security practices, but not privacy practices. It's not that they don't care; they're just not versed in what excellence looks like. The best way to get good at these things, of course, is for teams to automate. Yet if every team has to become domain experts, and build their own automation for each of these categories, it would take forever. That's where Jason's team comes in.

Jason defines his job, and that of the platform team—a group of about one hundred engineers across thirteen small teams—as "to provide software that will enable a traditional software developer to be successful in a DevOps culture without having a deep background in all of these specialized disciplines." They don't develop software that ships to customers. They make software that developers use to write, test, deploy, and monitor software. If anything about our process resembles an assembly line, this is probably the closest thing. Platform engineers are the people who design and optimize the "assembly line" that speeds innovation.

We wanted to make it easier and faster for developers to write code that achieves operational maturity with as little work as possible. Our solution was to build a platform that provides all of those functions in one place. Jason likens it to a big stained-glass window, a single pane of glass with many elements. Developers can access all of the tools they need through that single pane of glass. Their standards are high. "Software engineers are the most cynical, critical, curmudgeonly bunch on earth," Jason says. "I can say that because I am one of them. They're intellectually honest, but you get the most brutal feedback. The reason I'm building platforms is if you can build software that makes other software engineers happy, you can build software for anything."

JASON'S PRINCIPLES

When Jason joined Twilio, he drew up a list of principles and values to inform the way he builds and runs the platform. He had to walk a tricky line, striking a balance between giving developers freedom and autonomy while also persuading them to adhere to a set of standard ways of doing things. The standards help us have cohesion in almost all the parts of the codebase (as I stated in Chapter 6, guardrails, if done correctly, can set people free). But we don't want to be so rigid that we stifle innovation. We're constantly trying to get that balance right.

Here are the principles he landed on:

The Paved Path

The Admiral developer platform includes all of the tools a developer needs. But developers don't have to use them. If you love a particular testing tool and it's not in the platform, you can still use it. Jason calls this "off-roading" versus the "paved path," meaning if you want to use the tools we've chosen, your life will be easy, like driving on a paved road. However, you're free to go off-road and drive through the brush and dirt roads, too. You'll still get to where you need to be, but it might take longer. But if it's really that important to you, or if that special tool gives you some advantages, by all means go for it. One of Jason's favorite expressions is "We don't have rules—we have guardrails." But if you go off-roading, you're still on the hook for things like security and resiliency, which makes the paved path look all the more attractive.

Choose Your Language

Another example: We don't force developers to use only one language. Instead, we support four languages—Python, Java, Scala, or Go. A developer can use any one of those four languages and still get a fully supported platform. But as with tools, developers have permission to choose other languages, too. But again, it's about driving on the paved path versus going off-roading. "If you want to build something in C or some other language, by all means do it, because we're not here to tell you what you can or can't do," Jason explains. "Just know that you may have some heavy lifting to do, because you won't be able to use all of these tools in the platform."

Self-service

The goal is to provide developers with a menu and let them pick and choose what they want, whenever they want, without having to go through any gatekeepers. They also don't need to know how those processes work. They just choose what they want. It's like pressing a number on the vending machine and getting a Diet Coke. You don't care how the machine does that. "Developers just tell us what they need done, and we don't want them to care about how it gets done. You just tell us what you want, and we'll take care of that for you."

Opt In to Complexity

Admiral is set up so that each tool has a specified way of doing things—"an opinionated workflow," Jason calls it, meaning the platform engineers have certain opinions about the best way to use this tool. But, once again, developers don't have to follow those rules. "We allow developers to configure the software to perform more complex activities, or even to use the software to do things we hadn't considered when we were building it. Our mantra is 'The common should be easy and the complex should be possible.'"

Behave Compassionately but Prioritize Ruthlessly

"We never like to say no," Jason says. "But if one team has a request for something that would be cool to do, and another team has a project that will unlock $90 million in recurring revenue for the company, we're going to solve that one first and put the other request on our backlog."

Composable over Monolithic

Our software is based on a microservices architecture composed of hundreds of microservices. Each microservice performs a single function or capability. The advantage of microservices is that we can route around or absorb a failure. If one service fails, it won't bring down the entire Twilio voice system, for example. The services are all loosely coupled. They're all built by different teams, who can work independently. One microservice might be version one or two, and another might be on version five. But as long as they all "speak" to the API that connects them, that's fine.

PLATFORMS: THE SOFTWARE THAT MAKES THE SOFTWARE

In *Ford v Ferrari*, the film about Ford's quest to win the 24 Hours of Le Mans race, there's a great scene where Ford has finally managed to defeat Ferrari at Le Mans with an astonishing race car called the GT40. "She's a hell of a machine," Ken Miles, the driver, tells Carroll Shelby, the designer. But then, instead of basking in the glory, Miles and Shelby immediately start talking about ways to make the GT40 even faster.

That's the ethos of the software industry, too. Everyone feels relentless pressure to go faster, to do more work in less time with fewer people, to keep from falling behind. "Only the paranoid survive," was the mantra of Intel CEO Andy Grove, and the title of his memoir. We are all constantly paranoid.

At Twilio we've spent years incrementally building the "machine" that produces our software—the Admiral platform that Jason Hudak and his team designed—saving a little bit of time here, a little bit there, to try to stay ahead of this paranoia. I'm going to try not to get too far down into the weeds here, but I want to spend time describing the way this process works because it's so important to any modern software organization. A good platform will radically slash the time it takes for developers to get new code into production, letting fewer developers produce more code in less time.

The Admiral platform is based on the concept of "pipelines"—the process that kicks off when a developer commits new code. Every team has the ability to customize its pipeline based on the unique aspects of its product, but also for its working style—thus enabling autonomy. But there are several default, preconfigured pipelines that teams can start from. These represent the most "paved paths" for standard workflows, such as for websites, microservices, or database clusters. A typical pipeline starts by running unit tests—the most basic kind of code tests that developers write. Then it runs more sophisticated tests, like integration tests, which test how the software interacts with other services it depends upon. Passing those, the code runs through "failure injection testing," simulating real-world scenarios in which computers fail, such as network outages or hard disk failures. Then come the load tests, testing what happens when the volume of requests spikes, as well as durability testing, simulating sustained high loads to find memory leaks or other issues that arise only after a long period of stress. Passing all of these, the code moves into the "staging" environment for another set of tests—this is a complete copy of our real-world system, but used only for internal testing. Finally, if all is going well, the code is moved to the "production" cluster—the systems our customers actually use. The rollout to production, though, isn't instant.

Typically the code is phased in via a "canary deployment," as in "canary in the coal mine." A small percentage of requests are sent to the new software, and that percentage is slowly ramped up over time if no issues arise, until the new code is handling 100 percent of the production requests. If at any point issues are detected, the old code is rotated back in and engineers are notified so they can investigate the problem.

For most teams, this entire process is now automated. As you can imagine, doing this work manually would be excruciatingly slow, tedious, and error prone. But in reality, when this isn't automated, most teams will omit many of the steps, which incurs risks. The paved path is a powerful idea. Because so much of this infrastructure is ready and waiting, doing it right is also relatively easy. That allows teams to move quickly and confidently.

However, as awesome as I've made Admiral sound, teams are not required to use it. Small-team autonomy means that they're not forced to use a particular tool if they don't want to. Instead, they choose to use it. So Jason, like anybody "selling" a product, has to win over his customers: the internal developers at Twilio. That's where his principles really come into play.

With preconfigured pipelines, Admiral makes it easy for standard types of services to be built and deployed. However, for teams to adopt the tool, they have to be able to dive in and make changes if needed. Otherwise, they'd have to build their own tooling outside of Admiral, and lose the benefits. That's where one of Jason's other principles opt in to complexity—comes into play. While teams can take the default settings, they can also dive into the bowels of Admiral, and rewire it for the particulars of their project. Don't like the default unit testing framework? Developers can plug in their own, while still keeping all the benefits of Admiral and the rest of the pipeline. The same goes for all components. This gives teams autonomy to pick their tools, while making the defaults easy and attractive, helping to encourage adoption of Admiral. As of today, 55 percent of all deployments use the full pipeline functionality of Admiral. Most of the rest use parts of Admiral, but not the entire thing. And those numbers are growing all the time.

THE FALSE DICHOTOMY: FAST VERSUS GOOD

As I've noted, the cadence of software innovation is faster than ever before. Turning customer insights into products is happening at a lightning speed in this digital era. Yet there's often this question of whether teams should move quickly to capture opportunities and respond to customer needs, or whether they should move more cautiously, ensuring that everything works properly, scales well, and is bug-free. However, at really good software companies, this is a false dichotomy. Platforms like Admiral are what enable developers to quickly develop high-quality code, and move it to production with confidence that they aren't breaking the customer experience with every code deployment.

Jason's number one mission is to speed up every engineer at Twilio, while ensuring they meet the demands for quality, security, and scalability. Instead of six months, can we deliver a new feature in six weeks? Six days? Six hours? Jason reckons the platform does 80 percent of the work that a developer previously had to do. Some processes that previously took weeks or even months now can be done "with a few clicks in a few minutes." Today, Twilio releases new code to a production over 160,000 times per year—that's nearly 550 times every single working day.

MOVE FAST AND DUPLICATE WORK

Another tension that arises a lot in the world of building software involves the duplication of work versus synchronization of work between teams. By letting teams operate somewhat autonomously, and giving them a lot of leeway in picking how they build, you free them to sprint like a startup. But you run the risk that multiple teams will spend time building similar things. They're duplicating effort, solving the same problem in slightly different ways. It feels wasteful. Nevertheless, I don't lose sleep about this duplication of effort.

Werner Vogels of Amazon notes that this approach—where you're knowingly permissive of duplicated work—is often a non-starter at traditional companies, which tend to feel it's out of control or chaotic. "It's so counterintuitive for them because they're all about efficiency," he explains. "They're used to having top-down control, and in essence the hierarchy becomes more important than moving fast."

This may be part of why I'm often asked how we prevent duplicate work in our small, empowered teams culture. My answer is: we don't.

Here's why: Imagine two companies, each on the far ends of the spectrum between efficiency and autonomy. In one company, all teams are perfectly synchronized such that there is no duplicate work. Every team knows their role, what other teams they depend on, and if there's the possibility of duplicated work, ownership is assigned. This sounds great, but it rarely works out that way. In practice, teams would be waiting on their dependent teams frequently. When one team's road map slips, everybody else is impacted, and blame goes around for who's at fault. Sure, there's no duplication, but there's also no ownership for the outcome because there are so many people to blame when things don't go right.

Now let's look at the opposite company. Teams move quickly to serve their customers without much concern for whether another team is duplicating their work. All that team is incentivized to do is create successful products that drive customer adoption, customer satisfaction, and revenue growth. In that company, developers don't have to ask permission or coordinate at all with other teams. In your head, imagine each one of these teams works in a different physical space, has different email domains, and so on. They may as well be different companies. They're about as unsynchronized as you can imagine. So as you might expect, there's lots of duplicated work because teams aren't really working together all that much.

These two imaginary companies are extreme examples, but they're illustrative. Which of those companies would I rather build? I'd take company #2 any day of the week. A company where people feel empowered and accountable for the outcomes—that's the goal. Perfect synchronization necessarily removes autonomy and accountability.

Company #2 is basically a bunch of startups, each working to serve customers and drive revenue. One nice thing is the goals of each team will always bring them to want to leverage the work of other teams whenever possible. Why invent a new build system or security infrastructure if another team already has one that serves your needs? That's the shortest path to achieving your goals—growing customers and revenue—than going it alone all the time. But when there isn't something that meets their needs, they invent their own. Amazon also prefers speed and doesn't obsess about duplication, according to Werner Vogels. "We allow teams to just do a lot of things themselves, even if that duplicates some functionality. We're willing to exchange that for moving fast," Vogels says.

Other companies, most notably Microsoft, have become obsessed with stamping out duplication only to discover that the "de-duplication" effort eats up more resources than it saves. That's because keeping an eye out for duplication and/or spending time de-duplicating overlapping products means creating a new layer of oversight, which slows everything down. De-duplication usually involves looking at all the duplicates, choosing one as the winner, and then forcing everyone else to adopt that one.

By allowing teams to duplicate work if they need to, you also let the teams show you, with their valuable time and skills, where you need to invest. It's like that old story: An architect is asked to design a college campus. Upon presenting the final campus design, the regents point out that there are no walking paths. The architect's reply? "We'll let the students decide with their feet where the sidewalks should go. Within a year, it'll be obvious."

We allow our teams to charge ahead and lead the way. Then, as technical leaders and architects, we watch for the patterns to emerge. When we see multiple teams all inventing similar things you can step in, observe the trend, and staff a team to go solve that problem for everybody—thus achieving efficiency. That's the essence of platforms. But instead of trying to perfectly plan it out from the top, let teams organically show you the path.

Ultimately a lot of this is about making trade-offs for what you want to get versus what you're willing to give. That's kind of what culture is about. What are the unbreakable rules versus where do you want employees to use their talents in ways you couldn't imagine? Cultures that veer too far one way or the other don't work, but the balances and trade-offs you make somewhere in the middle really set the stage for the kind of innovation organization you'll have.

At Twilio, we have certain things we require every team to abide by, because they're existential for the company. Teams can't decide whether they want their software to be secure or not. They have to. Our customers demand it, our investors demand it, the market demands it, and it would be irresponsible to ship insecure code. So that's a rule. Now teams can use off-the-shelf "paved roads" as Jason says, to achieve security as easily as possible. But as long as they pass our bar, they can use other mechanisms to secure their code.

Same thing goes for reliability. We and our customers demand a minimum of 99.95 percent uptime of all of our services. That means no more than 43 seconds of downtime per day. The easiest way to achieve that stringent goal is for teams to use infrastructure, software platforms, and practices we've developed internally that they can take off the shelf and implement. But if a team has a unique requirement or a way that they believe is superior, and they can prove it, then they can go their own way. But they're still accountable for the uptime they deliver. So as you can imagine, the team would have to be very motivated by their solution to go it alone. But this sometimes leads to great innovation, too! Imagine a team invents a piece of software that helps them achieve 99.999 percent uptime—only 26 seconds of downtime per month! I bet a lot of other teams would be interested in using that! In fact, we're now close to achieving that, and the subtle competitive spirit between teams often drives great outcomes.

BITE THE BULLET

Some people might push back on the idea of spending money on infrastructure teams. We've had this argument nearly every year in our budgeting process. It's easy to get pulled into the trap of hiring more and more developers who work on customer-facing products, because that return feels more immediate—and their work translates more apparently into revenue. But infrastructure engineers make your entire development team more efficient. "Platforms are a force multiplier," Jason says. "It's like a fulcrum. For every dollar I put in I can return five dollars."

Here's an example. In 2018, it took our developers forty days to develop a new Java service. We wanted to speed things up. In theory, we could hire twice as many engineers, and they would produce twice as many services per year, right? (In fact, doubling our developer head count would not double our productivity, but for the sake of argument let's pretend it would.) But that would mean hiring hundreds of new developers. Instead, Jason grabbed two platform engineers, and they automated a bunch of steps in our development process. Their work slashed development time in half—from forty days to twenty days. The impact gets magnified because we develop about two hundred new Java services per year. Yes, we spent money on those two platform engineers. But their work saved us four thousand person-days per year. That's the argument for spending money on infrastructure instead of hiring more product developers. Instead of focusing on how much it costs to build a platform team, focus on the return those platform engineers can deliver. But also realize that these investments take time to pay off. Not only do you have to build the team, and have them build the infrastructure; the other teams need to adopt it. This cycle takes time, but it pays back in spades over a multiyear investment. It truly becomes a source of competitive advantage.

When we do hire new developers, they come up to speed much faster thanks to Admiral. "A few years ago it took us four months to get new engineers trained to the point where they could be a contributing part of a team," Jason says. "Today we can have them developing in a week." Again, it's all about the return on investment. Platform engineers punch way above their weight.

As huge as our gains have been, though, we think the platform can make even more dramatic improvements in speed. Jason wants to get the Java deployment process that got cut from forty days to twenty days down to one day—or even just a few hours. One of his thirteen teams is focused solely on optimizing the platform itself in these ways. They study how developers use the product, searching for places where developers get stuck or slowed down, and eradicating them. To measure the time developers spend fiddling with tools, Jason created a metric called Time Spent Outside Code (TSOC). Our average TSOC might never get to zero, but the goal is to get as close as possible.

"The future of platforms will be allowing software developers to focus only on their features and their customers, and not about all the underlying systems that are required to bring software from somebody's head to the cloud to a device and to an experience for a customer," Jason says.

The bottom line is that a modern development organization needs to use the best tools and methodologies, and a big part of that involves hiring infrastructure engineers to build a developer platform that automates as much of the software creation process as possible. It's all about speed and quality. No matter how fast we go, we can—and must—go faster, all without sacrificing the must-haves of reliability, quality, and security. Developer environments like our Admiral platform help us confidently build.

As you begin building a software development platform, ask your developers which processes have not yet been automated but should be. Which part of the development process is the most likely cause of your website or app's next outage, and is that something you should fix first? Find out how much work it takes developers to deploy code into production. Are they frustrated? Where are the bottlenecks and how could they be eliminated? Resist the urge to cut corners on platform investment—remember, money spent on platforms makes all of your developers more productive. Ask your technical leaders what percent of budget is being spent on platforms versus product development, and where the balance should be. Ask your leaders what ROI framework they use to justify the right level of platform investment.

EPILOGUE

In this book I've tried to explain why developers matter more than ever, how to understand and motivate developers, and how to create an environment where developers can do their best work.

Looking ahead, the companies that harness the power of software to deliver the best digital customer experiences will survive and thrive in the digital age. Build vs. Die means recruiting great developers, but more important, putting faith in those developers, turning to them not just for code but for creative problem-solving.

In other words, Ask Your Developer.

As I was finishing the book something happened that made this transformation far more urgent. The coronavirus pandemic that struck in early 2020 forced the world to reconfigure itself in real time as cities shut down, children learned at home, companies sent workers home, hospitals were overwhelmed with patients, and more. Suddenly digital transformation projects slated to take place over several years were happening in days or weeks. It was the great digital acceleration, not by choice but by existential necessity driven by the largest global pandemic in a century. As economic activity slowed to a crawl, it was literally Build vs. Die for companies across many industries.

The good news is, developers stepped up and delivered. In the course of a few weeks during March and April 2020 alone, many industries saw faster digital transformation than the entire previous decade. Zoom became our corporate conference rooms, and also the pub where we gathered after work. Google Classroom took the place of actual classrooms. Slack and other communication software became even more vital. Curbside pickup, meal delivery, and telehealth became the lifelines of retail, restaurant, and health care industries, respectively.

Like everyone else, Twilio sent our employees home and kept the company running with everyone working remotely. That was especially challenging because our business didn't drop off during the global shutdown. Our customers asked their developers to invent solutions to the onslaught of problems that COVID-19 brought them. Instead of taking it easy, our three thousand–plus Twilions were running harder than ever to handle a surge of demand from our existing customers and thousands of new customers who needed help—right away. From our front-row seat, we saw innovation that demonstrated so many of the principles I've written about in this book.

The city of Pittsburgh asked if we could find a way to keep its local 311 service, which lets people report non-emergency problems, up and running. The system was overwhelmed with so many calls that its dozen operators and seven IT support people could not cope. Things got even more difficult because operators and IT staff had to work remotely. Our engineers worked with their developers to build, test, and deploy a brand-new cloud-based contact center—in just four days.

But it wasn't just Pittsburgh. Across the United States, calls to 211 networks (which provide information about social services and emergency support) also skyrocketed during the pandemic, to 75,000 calls a day from 30,000 per day during ordinary times, according to United Way Worldwide, which runs the 211 program. Calls also lasted longer, with some taking as long as thirty minutes versus the usual four to six minutes, as many people were food or housing insecure for the first time and had no idea where to begin.

Ordinarily, if a disaster hits one region and the local call center gets overwhelmed, other call centers in other parts of the country can provide backup. But this time all of the 211 networks were swamped. To deal with the overload, developers at United Way used Twilio Flex to create a system that lets people in any part of the country call an 800 number and get routed to their local 211 service or go to an AI-assisted interactive voice response (IVR) system that answered commonly asked questions. The new system also enabled United Way to bring in volunteer service agents to handle the surge. Best of all, they got it up and running in just three days.

As schools shut down, kids not only had to find new ways to learn—but many faced the prospect of going hungry. Kinvolved, a company that helps school systems reduce chronic absenteeism, shifted its focus to distributing thousands of free meals—ten thousand on the first day—to students who depend on free or reduced-price lunch. Kinvolved used SMS to make sure that kids who lack Internet at home could stay in touch with teachers, find out about homework, and send PDFs to school. Usage tripled 200 percent during the pandemic shutdown. In March alone, 6 million messages were delivered among 300,000 teachers, students, and parents in eleven states, including 150 schools in New York City alone.

As shelter-in-place ordinances took effect, demand for telehealth soared, and virtual care became a new reality for providers and millions of patients around the world. In New York, we helped the Mount Sinai Health System launch a messaging system that let patients chat live with clinicians so patients wouldn't have to come to the hospital in person. Conversations started out on text messages but could escalate to video if necessary. Clinicians guided potentially COVID-infected patients into the hospital or set up remote monitoring for patients recovering at home. In one instance, live chat identified an elderly patient who needed immediate help, and clinicians dispatched an ambulance in minutes. In another case, clinicians via live chat identified an infected patient in a group home, and were able to notify the home, isolate the patient, and mitigate spread of the virus.

Epic, one of the largest electronic health record companies in the United States, with records on more than 250 million patients, built its own telehealth platform powered by Twilio's Programmable Video API in just a few weeks. Providers can launch a video visit with a patient, review relevant patient history, and update clinical documentation directly within Epic.

Not all of the new use cases involved life-and-death situations. In Brugherio, Italy, we helped QVC Italia, a TV-based shopping channel, remain in operation by deploying a Twilio-based call center that let its customer service agents work from home. The new system supports not just phone calls but also SMS and WhatsApp—and took less than a week to get up and running. Back in the States, we helped Comcast integrate Twilio Video into their internal customer database so technicians could help a customer whose critical TV or Internet connection wasn't working, without having to step foot in the customer's house.

In our own small way, Twilio was helping to keep people safe and the economy running. I was awestruck by folks at Twilio who understood that this was about more than just business, that this was about our mission of serving others, enabling developers to do their best work. For weeks, our teams worked nonstop, nights and weekends, all while dealing with their own stress and anxiety and challenges of working remotely. The experience left me humbled—and grateful to have such amazing colleagues. To every single Twilion I cannot say this enough: thank you.

These quick rollouts also taught us a few things. First was how great things can happen when people stop worrying about making mistakes or not getting everything perfect the first time around. During the COVID-19 crisis, change was free. There were no alternatives, no office politics, and no fear of mistakes—because the alternatives were far worse. It's what happens when management doesn't have time to hold a bunch of meetings, to send requests and approvals up and down the chain of command or to insist on huge master plans that never end up being what you build anyway. Under pressure-cooker conditions, management and developers could quickly come to alignment, and then let developers problem-solve and invent solutions.

The crisis also showed how much faster it has become to build and deploy software. Software building blocks, microservices, and APIs have radically accelerated the process. For this we can thank thousands of developers who created those tools. Without all that modern infrastructure, the response to COVID-19 would have been far slower and less effective at so many organizations.

Finally, these overnight rollouts demonstrated the incredible human creativity and adaptability of developers who work inside corporations. Many were using these new tools for the first time and under great duress—and yet they figured things out and got everybody up and working. We were inspired by their heroic efforts and honored to be working alongside them.

Now it's time to build on the foundation and to keep working with the same level of urgency. These new ways of working are not only critical now. I believe that work and customer engagement have changed fundamentally during the pandemic and will never go back to the old way again. Millions of people have embraced new technologies; they will not want to go back. This was largely a one-way acceleration toward digital. Customers will become accustomed to these digital experiences, and expectations will just continue to rise quickly. Companies that get this right will have loyal, engaged, productive customers. Those that don't will struggle even more than before the COVID-19 crisis.

But the good news is—you got this. I hope this book helped show you the path to partnership with software developers. Together, with great mutual respect and understanding, you too can build the future.

Onward!

ACKNOWLEDGMENTS

I've received wisdom, mentorship, and friendship from so many people who have enabled me over the years to write code, build companies, and ultimately write this book. You've met most, if not all, of these characters through the course of reading the book, but I'd like to thank them again here.

To Mr. Bowers, my high school radio teacher, who let a bunch of high school students run "Metro Detroit's most powerful high school radio station, 88.1FM WBFH: The Biff." Thank you for letting us make mistakes. That's truly what learning is all about.

Kevin O'Connor, thank you for being an entrepreneurial mentor and Hamptons landlord. You truly created the "startup school of the hard knocks" that helped me become the founder I am. Sorry I never made you any money, though.

Thank you to Matt Levenson, my partner in building Versity, StubHub, and Nine Star. Thank you for inspiring the Ask Your Developer mindset. You taught me how to use software to solve great business problems. I loved building those businesses with you!

As you can tell, my time at Amazon was incredibly influential. Thank you, Andy Jassy, for investing in me when AWS was your baby. Thank you to Charlie Bell, who's given me so much mentorship and advice over the years on how to build a great R&D culture. And thank you to Rick Dalzell for your guidance in building the Twilio R&D organization, and for being a fantastic board member.

To Marc Benioff, thank you for instilling in me the greater sense of purpose that companies should carry, and for showing me that we can build great companies while strengthening our community and society around us.

Mitch Kapor and Freada Kapor-Klein, thank you for investing in Twilio so early on, but more important, for helping me make diversity and inclusion key pillars of Twilio's culture.

To Albert Wenger, thank you for teaching me the practice of long-term thinking, and the value of maximizing future optionality. Twilio wouldn't be where we are without your early coaching of our young team.

Byron Deeter, you've been supporting Twilio as an investor, board member, friend, and cycling partner for more than a decade now. Thank you—I've never met such a devoted supporter as you've been.

Jerry Colonna, you make me cry. In the healthy way. Thank you for your wisdom through the years. I hope you enjoy this book as much as I've loved yours.

Thank you, Jeff Immelt, for so openly sharing your learnings and wisdom from GE. I enjoyed our time comparing notes on our respective book-writing journeys, and thank you for being a good critical reviewer. I hope I returned the favor!

Hollis Heimbouch—thank you for taking a bet on me and, particularly, on this topic. The relationship between businesspeople and developers may not be the most obvious, but you took a bet that the world's organizations would be better if these groups spoke the same language. Thank you!

Christy Fletcher—thank you for your counsel throughout the publishing process. I didn't know what I didn't know about writing or publishing a book. I would have been lost without your wisdom.

Dan—your partnership in this book was crucial, thank you for all of the work you poured into *Ask Your Developer*. And Melanie, thank you for stepping in to give us a boost when we needed it.

Eric Ries—thank you for writing *The Lean Startup*, which changed the way we build products at Twilio. Your feedback and advice in the process of writing this book have been instrumental. And thank you for framing this book so eloquently in the foreword!

Thank you to those who were so generous with their time and ideas that helped me flesh out the concept of *Ask Your Developer*: Theo Frieswijk, Kevin Vasconi, Ali Niknam, Josh Hoium, Ashton Kutcher, Jason Fried, Werner Vogels, Patio11, "Jazzy" Chad Etzel, Leah Culver, Ryan Leslie, Kaya Thomas, and Danny Meyer.

Sara, Jessica, Chee, Kho, Stevie, Emma, Jason, Andres, Patio11, Donna, Jeff E, Erika, Elena, Danny, and Doug—thank you for reviewing early drafts of this book. You gave me incredible feedback through versions 0.1, 0.2, and 0.3 of this book. I wouldn't have a 1.0 without you!

To George Hu, thank you for being a great thought partner, and helping me structure and restructure this book for maximum impact. I truly cherish your partnership!

Andres Krogh, Nathan Sharp, and Sean McBride—through many iterations and my senseless feedback, you nailed the cover for this book! (As you always do.)

Thank you to the great team who's helping to get the *Ask Your Developer* word out: Caitlin Epstein, Tim Schraeder, and Billy Hackenson.

Kat McCormick-Sweeny, my chief of staff, thank you for keeping me on track. This book would be nowhere without you. You're the best boss a CEO could have.

To Evan Cooke and John Wolthuis, my Twilio cofounders: nothing is as satisfying as checking off to-do items from the lid of a pizza box. I'm so appreciative of all of the debate, thought wrangling, and seeds we planted in those early days that still grow today.

To all Twilions past and present, your passion to invent and to serve customers is infectious. You consistently remind me that, indeed, every day is Day 1 of our journey.

Thank you to those organizations who are helping to create the next generation of developers. Proceeds from this book will be donated to organizations that help underrepresented populations learn how to code to support this important work. Check out askyourdeveloper.com/proceeds to learn more.

Mom, thank you for teaching me to learn, and inspiring me to leadership.

Dad, thank you for building "projects" with me, and not getting too discouraged when they "didn't actually work." You made me a builder.

To M&A, my boys, thank you for always reminding me to play Magic the Gathering, bunny theater, and trampoline. And yes, it's not fair that adults get more screen time than kids.

Erica, my wife, thank you for putting up with my shenanigans for all these years. "I love you more than I have ever found a way to say to you."

ABOUT THE AUTHOR

JEFF LAWSON is cofounder and CEO of Silicon Valley–based Twilio, one of the world's fastest growing technology companies. A lifelong software developer, Jeff founded Twilio in 2008 with the belief that empowering developers was key to unlocking innovation within nearly every kind of business. Millions of software developers and hundreds of thousands of companies use Twilio's platform to add communications to the websites and apps you use daily. A serial entrepreneur, Jeff also founded Versity.com and Nine Star, was the founding CTO of StubHub, and was one of the first product managers at Amazon Web Services. He lives in San Francisco with his family and still makes time to hack on new software and hardware projects.